Cultural Foundation
in Latino/a Mental H

KDE Plasma

This is one of the most engaging, thorough and practical books on Latino/a Mental Health.
–Martin La Roche, Associate Professor,
Harvard Medical School, USA

Superb! *Cultural Foundations and Interventions in Latino/a Mental Health* is a must read for anyone interested in Latinas/os. Hector Adames and Nayeli Chavez-Dueñas weave psychological theory, research, and practice into a healing *arpillera*. This invaluable book is a timely and essential contribution to the field.
–Lillian Comas-Díaz, Executive Director & Clinical Professor,
George Washington University School of Medicine and
Transcultural Mental Health Institute, USA

This book offers a major contribution to understanding and effectively working with Latino/a students, families and mental health clients. It presents an excellent history of the journey of Latinos/a in the United States and their ability to maintain hope, dignity and connection to the past and future. The authors offer a powerful discussion of the role of skin color in Latino/a ethnic and cultural identity.
–Joseph L. White, Professor Emeritus of Psychology and
Psychiatry, University of California, Irvine, USA

Advancing work to effectively study, understand, and serve the fastest-growing U.S. ethnic minority population, this volume explicitly emphasizes the racial and ethnic diversity within this heterogeneous cultural group. The focus is on the complex historical roots of contemporary Latinos/as, their diversity in skin color and physiognomy, racial identity, ethnic identity, gender differences, immigration patterns, and acculturation. The work highlights how the complexities inherent in the diverse Latino/a experience, as specified throughout the topics covered in this volume, become critical elements of culturally responsive and racially conscious mental health treatment approaches. By addressing the complexities, within-group differences, and racial heterogeneity characteristic of U.S. Latinos/as, this volume makes a significant contribution to the literature related to mental health treatments and interventions.

Hector Y. Adames is Associate Professor and Neuropsychologist at the Chicago School of Professional Psychology, USA.

Nayeli Y. Chavez-Dueñas is Associate Professor and Clinical Psychologist at the Chicago School of Professional Psychology, USA.

Explorations in Mental Health Series

For a full list of titles in this series, please visit www.routledge.com

Books in this series

Cultural Foundations and Interventions in Latino/a Mental Health

History, Theory, and Within-Group Differences

Hector Y. Adames and
Nayeli Y. Chavez-Dueñas

Routledge
Taylor & Francis Group

NEW YORK AND LONDON

First published 2017
by Routledge
711 Third Avenue, New York, NY 10017

and by Routledge
2 Park Square, Milton Park, Abingdon, Oxon, OX14 4RN

First issued in paperback 2017

Routledge is an imprint of the Taylor & Francis Group, an informa business

Library of Congress Cataloguing-in-Publication Data
Names: Adames, Hector Y., author. | Chavez-Dueñas,
    Nayeli Y., author.
Title: Cultural foundations & interventions in Latino/a mental
    health : history, theory, and within group differences / by
    Hector Y. Adames and Nayeli Y. Chavez-Dueñas.
Other titles: Cultural foundations and interventions in
    Latino/a mental health | Explorations in mental health series.
Description: New York : Routledge, 2017. | Series: Explorations in
    mental health series | Includes bibliographical references and
    indexes.
Identifiers: LCCN 2016008909 | ISBN 9781138851535 (hbk) |
    ISBN 9781315724058 (ebk)
Subjects: | MESH: Hispanic Americans—psychology | Hispanic
    Americans—ethnology | Mental Health—ethnology | Mental
    Health Services | Culture | United States—ethnology
Classification: LCC RC451.5.H57 | NLM WA 305 AA1 | DDC
    616.89008968/073—dc23
LC record available at http://lccn.loc.gov/2016008909

ISBN 13: 978-0-8153-8637-7 (pbk)
ISBN 13: 978-1-138-85153-5 (hbk)

Typeset in Sabon
by Apex CoVantage, LLC

To all those who continue to resist and defy oppression by creating their own narratives. . .

Contents

Tables

Figures

Foreword

There Is No Time to Waste: The Latinization of the United States Is Underway

Self-authorization, self-definition, multidimensionality, and truth telling are cross-cutting themes throughout *Cultural Foundations & Interventions in Latino/a Mental Health: History, Theory, and Within-Group Differences*, emphasizing the complexity and heterogeneity of this powerful multicultural and multiracial collective of Latina/o peoples. As the authors state, this is the "fastest-growing" sector in the United States (U.S.) population embodying heterogeneity, differences, and similarities grounded in many dimensions of history, identity, and at the same time, often viewed only through stereotypes. When preparing mental health practitioners for culturally responsive care, images of nachos, sombreros, and *quinceañera* celebrations are insufficient, yet they are far too common. As well, often discussed is the idea that acculturation to dominant cultural values and behaviors are an indication of adjustment and success for Latinas/os. In reality, this notion only contributes to the status quo's assumption that ethnic minorities and immigrants must change and give up who they are in order to live the proverbial "American dream." Adames and Chavez-Dueñas discuss the flaws and harm these perspectives have when treating or studying Latino/a individuals, families, and communities. In 2016, and heading to 2040 when Latinas/os will be 40% of the U.S. population, there is no time to waste— the Latinization of the country is underway.

Part I of the text reflects the sociocultural foundations designed to help the reader become familiar with the history, complex racial background, and patterns of immigration of Latinas/os in the U.S. This lens or approach is essential to understand fully the lived history, historical context, and the evolution of any cultural group across geographical settings and time. In this case, the authors describe the rich and complex Latina/o history beginning in the pre-Columbian era, thereby acknowledging that the Indigenous peoples whom the Spaniards exploited and annihilated were prodigious scientists, artists, and loyal family/tribal members. In other words, they were peoples with civilizations informed by science, strong spiritual beliefs, and principles grounded in respect for self, others, and nature. Although not perfect societies, Indigenous groups were shaping history through their creativity, innovation, and determination. Their history and legacy lives on through the lifeblood of their multiracial descendants—today's Latinas/os.

The Latina/o history is well captured by discussion of the contributions of the Aztecs, Mayans, Incas, Tainos, and Caribs, the original people of the Americas. The tragic transatlantic slave trade brought many peoples from Western Africa to the Americas, enriching the cultural and racial heterogeneity of existing Indigenous empires. In explicit terms, the authors affirm that the history of Latina/o peoples reflects their multicultural and multiracial dimensions of identity, specifically that of skin color. Chapter 2, "Skin-Color Differences Within Latinos/as," is very powerful in this respect. Adames and Chavez-Dueñas introduce candid facts, ones often ignored or unknown among most Latinas/os today. Through the use of tables and figures, they illustrate the social stratification based on skin color in Latin America, the relationship between skin color and stigmatization, and "concealment strategies" that promote misinformation about Latinas/os. From this chapter flows many of the perspectives that need to be accounted for in the education, research, and practice of Latina/o psychology.

The attention to skin color, race, and colorism is one of the key features of this text. Far too often, skin-color privilege is simply accepted as a fact of life. However, the authors provide examples of how intergroup racial biases and internalized racism affect members of Latina/o families. Skin color, as discussed, is also embodied in the concept and reality of *mestizaje* (the mixing of the races), which directly leads to discrimination, marginalization, and other forms of oppression. Examples from the U.S. invasion of Mexican territory illustrates how Mexican people became tenants in their own land and also were subjected to discrimination in schools, employment, playgrounds, restaurants, and military veteran recognition. Thus colorism and prejudices based on skin color have led to both within-group and majority-group discriminatory and oppressive practices.

The role of skin color in the examination of immigration policies is also raised as a contributing factor to groups that have succeeded and reached the "American Dream" and those continuing to be demonized. The 2016 presidential election provides vivid testimony to the xenophobia, hate, and vagueness of knowledge about Latinas/os in the U.S. Regardless of immigration status and historical roots, Latinas/os have been and will continue to be contributors to the success of the U.S. Failure to recognize this fact suggests future leaders are out of touch. Of course, individuals in the mental health profession witness this type of demagogic behavior and discourse from educators, researchers, practitioners, and organizational leaders. Adames and Chavez-Dueñas provide excellent testimony about why it is important to know the stories of Latinas/os from Latinos/as who have strong and healthy racial and ethnic identities. Latinas/os are not one and the same; rather, they are multiracial, multidimensional, and complex. As the text proclaims, Latinas/os are indeed heterogeneous in multiple ways, including ethnicity, skin color, nationality, gender, level of acculturation, and the like. Thus to understand within-group differences requires a shift in worldviews. Adames and Chavez-Dueñas dedicate the second part of the text to understanding within-group Latino/a differences. As a prelude to examining differences, and consistent with Guidelines One and Two of the American Psychological Association (APA) Multicultural Guidelines (American Psychological Association, 2003; Fouad & Arredondo, 2007), readers are reminded that 1) there is a need to recognize biases and assumptions about Latinas/os, 2) question the source of these beliefs, 3) recognize how these cognitions affect their emotions and working relationships with Latinas/os, and 4) commit to becoming knowledgeable about the breadth and depth of Latinas/os so as to do no harm (APA Ethical Principles of Psychologists and Code of Conduct, 2010).

Part II also examines the intersection of identity development and acculturation processes, drawing from other disciplines such as anthropology and sociology. The static nature of the social construction of gender is underscored. In direct relation, the cultural concepts of *marianismo* and *machismo* are introduced as both conscious socialization processes and internalized worldviews that inform self-beliefs and expectations. The explanation of the gender spectrum in these chapters is also a refreshing approach to discussing gender orientation(s) more holistically and inclusively. Not only is this approach relevant to understanding Latinas/os, but it also provides a template for understanding people in general. As mentioned, an in-depth discussion of acculturation is also included in this section of the text. Acculturation has been associated with Latinas/os without consideration of the status of the individual and using either-or models with a focus primarily on behavior. In this section, Adames and Chavez-Dueñas review the shortcomings of these models. The authors then propose an ecological systems perspective, one that examines the complexity of acculturation processes of change. Other research on acculturation has looked primarily at ethnic identity development status as the independent variable. Of course, it is not quite so simple. These studies, as has been noted, have often been done with a limited cohort of adolescent immigrants with no consideration of their heterogeneity. Furthermore, the cognitive and emotional dissonance that occurs during the acculturation process and other contextual factors are examined, which are often overlooked in existing literature. In contrast, as the authors discuss, the ecological perspective is more embracing of how history, legislation, and political climate affect individual acculturation.

Part III of the book introduces a broad canvas to depict the multiple factors that may affect culturally responsive and racially conscious clinical practice with Latinas/os. In this section, the traditional cultural values including *familismo, respeto, dignidad, confianza,* and *personalismo* (Santiago-Rivera, Arredondo, & Gallardo-Cooper, 2002) are discussed. Adames and Chavez-Dueñas identify and describe eight additional cultural values: *vergüenza, amabilidad, lealtad, obediencia, responsabilidad, ser trabajador, honestidad,* and *humildad* while discussing how each value is manifested among Latinos/as. These values transcend generations, gender, age, and language differences. Overall, Adames and Chavez-Dueñas masterfully integrate the content presented in Parts I and II of this text to develop a culturally responsive and racially conscious treatment modality titled CREAR-CE (*Culturally Responsive AND Racially Conscious Ecosystemic Treatment Approach*).

In closing, the last section of the book is powerful because it provides authentic, soulful narratives prepared by graduate students and professionals trained in Latina/o psychology. The theme of awakening runs throughout the narratives of the nine essays. The narratives describe powerful emotions related to racial and ethnic identity development, reflections on personal and collective group history, and the overall responsibilities to be ethical practitioners, scholars, and advocates for systemic change. These essays should be required reading for all graduate students and professionals who believe they are fair-minded, culturally aware, and racially conscious.

Cultural Foundations & Interventions in Latino/a Mental Health: History, Theory, and Within-Group Differences is simply remarkable and to be celebrated! It is a scholarly statement about knowledge-building, honoring the shared history among Latinas/os and all humanity, confronting race, colorism, and color-blind ideologies, as well as its perpetuation by academics, while setting expectations for culturally, racially, and ethically responsive practice. Adames and Chavez-Dueñas have opened new pathways that respect and celebrate the racial and cultural diversity among Latinas/os and honor the history, individuality, and continuing contributions of Latinas/os to these United States of America!

Patricia Arredondo, Ed.D.

References

American Psychological Association. (2003). Guidelines on multicultural education, training, research, practice, and organizational change for psychologists. *American Psychologist, 58*(5), 377–402. doi:10.1037/0003-066X.58.5.377

American Psychological Association. (2010). *Ethical principles of psychologists and code of conduct.* Retrieved from http://apa.org/ethics/code/index.aspx

Fouad, N. A., & Arredondo, P. (2007). *Becoming culturally oriented: Practical advice for psychologists and educators.* Washington, DC: American Psychological Association. doi:10.1037/11483-000

Santiago-Rivera, A. L., Arredondo, P., & Gallardo-Cooper, M. (2002). *Counseling Latinos and la familia: A practical guide.* Thousand Oaks, CA: Sage.

Acknowledgments

We are nothing if we walk alone,
We are everything if we walk together . . .

We are thankful to so many people who contributed to making *Cultural Foundations & Interventions in Latino/a Mental Health: History, Theory, and Within-Group Differences* a reality. We want to recognize and thank those who came before us and laid the groundwork so that today we, two immigrants and first-generation College Students of Color can write these pages. We thank our Indigenous and African people from whose history and role modeling we learned to resist and persist even during the most oppressive and difficult times. Because of your struggles we live; because of your resilience we survive.

We would like to acknowledge a number of Psychologists of Color who are pioneers in the field and have mentored and believed in us. We are indebted to Dr. Patricia Arredondo for paving the way for so many Latina/o psychologists and for being an inspirational and guiding force in our careers. We owe a great deal of gratitude to Dr. Kurt C. Organista who provided invaluable feedback, countless check-ins, and encouragement throughout the process. Your attention to detail, your honest feedback, and your supportive mentorship has been instrumental in our development as scholars. To Dr. Joseph L. White, you have appeared in our lives and brought us smiles, courage, and hope. You have been a true, magical, and spiritual blessing in our lives. Thank you for the mentorship, for gently pushing us to write this book, and for believing we could do it. Lastly, we want to express our heartfelt appreciation to our academic *madrina* (godmother), Dr. Lillian Comas-Díaz, for inspiring us to write about our Black and Indigenous roots with love and pride. Your work, spiritual energy, and healing powers have shaped our academic careers. Thank you for blessing our work. Without each of you, our book would not have been written, completed, or produced in the form that it encompasses today.

We want to thank our graduate students and mentees Jessica G. Perez-Chavez, Silvia P. Salas-Pizaña, Shanna N. Smith, Robert L. Mendez, Danielle

Alexander, Minnah W. Farook, Mackenzie T. Goertz, Chelsea L. Parker, and Leah Hirsch for contributing their voices to this project. We know your journey through the realities and ugliness of racial injustice, xenophobia, and inequality has not been easy, yet you have persisted. You are the reason why we teach and love what we do. Thank you for allowing us to witness your struggles, growth, and triumphs. We also wish to acknowledge our colleagues Dr. Martin J. La Roche, Dr. Elisa Velasquez-Andrade, Dr. Hector L. Torres, Dr. Edil Torres Rivera, Cathleen Palubicki, Frances McClain, and Anita O'Conor who have provided support and encouragement throughout the completion of this project.

Lastly, we would like to thank our *familia* and friends who have taught us about dedication, hard work, excellence, and love of our Latino/a roots.

Dr. Nayeli Y. Chavez-Dueñas Writes

Mi familia biológica y escogida ha sido indispensable para hacer este sueño una realidad. A ellos mi mamá (Delfina Dueñas), mi papá (Pablo Chavez) hermanas (Ernestina, Araceli, María y Veronica), hermanos (Flavio, Eraclio, Gilberto, y Sigifredo), sobrinas (Janeth, Marisol, Elizabeth, Guadalupe, Anael, Edith, Aide, Itzel), y sobrinos (Carlos, Flavio, Andres, Juan, Fernando, Miguel, Jorge, Antonio, Alexis, Giovani y Victitor) les agradezco por su paciencia, apoyo y cariño y espero representar a la familia con orgullo. Mis triunfos son más suyos que míos porque las lecciones que he aprendido de cada uno ustedes me han permitido seguir adelante a pesar de las dificultades. También quiero agradecer a mi mamá Delfina Dueñas porque no podría haberle pedido a la vida una mejor madre que tu; fue a través de tu ejemplo de lucha, y determinación que aprendí el valor del trabajo y perdí el miedo a soñar con lo que parecía imposible. A ti mamá, le debo mucho más que la vida, te debo mi fuerza, mi esperanza y mi fe en un futuro mejor. To my chosen family, mis amigas y amigos who have allowed me to be me and still love me, thank you; I know that is not an easy task. I owe a special thanks to my academic brother, Dr. Adames, who has not only shaped and marked my career but also my personal life. I am very grateful to the creator for putting you on my journey. Lastly, I would like to acknowledge Dr. Joseph L. White who has been a special spiritual and paternal force who has transformed my life. Thank you Dr. White, for your selfless support, guidance, and dedication. Your example of love and dedication to the fight for social justice has left an everlasting imprint on my soul. In addition to the people who have walked and sometimes ran with me through the marathon that has taken me to this beautiful place in my career, I am grateful to the spiritual forces that have given me the strength, perseverance, and ability to get to the finish line. I am thankful to La Virgen de Guadalupe who has been a symbol of motherly love, acceptance, and pride in my Indigenous roots. I am also thankful to the God, Quetzalcoatl, who has been my companion through the twisted yet exciting labyrinths of academia. They have both lighted the dark roads and removed many of the barriers and shadows that have threatened to stop my steady walk, run, and sprint to the finish line. It has taken your supernatural and powerful forces to get someone from where I started, a little girl growing up in a humble Mexican family, to where I am today, a proud Mexican immigrant who is in love with her roots, works as an associate professor, is a scholar, an author, and a mentor. Gracias infinitas.

Dr. Hector Y. Adames Writes

I could not be where I am today without the unwavering support and love of so many individuals. I am indebted to my *familia* who were my first teachers and continue to teach me how to thrive, despite the many foreign barriers we face in a land often not welcoming of people who look, speak, and dance like we do. You have in your own special ways supported me personally and professionally. *A mi mami Rosa Adames y a mi papi Angel-Manuel Adames cuya energía, fuerza, y cariño me han convertido en la persona que soy. Es un honor ser la inversión de su sacrificio.* To my *abuelita* Basilia Ramos, *hermana* Johansi Matos, and brother Angel Adames who always see me for who I am and love me despite my flaws. To my soul sisters Dr. Janette Rodriguez, Wendy Y. Blanco, and Dr. Shweta Sharma for being soft and strong when I needed it the most throughout the years. You're simply beautiful. To my extended family Dulce Matos, Luis Ney Matos, Luis Matos, Rosanna Matos, Deiby Marte, Alexandra De La Cruz, Jeancarlos Paulino, Carmen De La Cruz, Nancy Adames, and Zunilda Adames who have taught me the importance of honoring, embracing, and celebrating my Latino roots. *"Dominicano soy, de mis raices yo no voy a olvidarme; soy de una raza tan humilde y tan grande, que de su espera se hacen rayos de sol"* (Fernando Villalona, n.d.). I express my gratitude to my chosen family Dr. Arianne E. Miller, Dr. Milton A. Fuentes, Dr. Erendira Lopez-Garcia, Dr. Michelle S. Schultz, and Gary Scaife for patiently listening to me and my many unconventional ideas and *locuras* throughout the years. I cherish the many passionate debates, laughs, and tears we have shared. To Dr. Elizabeth L. Haines for her mentorship during my early academic years and her contagious passion for the study of bias, power, and privilege. A big heartfelt thank you to my academic sister, Dr. Nayeli Y. Chavez-Dueñas, for embarking on this arduous yet exciting book project journey. Your imprint on my life as a person and a racially conscious scholar is everlasting. Lastly, to every single one of you I say *mil gracias* and *In Lak'ech . . . Tú eres mi otro yo (you are my other me).*

Preface

The latest Bureau of the Census report (2011) demonstrates that in the last decade, the United States (U.S.) has experienced an unprecedented change in its demographic makeup. Latinas/os, one of the groups contributing to this shift, are currently the largest and fastest growing ethnic minority group. As of 2010, there were 55.4 million Latinas/os living in the U.S., comprising 17% of the total population (U.S. Census Bureau, 2011). Moreover, demographic projections suggest that the proportion of Latinas/os will continue to increase. In fact, it is expected that by the year 2030, 20% of the total U.S. population will be of Latina/o descent (U.S. Census Bureau, 2004). As the proportion of Latinas/os in the U.S. continues to grow, there will be a higher need for practicing mental health providers to be adequately prepared to meet the needs of this growing segment of the U.S. population and understand the complexities within this racial and ethnic group. Despite the increased demographic representation of Latinas/os in the U.S., there continues to be a dearth in the psychological literature that explicitly emphasizes and addresses the racially and ethnic differences within this population.

In an effort to prepare students, supervisors, and mental health professionals to effectively study, understand, and serve Latinos/as, the volume *Cultural Foundations & Interventions in Latino/a Mental Health: History, Theory, and Within-Group Differences* is an addition to the few books presently available in Latina/o psychology. Unlike other texts that provide broad coverage of the U.S. Latina/o population, this book is an up-to-date reference that explicitly emphasizes the racial and ethnic diversity within this heterogeneous cultural group. The volume focuses on the complex historical roots of contemporary Latinas/os, their diversity in skin color and physiognomy, racial identity, ethnic identity, gender differences, immigration patterns, and acculturation. The complexities inherent in the diverse Latina/o experience become critical elements of culturally responsive and racially conscious treatment approaches with Latinas/os. No other book covering topics related to mental health singularly addresses the complexities, within-group differences, and racial heterogeneity characteristic of U.S. Latinas/os.

The volume is comprised of ten chapters organized into four sections. Part I, "Sociocultural Foundations," is designed to orient readers to Latina/o cultural and racial backgrounds, history, and patterns of immigration to the U.S. In order to help students and professionals understand the cultural and racial roots of Latinas/os, Chapter 1 describes and examines the history of the four main Indigenous groups: the Aztecs, Maya, Inka, and Tainos/Caribs. A description on the legacy of each Indigenous group and their contributions to contemporary Latin American culture is provided. The devastating effects of the historic periods of the conquest and colonization for Indigenous people and their culture is also discussed, followed by a brief summary of the history of Africans in Latin America. The chapter concludes with recommendations for the integration of collective group history into Latino/a mental health by introducing and describing seven psychological strengths. Chapter 2 examines the role of skin color and colorism, a form of within-group racial discrimination, on the lives of Latinas/os. Overall, the mental health literature on racial differences within the Latina/o community and colorism is sparse. In an effort to contribute to this understudied area and highlight its significance, a concise and selective review of the history of colorism in Latin America is provided. Specifically, three historical eras (i.e., conquest, colonization, and post-colonization) are summarized. In each era, the establishment of racial and ethnic stratification and their consequences for Latinas/os of Indigenous and African descent are discussed. Connections between today's color-blind racial ideologies and *mestizaje*, or the mixing of races, is underscored to demonstrate how these strategies have been used, historically and in contemporary times, to deny and minimize skin-color privilege. The chapter culminates with questions to help mental health practitioners and researchers reflect and engage in dialogue about colorism. In Chapter 3, we provide a brief overview of Latina/o history in the U.S. The chapter focuses on the immigration patterns of the four largest U.S. Latina/o groups: Mexicans, Puerto Ricans, Cubans, and Dominicans. The chapter highlights the specific features that characterize contact with U.S. These features include demand for immigrant labor, transnational labor-recruiting networks, wage differentials, and international laws and policies that have propelled individuals to emigrate from Latin America to the U.S. To help contextualize the impact that immigration has on U.S. Latinas/os, an analysis of the complex interplay between immigration policies, general public perception of immigrants, and the economic, cultural, and social contributions of Latinas/os is provided. The chapter ends by reviewing the social, economical, and psychological impact of immigration laws on Latinas/os.

Part II, "Understanding Within-Group Latino/a Differences," provides theoretical and practical approaches to understand the heterogeneity and differences within the Latina/o population, including racial and ethnic identity models, gender, acculturation, and history of immigration. In Chapter 4, the social construction of gender and the role that it has played in the lives of Latinas/os throughout history is reviewed. The chapter provides a brief overview on how gender was introduced into the lexicon of academia as a prelude to reviewing various constructs that communicate gendered identities and expression. The chapter continues with a review of the historical development on *machismo* and *marianismo*, the two cultural gendered ideologies associated with traditional Latina/o culture. The chapter integrates information from various disciplines in the social sciences to provide a rich historical and contemporary contextual account on the effect of *marianismo* and *machismo* on the lives of Latinos, Latinas, Latin@s, Latinxs, and Queer Latin@s. The chapter concludes with treatment recommendations for Latin@s across the gender spectrum. In Chapter 5, an overview of the dynamic and complex process of acculturation experienced by many Latinas/os in the U.S. is provided. A brief history of the theories of acculturation followed by an overview and critique of the three main acculturation models, *unidirectional*, *bidirectional*, and *multidirectional*, are discussed. The chapter concludes with an ecological systems perspective on the acculturation of Latinas/os as a prelude to implications on the health and social mobility of Latinas/os in the 21st century. This section ends with Chapter 6, which concentrates on the development of racial and ethnic identity, two paradigms situated within the larger umbrella of the study on social identities. The definitions of terms pertinent to the study of race and culture are provided as a foundation for understanding the complexities inherent in the existing ethnic and racial identity development models and literature. The chapter also provides an in-depth view of the current models on Latina/o ethnic identity. The impact on practice and research regarding the common practice of interchangeably using race and ethnicity in the study of Latina/o social identity is discussed. Lastly, a new conceptual framework titled, C-REIL (*Centering Racial and Ethnic Identity for Latinos/as Framework*), which integrates *both* race and ethnicity in the understanding of these two social constructs among Latinas/os is provided. The chapter concludes with implications for research and practice.

Part III, "Culturally Responsive and Racially Conscious Clinical Practice With Latinos/as," offers strategies for clinicians to apply the information provided in Parts I and II of this volume. In Chapter 7, specific barriers that racially and ethnically diverse Latinas/os may experience when seeking mental health services are identified. Some of these challenges include systemic and individual barriers, which may impact access to mental health services by individuals in the Latina/o community. Overall, the aim of this chapter is to provide a framework that illustrates the factors that contribute to the maintenance of service underutilization among Latinas/os, while highlighting the impact of within-group differences (e.g., language, socioeconomic factors, documented status, skin color, physiognomy) and sociohistorical context on the mental health utilization of diverse individuals. Chapter 8 centers on helping the reader gain knowledge and understanding of traditional Latina/o cultural values that can serve to inform the development of culturally congruent treatment interventions. The chapter provides an overview of the five main traditional Latina/o cultural values followed by a brief overview of the available research in this area. Additional Latina/o cultural values that are not as well researched or documented in the mental health and social science literature are outlined and reviewed. A discussion regarding the importance of considering Latina/o within-group differences when applying traditional cultural values to Latinas/os is offered. The chapter ends with specific ways in which providers can integrate the cultural values into mental health treatment. Chapter 9 provides a review of the literature on Empirically Supported Treatments, Evidence-Based Practice, and Culturally Adapted Psychotherapies with a particular focus on the congruence of those modalities with Latinas/os of diverse racial and ethnic backgrounds. In an effort to apply the material presented in Parts I, II, and III of this volume, an interventional framework titled CREAR-CE, which stands for *Culturally Responsive AND Racially Conscious Ecosystemic Treatment Approach* is offered.

Lastly, Part IV, "The Impact of Latino/a Psychology on Racially and Ethnically Diverse Students and Professionals," seeks to highlight the ways in which studying Latina/o mental health can influence the personal and professional lives of people. To accomplish this goal, Chapter 10 offers the narratives of nine racially and ethnically diverse individuals (i.e., three Latina/o, two African American, one South Asian, and three European American individuals) who have studied and applied the content presented in this volume. Each narrative outlines how learning about Latina/o psychology can lead to personal and professional growth. In closing, we hope this volume helps us all envision a healthy, welcoming, and accepting world "where many other worlds will have a place . . . the community we want to build is one where all people fit with their own languages" (Subcomandante Marcos, 2001, p. 80), their own shades of color, histories, contributions, and strength.

References

Villalona, F. (n.d.). *Dominicano soy.* Retrieved from http://www.albumcancionyletra.com/dominicano-soy_de_fernando-villalona___271963.aspx

Subcomandante Marcos. (2001). *Our word is our weapon: Selected writings.* New York, NY: Seven Stories Press.

U.S. Census Bureau. (2004). *U.S. interim projections by age, sex, race, and Hispanic origin.* Retrieved from http://www.census.gov/ipc/www.usinterimproj/

U.S. Census Bureau. (2011). *The Hispanic population: Census 2011 brief.* Retrieved from http://www.census.gov/compendia/statab/brief.html

Part I
Sociocultural Foundations

1 The Diverse Historical Roots of Today's Latinos/as

Learning From Our Past to Move Into the Future

Our people were born dignified and rebellious . . . Survival, resistance, dignity, and defiance have been the only means of survival.

–Marcos, 2001, p. 33

A fundamental aspect of self-knowledge involves individuals having a strong sense of who they are in two main areas: *personal identity* and *group identity*, which undoubtedly shape an individual's personal history. *Personal identity* refers to the adoption of idiosyncratic individual attitudes, emotions, feelings, personality characteristics, and behaviors of the self. It involves the process of answering two important questions: "Who am I at the core of my being?" and "What are my personal standards, morals, and values?" (White & Cones, 1999). Alternatively, *group identity* is defined as the process of learning the *collective group history* and identifying with a larger social group of people with similar values, characteristics, worldviews, beliefs, and practices.

In the literature, *collective group history* has been described as having several protective functions for individuals. First, it contributes to the development of a strong sense of group membership, allowing individuals to understand and connect with their ancestral roots and cultural heritage (Parham, Ajamu, & White, 2011). Second, ancestral knowledge, skills, and achievements are transmitted to a new generation and help provide self-affirmation for Youths of Color (Akbar, 1998; White & Parham, 1983; Woodson, 1990). Such knowledge, skills, and achievements also provide Youths of Color with a blueprint with which they can begin to internalize and believe that they have

a legacy of greatness and accomplishment that they are required to continue. It is the images of greatness, which resemble them which serve to inspire young people to become the great scientists, scholars, and artists which continue to fearlessly explore the world and develop new ideas and concepts which advance themselves and the rest of humanity.

(Akbar, 1998, p. 8)

Lastly, *collective group history* can serve to transmit the *acquired immunities* or knowledge regarding the successful ways that an individual's ancestors have used to cope and navigate life's difficulties, challenges, and transitions (Akbar, 1998).

Overall, knowledge of history is necessary for mental health providers in the therapeutic setting. In fact, mental health practitioners are trained to take a detailed personal history of their clients. The information gathered from the client's history helps shape how providers understand the impact of past events and experiences on their client's presenting difficulties and adjustments. This information further provides context regarding the unique ways in which clients discuss and experience problems in daily living, including their mental health symptoms. We argue that in addition to personal history, it is pivotal for mental health practitioners to learn and understand their clients' *collective group histories*. Without an integration of both the personal and collective history, clinicians would be left with a fragmented and incomplete view of their clients. Unfortunately, while many providers receive training that helps them to understand their clients' personal histories, many lack knowledge regarding the collective group histories of the clients they serve.

In an effort to help address the gap in training, this chapter aims to assist mental health providers and researchers studying or working with Latinos/as become familiar with the *collective group history* of this racially and culturally diverse population. The chapter begins with a brief review of the history of the four main Indigenous groups that flourished in the Americas: the Aztecs, Maya, Inka, and Tainos/Caribs. A description of the legacy of each Indigenous group and their contributions to contemporary Latin American culture is provided. The devastating effects of the historic periods of the conquest and colonization for Indigenous people and their culture is also discussed, followed by a brief summary of the history of Africans in Latin America. The chapter concludes with recommendations for the integration of *collective group history* into Latino/a mental health.

The Aztecs

One of the most advanced Indigenous civilizations of the central Valley of Mexico was developed by the Aztecs, people also known as the Mexica (Ferguson, 2000; Meier & Ribera, 1993). The group who later formed the Aztec Empire is believed to have originated in a mythical place called *Aztlan*. This mythical place is believed to be located in what is today known as the southwest region of the United States (Ferguson, 2000; Meier & Ribera, 1993). Interestingly, in contemporary times, the descendants of the Aztecs are the numerical majority in the southwest, the very same lands where ancestors are believed to have originated from.

According to the legend, the Aztecs migrated south of *Aztlan* looking for their promised land. After hundreds of years of migration, the Mexica settled in the middle of a muddy island surrounded by water where they eventually built the center of their civilization, which they named Tenochtitlan and which served as their capital. Here the Aztecs built one of the most complex and intriguing civilizations that has ever existed. The capital city of Tenochtitlan had approximately 200,000 to 300,000 inhabitants, making it one of the largest cities of that historical time period (Ferguson, 2000; Meier & Ribera, 1993).

The Aztec civilization thrived and prospered in the central Valley of Mexico, and by the time the Spaniards arrived in 1519, their empire had achieved a vast and remarkably advanced knowledge of technology, architecture, farming, and medicine. They had developed a system of public health, public sanitation, and a sewage disposal unparalleled by any other existing city during that historical era (Ferguson, 2000). The Aztec Empire was also economically successful and had a powerful army, which eventually ruled the majority of other Indigenous groups inhabiting the central Valley of Mexico (Meier & Ribera, 1993). This section provides a brief review on the history of this advanced civilization, including their origins, social organization, and spirituality. The section ends with a brief discussion regarding the contributions of the Aztec civilization to contemporary Mexican and Latino/a culture.

Origins

Mystery and ambiguity mark the history and origin of the Aztec civilization. Such lack of clarity regarding this successful civilization stems from the destruction of important Indigenous records by the Spaniards. Specifically, the Spanish conquistadors, who were unable to understand the complexity and level of advancement achieved by the Aztec civilization, considered native records the works of the devil (Davies, 2001). As a result, during the historic period of the conquest, the Spaniards destroyed all existing records, including the Aztec codices, which pictorially documented information pertaining to the origin, culture, and scientific advances of this civilization (Duran, 1967). Thus what is known today about Aztec history and culture has mainly been compiled from a combination of sources, including depictions found in monuments, in pyramids, and in works of art made by the Aztecs themselves that survived colonization. In addition, historical information passed orally by the Aztecs from generation to generation, research gathered by scholars (e.g., historians, anthropologists, archaeologists), as well as data collected from letters and documents written from the perspective of the Spanish conquistadors contribute to knowledge about the Aztecs. Although information regarding the Aztec Empire and its accomplishments can be more readily identified, less is known about the origin, the culture, and the people who developed such a complex civilization.

As previously stated, the Aztec began their migration from *Aztlan* approximately in 1111 AD. They traveled south for hundreds of years, following the orders of their God, *Huitzilopochtli*, eventually reaching a place called

Coatepec located near the city of *Tula,* approximately 40 miles away from what would be their final destination (Davies, 2001; Escalante Gonzalbo, 2010). In *Coatepec,* the Aztecs commemorated the first New Fire of migration, which marked the beginning of the first 52-year cycle in the ritual calendar of ancient Mexico. Here, in the city of *Coatepec,* the birth of *Huitzilopochtli* as a God is believed to have taken place (Davies, 2001). Thus *Huitzilopochtli* is thought to have been a human leader of the Aztecs prior to their migration from *Aztlan.* He later became a legend after his death and was declared a God in *Coatepec.* The Aztecs left *Coatepec* around 1168 AD and proceeded to their final destination guided by dreams and visions from their *God Huitzilopochtli* (Davies, 2001; Escalante Gonzalbo, 2010).

Despite the short distance between *Coatepec* and the central Valley of Mexico, it took the Aztecs hundreds of years to arrive there. They eventually reached a place located about a mile away from *Tenochtitlan* where the God *Huitzilopochtli* appeared to one of his priests and told him that they should continue until a "place where you find the cactus plant, with the eagle perched upon it, and give it the name *Tenochtitlan*" (Davies, 2001, p. 13). The following morning, the Aztecs found the cactus plant with an eagle standing on it eating a snake; it was in this precise magical location, an island surrounded by water, where the Aztecs founded their magnificent city, *Tenochtitlan.* The Aztecs established themselves in the Valley of Mexico on the New Fifth Fire or the year 1345 (Escalante Gonzalbo, 2010). Although the location reportedly chosen by the *God Huitzilopochtli* did not seem ideal for the establishment of a civilization, the Aztecs quickly learned how to take advantage of every natural resource available. They eventually became masters of the region surrounding *Tenochtitlan.*

Social Organization

A rich combination of the traditions, culture, and spiritual beliefs of various Indigenous groups (e.g., *Toltecs, Teotihuacanos*) formed the Aztec culture. Initially, the Aztecs followed a tribal social organization that eventually transformed itself into an empire with a complex system of social stratification, including a powerful army. At the head of the state was the *Tlatoani,* whom the Spaniards later called the emperor. Under the *Tlatoani* were the priests, nobles, merchants, free peasants, and slaves. More specifically, the Aztec society was made up of two main social classes that included the *pilli* (nobility) and the *macehualli* (commoners). Each group was further subdivided into social groups with different statuses. At the bottom of the system were servants who have been referred to as "slaves." However, the concept of slavery for the Aztec was different from how it was later conceptualized by the Europeans. For instance, slavery for them was not based on hereditary and children of slaves were born free members of the civilization. Moreover, it was possible for "slaves" to gain their freedom (e.g., by buying it; Davies, 2001; Escalante Gonzalbo, 2010; Ferguson, 2000).

A particular characteristic of Aztec society was its value and emphasis on the education of its citizens. In fact, for the Aztec people, education was mandatory for everyone regardless of gender and social class. Although the education offered was very similar for all children, they were eventually divided into two different tracks. The first track, called the *calmecac*, was available to the children of nobility. Noble children received the training and education necessary to become the leaders, doctors, teachers, and priests of the empire. The second track, known as the *telpochcalli*, was provided to children of the commoners. On the *telpochcalli* track, children were taught skills necessary to become part of a wide variety of trades (e.g., farmers, merchants, artisans) and gender specific skills (e.g., weaving, hunting), as well as the Aztec culture and religious/spiritual beliefs (Davies, 2001; Escalante Gonzalbo, 2010).

An important part of the Aztec civilization and success was its powerful army with strong warriors who eventually conquered a large territory of the central Valley of Mexico. The Aztecs fought several wars, eventually establishing a triple alliance with the neighboring kingdoms of *Texcoco* and *Tlacopan*. This alliance helped the Aztecs gain the stability and power necessary to become the most influential empire in the central Valley of Mexico (Escalante Gonzalbo, 2010). In fact, it has been estimated that at its peak, the Aztec Empire had a population of 10 million people, with each group conquered being forced to pay tribute (e.g., taxes). The taxes paid to the empire by all conquered groups were a significant component of the Aztec economic success, allowing this empire to maintain power for many years thereafter (Davies, 2001; Escalante Gonzalbo, 2010).

Spirituality

Aztec religion was a complex and fascinating mixture of the beliefs and Gods of the many Indigenous groups they had conquered. Overall, the Aztecs were polytheistic with a number of deities being worshiped, including three main Gods: *Quetzalcoatl* (The Creator), *Huitzilopochtli* (Sun God), and *Tezcatlipoca* (The Chief God). The Aztecs were deeply religious and superstitious people whose religion permeated every aspect of their society (e.g., celebrations, holidays, rituals, and sacrifices). One of the main objectives of Aztec spirituality centered on the desire to keep nature in balance to prevent its destructive forces from ending the world (Ferguson, 2000).

Creation of the World

According to the Aztec religion, time was divided into five eras or suns, and during the Aztec era, they were living in the fifth sun. Based on their beliefs, it had taken the Gods five attempts to create the world and each previous world had been destroyed due to conflict among the different Gods. For instance, the God *Tezcatlipoca*, who created the first world, was overthrown by other Gods from his honored position as the creator. In vengeance, the God *Tezcatlipoca* turned himself into a jaguar and destroyed the world he had created. As a result, the world was recreated three times and consecutively destroyed by the wind and floods. Each time the world was destroyed, the new God would become the sun. Finally, during the last attempt at creating a long-lasting world, all the Gods came together to decide how to proceed. During this encounter, the Gods agreed that one of them would sacrifice themselves to become the new sun. Sacrification involved the Gods throwing themselves into the fire. As a result, a humble God named *Nanahuatl* sacrificed himself and became the new sun or the fifth sun. However, the new sun did not move, posing a problem for the newly created world. It was decided that four additional Gods would also have to sacrifice themselves, which would then allow the fifth sun to move. As a result of the Gods' sacrifice, the wind arose and began moving the sun. Unfortunately, the sacrifices came at a high cost to humans who for the entire history of the Aztec Empire would carry the responsibility of helping the sunrise every morning by performing rituals and sacrifices (Davies, 2001; Ferguson, 2000). Thus Aztec religion and social life emphasized the need to keep nature in a state of equilibrium, as they believed that a battle between light and darkness was constantly being fought. They also believed that the Gods needed human blood in order to win the battle against darkness. As a result, humans used bloodletting rituals and/or human sacrifices to help the God *Huitzilopochtli* win the constant battles against darkness. They believed that those who sacrificed themselves to the Gods would rise to the heavens to fight with God *Huitzilopochtli* for the continuation of the world and humanity. For the Aztec people, blood was the essence of life and the substance that fueled the continuation of life and the world. Human blood and human life were the most sacred gifts that the Aztec/Mexica could offer to their Gods who had created them and to whom they were eternally indebted to (Davies, 2001; Ferguson, 2000).

Creation of Humans

Based on Aztec religion, once the fifth sun was moving across the sky, the Gods realized that they, once again, needed to create humans to populate the earth. Although human beings had previously been created four times, they had also been destroyed and their remains sent to the underworld. This fifth and final time, the God *Quetzalcoatl*, decided to go into the underworld (*Mictlan*) to retrieve the bones of the humans previously destroyed. The legend posits that as *Quetzalcoatl* fled from *Mictlan* with the bones, he tripped and the bones were shattered into different pieces. According to the Aztec/Mexica, this is the reason why people are of all different shapes and sizes (Taube, 1993). Upon retrieving the shattered bones, the God *Quetzalcoatl* took them to *Cihuacoatl* (the Snake Woman) who "ground them [bones] like cornmeal into a fine powder, which she poured into a pot" (Ferguson, 2000, p. 34). One by one, the Gods came and pierced their bodies and allowed their blood to drip onto to the "bonemeal" (Ferguson, 2000, p. 34). Thus the new human beings were formed from a mixture of the bones from their ancestors and the blood of their Gods.

View of Time

The Aztec religion was also centered on the calculation of time. In fact, Aztec/Mexica society used two calendars: 1) a solar calendar consisting of 365 days called the *xiuhpohualli*, and 2) the sacred calendar referred to as the *tonalpohualli*. The solar calendar was used to determine the best times to prepare and cultivate the land in order to have successful harvesting seasons. The sacred calendar consisted of 260 days. Each day was named by using a combination of 23 signs followed by a number from 1–13. This calendar was used for religious holidays as well as a way to determine the names given to children. Names were chosen based on the number and sign of the day that individuals were born. According to Aztec spiritual beliefs, the name of a child could determine whether their fate would be good, bad, or neutral. However, a "bad" fate could be prevented by postponing bathing and by having an Aztec priest conduct a ritual. In such cases, the child could be named after a date with a more auspicious fate (Davies, 2001; Taube, 1993). Many of these practices were later combined with those imposed by the Spaniards and brought by the Africans, creating a rich and unique Mexican culture.

Perspectives on Death and the Afterlife

The Aztecs did not see death as a final point, but rather as a transition into a different sphere of the universe. According to their religious beliefs, the way in which a person died was more important than how that individual had lived his or her life when determining whether the deceased would go into the heavens or the underworld. Since the Gods sacrificed themselves to create the world, the Aztecs believed that people would go to the heavens only if they sacrificed themselves or were sacrificed to the Gods. For instance, a person who died from natural causes would not go to the heavens and instead would go the *Mictlan* (i.e., the underworld; Furst, 1995; López, 1980). Upon their deaths, the remains of individuals who died of natural causes would be carefully prepared for their long journey by being dressed in paper vestments and wrapped in a cloth bundle. The remains were then cremated along with a dog, who was believed to serve as the guide to the *Mictlan*. There was another destination called *Tlalocan* or the afterworld (the paradise of the God of rain and water) for individuals who had died from particular diseases (e.g., gout) or those who died as a result of lightning or drowning (Furst, 1995; López, 1980). *Tlalocan* was believed to be a place of eternal spring and wealth; people making the journey there were not cremated, but were instead buried whole with images of Gods.

The last destination was reserved for people who had sacrificed themselves to the Gods, warriors who had died in battle or women who had died while giving birth. It was believed that the souls of these individuals would follow the sun to the heavens. In preparation for their journey, the bodies of the deceased were burned in warrior bundles with butterflies signifying their courageous souls. Contrary to *Mictlan* (underworld) and *Tlalocan* (afterworld), the privilege of spending eternity in the heavens was related not only to the manner in which one had died but also to how one had lived on earth. For the Aztecs, the virtues of bravery and self-sacrifice were essential to the survival and success of the entire human species (Furst, 1995; López, 1980). These traditional cultural values rooted in the Aztec culture can be clearly observed today among their descendants. For instance, the Mexican culture continues to place a strong emphasis on the need to sacrifice oneself for the well-being of one's family and community and showing bravery and valor even under the most difficult circumstances (e.g., disease, immigration, experiences of racial discrimination).

The Day of the Dead

The Aztecs honored and celebrated the dead with a series of rituals that lasted an entire month. Such celebrations took place during the ninth month of the solar calendar. The month-long celebrations, which were presided by *Mictecacihuatl* (the Goddess of death), included elaborate rituals with offerings of food and drink for the spirits of the dead, who were believed to be coming back from the afterlife to visit the loved ones they had left on the earth. Contrary to the Spaniards who feared death, the Aztecs celebrated and embraced death. Thus it is of no surprise that the conquistadors, who were horrified by the rituals of the Day of the Dead and perceived its celebration as sacrilegious and barbaric, prohibited the Aztecs/Mexica from carrying out these spiritual rituals. In an attempt to maintain their tradition, the Aztecs/Mexica moved the Day of the Dead to coincide with the Catholic holidays of All Saints Day and All Souls' Day (November 1st and 2nd). They also added Catholic elements such as prayers and masses to the Day of the Dead rituals.

Contemporary celebrations of the Day of the Dead include elements grounded in Aztec traditions, such as beautifully decorated offerings (*ofrendas*) built to commemorate the life of the spirits of the dead who come back from the afterlife to visit their families. Traditional *ofrendas* can be vertically built with two, three, or seven levels. *Ofrendas* with two levels represent the division between the earth and the heavens. Those built with three levels signify the heavens, the earth, and the underworld, and *ofrendas* with seven levels represent the seven steps individuals must travel through to reach the heavens or the underworld. In addition to the specific levels, *ofrendas* often include common elements such as the favorite foods and drinks of the deceased; *flores de cempasuchil* (marigold flowers) whose strong essence and bright colors are believed to attract the spirits of the dead; a bowl with clean water, soap, and a towel for the spirits to clean themselves after their long and trying journey from the afterlife; and items representing the four elements: fire (represented with candles which light the spirits' journey), air (symbolized with crepe paper cutouts/*papel picado*), earth (exemplified by fruits and grains), and water (represented in the drinks and clean water).

Besides the *ofrendas*, Mexicans prepare for the celebration of the Day of the Dead by cleaning the graves of their deceased loved ones a day or two before the actual holiday. On the Day of the Dead (November 1 for children and November 2 for adults), people visit the graveyards and decorate them with marigolds and bring food, drinks, and music. They spend the night at the cemetery singing, praying, and waiting for the dead to come back to earth. For centuries, the tradition of the Day of the Dead has allowed Mexicans to see and understand death as an unavoidable transition of the physical body, which is not to be feared but instead celebrated with dignity and reverence. Rituals related to the Day of the Dead further serve to provide *consuelo* (comfort) to Mexicans who have lost a loved one by maintaining the dead alive as an integral and active member of the family and community through their *consejos* (advice) dreams, visits, memories, and expectations, as well as through the rituals conducted in their honor (religious and spiritual services for the deceased, offering of their favorite food, music, poetry, books, flowers, and scents). These traditions have been adopted and are practiced by many other Latino/a groups today in contemporary times.

The Aztec Legacy

Many elements of the rich Aztec ancestral civilization survived despite the Spaniards explicit attempt to eradicate their culture. For instance, the Aztec experienced the burning and destruction of their codices by the Spaniards. The Indigenous people were also prohibited from practicing their traditions (e.g., Day of the Dead). Nonetheless, the legacy left by the Aztec can be readily observed in many aspects of contemporary Mexican culture and has broadly influenced society at large, including the arts, sciences, and culinary practices. For instance, in the sciences, the Aztec had a superior knowledge of math, medical care, public health, astronomy, farming, and architecture (Padilla, 1984; Thomas, 2004). They had an in-depth knowledge of farming and learned to build *chinampas* (small artificial islands where crops could be grown above the waterline in a muddy environment) as a way to maximize their resources and space.

They were also experts in the healing properties of many plants and herbs native to the region where they lived, as well as plants and herbs imported from locations that were hundreds of miles away (e.g., South America). Botanical gardens were used to develop complex systems of plant classification and research to examine their medicinal properties (Keoke & Porterfield, 2001). Additionally, the Aztec/Mexica developed intricate and highly effective sewage disposal systems. They also built magnificent and detailed structures using *tezontle* (a light and porous volcanic rock that is mixed with rocks and pebbles). Structures and buildings made with *tezontle* were strong and durable, yet light in weight, which enabled temperature to be regulated (e.g., conserving warmth during winter months and coolness during the summers; Saragoza, 2012).

In the arts, the Aztec/Mexica are known as skilled musicians and dancers using a variety of native Mexican instruments such as the *huehuetl* (a single-headed cylindrical upright drum played with bare hands), *teponaztli* (log drum), and different types of flutes known as *axayacatl* and *huilacapitztli* (Cresson, 1883; Gallop, 1939). With regard to their culinary practices, traditional Aztec/Mexica foods include chocolate, vanilla, avocados, tomatoes, and corn, all of which are staples of the Mexican diet (Long-Solis & Vargas, 2005; Padilla, 1984; Schendel, 1968). During colonization, these foods were appropriated by the Spaniards and imported to Europe, becoming popular worldwide soon thereafter. In the area of education, the Aztec/Mexica were one of the first civilizations to have mandatory education for everyone, a practice that has become universal among developed countries. Lastly, in the area of mental health, the Aztecs/Mexicas demonstrated in-depth and advanced (for their time) comprehension of the human psyche. They divided psychopathology into passive (*tlahuiliscayotl*) and active (*xolopeyotl*) insanity, where *tonalpouhqui* (healers) provided mental health treatments in ways that are similar to what is known as talk therapy, counseling, or psychotherapy (Padilla, 1984; Schendel, 1968).

For Latinos/as of Mexican descent in the U.S., the legacy of the Aztecs can serve as a counternarrative to the negative images often portrayed in the media about people from this ethnic background, particularly those of Indigenous heritage. In such portrayals, Indigenous Mexicans are often depicted as unintelligent, lazy, and aggressive, with their culture often portrayed as primitive "third" or "developing" world. Contrary to these harming and oppressive stereotypes, the history of the Aztecs demonstrates that Indigenous Mexicans are the descendants of one of the most impressive, advanced, and rich cultures in history. Learning about their collective group history can help Mexican people be proud of their roots and ancestors who were great scientists, mathematicians, and astronomers, as well as prodigious artists, musicians, healers, and cooks whose traditional cuisine includes some of the most delectable and heavenly flavors Mother Earth has to offer.

The Maya

One of the most magnificent and intriguing civilizations known to humankind originating in the American continent are the Maya who reached high levels of sophistication and advancement. The Maya civilization prospered in particular geographical areas south of Mexico, Guatemala, Belize, and

Honduras that are not optimal for the establishment of an empire (Ferguson, 2000; Meier & Ribera, 1993). Nonetheless, through their creativity and innovation they were able to establish a powerful empire in the middle of tropical rain forests, which is a notable accomplishment given that most great civilizations of that time were built in regions with drier climates, where it was easier to manage natural resources (e.g., through irrigation). The Maya people were also skillful at learning how to utilize the natural resources available to them such as limestone (used for construction), obsidian (volcanic rock used for tools), jade and quetzal feathers (used for decorations, garments, accessories), and marine shells (used as trumpets). In addition to mastering their physical environment, the Maya are most well known for their advances in mathematics, astrology, astronomy, and architecture. For instance, they are thought to be the first civilization to utilize the concept of zero; they also developed their own writing system consisting of logographs to signify phonemic sounds and semantic symbols (Ferguson, 2000; Meier & Ribera, 1993). Their architectural skills are observed in the magnificent cities they built for ceremonial government, trade, and learning centers that were linked by a complex road system. Thus it is of no surprise that on the American continent, the Maya is thought to have developed one of the most advanced civilizations (Ferguson, 2000; Meier & Ribera, 1993).

Origins

Although precise information regarding the origin of the Indigenous people who would later be called the Maya is not available, it is hypothesized that they began to settle in the Yucatan Peninsula of Mexico between 2600 BC and 1800 BC. This civilization developed within the geographical area known as Mesoamerica, which covers a region that spreads from Northern Mexico southward into Central America (Hammond, 2000). More specifically, the Maya were centered in the geographical region of what today is considered southeast Mexico, including the Yucatan Peninsula, parts of the states of Tabasco and Chiapas, as well as the countries of Guatemala, Belize, and the western part of Honduras and El Salvador. Within this area, the Maya were located in three separate subareas with diverse environmental and cultural differences: 1) the northern Maya, who lived in the lowlands of the Yucatan Peninsula; 2) the southern Maya, who were located in the lowlands of the Peten district of northern Guatemala, and adjacent portions of Mexico, Belize, and western Honduras; and 3) the southern Maya of the highlands, who were situated in the mountainous regions of Guatemala (Hammond, 2000). The Maya built entire cities and sumptuous pyramids in these regions without any help from draft animals or wheeled carts. Given the complex and extensive Maya history, scholars have divided the Maya civilization into three main periods known as the 1) *Preclassic/ Formative*, 2) *Classic*, and 3) *Postclassic* periods, which are briefly reviewed in the following section.

*An Empire Emerging: The Early Maya of the
Preclassic/Formative Period*

The earliest Maya settlements date back to approximately 1800 BC, in what
is known as the *Preclassic* or formative period. During this period, the Maya
were primarily farmers who cultivated corn, fruits, cacao, squash, and cassava (yuca roots). Their social organization was simple and centered on
family activities revolving around the acquisition of goods necessary for survival (Mesoamerican Research Center, 2010). As the population began to
expand, the Maya civilization became more complex with evidence of public architecture. Toward the end of the *Preclassic* period, the Maya began
to build monuments, pyramids, and cities, including the splendid city of
Mirador located in northern Peten, Guatemala (Hammond, 2000; Mesoamerican Research Center, 2010).

*The Beginning Collapse of a Flourishing Empire:
The Maya of the Classic Period*

The *Classic* period, also known as the Golden Age of the Empire, is believed
to have started around 250 AD. During this period, the Maya attained the
greatest level of sophistication (Hammond, 2000; Mesoamerican Research
Center, 2010). Some of the developmental characteristics of this era include
unique writing and calendar systems, polychrome ceramic work, corbelled
vault architecture, and major public architecture, including pyramids, monuments, palaces, and ball courts (Hammond, 2000; Mesoamerican Research
Center, 2010). As of today's date, the first stone inscriptions carved using
hieroglyphics were found from this era (Hammond, 2000). In the *Classic*
period, the Maya civilization grew to include approximately 40 magnificent
cities and complex centers, such as Copan, Palenque, and Tikal, which has
pyramid temples that are more than 200 feet high. The typical prototype
of a *Classic* Maya city included a central square or plaza, palaces, temples,
pyramids, and ball courts. Characteristic of many of the temples and palaces built during this era is a stepped pyramid shape adorned with elaborate inscriptions (Hammond, 2000). At the beginning of the *Classic* period,
each of these cities had populations ranging between 5,000 and 50,000. At
its peak, the Maya population is estimated to have reached approximately
2 million individuals (Hammond, 2000).

The beginning of the *Classic* era is known as a time of expansion and
prosperity; however, between the late 8th and 9th centuries, the Maya experienced a series of changes that led to a massive exodus of people from the
cities in the southern lowland region (Nalda, 2010). This exodus eventually
resulted in the collapse of the Maya Empire. There are many theories regarding the reasons leading to the collapse of the Maya Empire. For instance,
scholars have pointed to a number of causes, including the exhaustion of
natural resources by overpopulation, overuse of land, catastrophic climate

changes that produced extreme drought, a breakdown in alliances, decline in trade between cities and states, and/or the increase of interstate conflict resulting in endemic warfare (Coe, 1999; Ferguson, 2000; Hammond, 2000; Stuart & Swanson, 1992). Although no one theory is universally supported as a main contributor to the collapse of the region, historians agree that the changes experienced by the Maya of the southern lowlands were of catastrophic proportions (Nalda, 2010). Such changes led to the rapid abandonment (within a period of 50–100 years) of cities with the largest populations (Hammond, 2000; Nalda, 2010). Following this period, a shift of activities was made to northern cities of Chichén Itzá and Uxmal (Martin & Grube, 2000). These cities continued to prosper long after the southern lowland area had completely decimated (Becker, 2004).

Struggling for Survival: The Maya of the Post-classic Period

The historic time following the collapse and abandonment of the cities in the southern lowland region is known as the *Post-classic* period. This period begins with a shift of activity from southern to northern cities. The *Post-classic* period concludes with the greatest disaster ever experienced by the Indigenous people of the Americas: the arrival of the Spanish conquistadors (Ferguson, 2000; Hammond, 2000). Although the prominence of the Maya Empire had declined by the *Post-classic* period, cities located in the highlands of the Yucatan Peninsula such as Chichén Itzá, Uxmal, and Mayapan continued to prosper during this time (Hammond, 2000). For instance, the city Chichén Itzá was built in the *Post-classic* era. Chichén Itzá is considered to be one the greatest and most opulent cities ever built by the Maya and is listed as a World Heritage Site according to the United Nations Educational, Scientific, and Cultural Organization. This city is home to the great Pyramid of Kukulkan, one of the most prominent and magnificent historical buildings of the world (Ferguson, 2000; Hammond, 2000). The pyramid is 30 meters tall or 98.4 feet high, and it was designed to represent specific information on the Mayan calendar. For instance, it contains 365 steps, one for each day of the calendar, with 91 steps in each of the four stairways, except the northern side, which consists of 92 steps. The Pyramid of Kukulkan was built with such geographical precision that twice a year, during the spring and fall equinoxes, triangular shadows from the different levels cast onto the sides of the pyramid giving the illusion that, as the sun sets, a giant snake descends its steps. This event represents the descent of the God *Kukulcan* (the feathered serpent) to whom the pyramid is dedicated (Hammond, 2000; Nalda, 2010). Despite their opulence, the Maya cities of the *Post-classic* period eventually had the same destiny as those of the earlier eras. In fact, it is estimated that by the year 1448, the city of Mayapan had been abandoned due to social and environmental changes similar to those experienced by the Maya of the southern lowlands (Hammond, 2000; Nalda, 2010). The fall of Mayapan was followed by a long period of warfare that ended just before the arrival of the Spaniards. Thus by the time the Spaniards arrived in the Americas, the Maya had abandoned their grand cities and were living in small agricultural villages.

Social Organization

The organization of the Maya social structure at the peak of the civilization included a king or emperor, who was also known as the *Kuhul ajaw* (the holy lord) who was situated at the top of the Maya's system of stratification. The *Kuhul ajaw* was considered to be related to the sun God and adhere to a hereditary succession (Hammond, 2000; Nalda, 2010). Given their strategic placement between the Gods and humans, emperors served as mediators and representatives of humanity to the creators. Thus the *Kuhul ajaw* was responsible for performing elaborate religious ceremonies and rituals characteristic of the Maya culture and spiritual beliefs. In addition to their spiritual duties, they were also in charge of more mundane governmental activities such as the imposition of taxes, supervision of justice, foreign relations, and decisions regarding warfare (Hammond, 2000; Nalda, 2010). The *Kuhul ajaw* was assisted by a council of priests and nobles, followed by commoners who made up approximately 90% of Mayan civilization. Commoners were individuals not born from noble families and thus had a nonelite status (Marcus, 2004); however, they were required to pay tribute to the elite (Foias, 2014). The commoners included individuals engaged in the production of food and woods consumed (e.g., farmers, craftsmen) by the elite (Foster, 2002; Masson & Peraza Lope, 2004).

Spirituality

The Maya held deep religious polytheistic convictions, and religion permeated all aspects of their life. For instance, laws were based on religious principles and the tribute (taxes) paid by members of the empire was considered religious offerings. Formal education was established to predominantly train priests. They worshiped Gods related to nature (i.e., *Kinich Ahau*, Deity of the Sun; *Ix Chel*, the Goddess of the Moon); however, their main God was *Itzam Na* (also known as Iguana House), the creator and farmer of the universe. Although much has been written about religious rituals practiced by the Maya, including human sacrifice and bloodletting, this section underscores other aspects of Maya history and spirituality, which are not referenced as often. For instance, an interesting aspect of Maya religion included the reverence and respect of their ancestors. In fact, important Maya cities such as Tikal and Palenque built several pyramids over the burials of rulers (Hammond, 2000). Another important value permeating throughout the Maya religion was the belief that humans and animals were equally sacred and deserving of respect and dignity. Although humans and animals were viewed as equal, the serpent was thought to be the most sacred of all animals given that the God *Kukulan* was represented by this one creature. Interestingly, the traditional cultural values held by the Maya (e.g., respect, dignity) are principles that are easily observed today among their descendants. These cultural values have also influenced contemporary Mexican and Central American culture where individuals are raised to demonstrate a strong regard and deference to their ancestors and elders, coupled with having a strong connection with and respect for all living animals.

Maya Legacy

The Maya developed one of the most advanced, sophisticated, and complex preindustrial civilizations of their era. They were skilled engineers and architects who produced a vast array of incredible pyramids, buildings, and structures and have left an extensive architectural legacy.

They were also gifted artistic sculptors, painters, and potters. However, the Maya are most well known for being sophisticated scientists with advanced knowledge of astronomy. For instance, one of their greatest advances in the sciences was their complex, yet accurate calendar, which was capable of recording lunar and solar cycles, including the eclipses and movements of the planets. They used the calendar system to keep track of important dates as well as for astronomical discoveries. Additionally, they were advanced mathematicians who invented the concept of zero well before other civilizations (Nalda, 2010). The Maya were also pioneers in the area of language. For instance, they developed a written language consisting of an intricate and sophisticated writing system, inclusive of logographs used to signify phonemic syllables and semantic symbols (Sharer & Traxler, 2006). Many of their writings have been found in buildings as well as in their books (codices), which were made from paper created from tree bark (Ferguson, 2000; Meier & Ribera, 1993).

Overall, the vast accomplishments made by the Maya can serve as a reminder for Latinos/as about the surmountable possibilities that exist when a group of people is determined to overcome adversities. Latinos/as come from a legacy of people who created one of the most impressive civilizations, which included advanced mathematicians and scientists who thrived in an environment often viewed and experienced as dangerous and inhospitable. Their perseverance, strengths, and abilities can serve as a source of inspiration to new generations of Latinos/as who may feel overwhelmed by the challenges they face as members of a cultural and racial minority group, particularly in foreign lands. It is indeed important for Latinos/as to know or be reminded that they come from a long legacy of adaptable, determined, and hardworking people who invented concepts and ideas that have benefited humanity as a whole (e.g., concept of zero, design and construction of complex pyramids, prediction of solar events without the help of the type of technological advances available to scientists today).

The Inka   *Chile/peru -Andes*
1300 - 1572

The Inka is another extraordinary empire that marked the history of Latin America; they flourished and ruled many parts of South America. Although the name Inka is the most common term used when referring to this empire, *Tawantinsuyu* or the *Four Regions*, is the name the people of this civilization gave to themselves. The Inka are well known for their immense wealth, advanced architecture, and sophisticated metallurgical skills, as well as their remarkable ability to thrive at very high altitudes (Davies, 1995).

The Inka Empire encompassed 2,500 miles north along the high mountains of the Andes, reaching from what is known today as Colombia to Chile and west from the arid lands of the Atacama Desert to the rain forest of the Amazon. The Inka civilization included large portions of western South America, including Peru, Ecuador, eastern and south central Bolivia, northwest Argentina, north central Chile, and southern Colombia. The Inka Empire was so immense that its population peaked at approximately 10 million people. It is believed that they were the largest pre-Columbian empire, the largest native nation to have existed in the western hemisphere, and the largest in the world at that time (Davies, 1995; Ferguson, 2000).

Origins

Knowledge regarding the Inka's history and origin comes from a variety of sources, including hand-painted pottery and ceramics, stone carvings, and narratives produced by the Spanish chronicles during colonization. The Inkas spoke the *Quechua* language, but they did not develop a system of writing; instead, they used *quipu*, a method consisting of a cord with different color strings and lengths, which was used to record important statistical information such as troops, supplies, population data, and agricultural inventories (Davies, 1995; Ferguson, 2000). Because of the lack of written information available regarding the Inka, their history has been chronicled by the Spaniards (Davies, 1995). For instance, a Spanish conquistador named Cieza de León, who arrived in Peru in 1547 and traveled extensively throughout the country, documented and recorded the stories that were shared with him by the natives. His work was published in 1553 and 1554 and it is known as the *Crónica del Perú*. Another Spaniard, Juan de Bentazos, who "married" (Indigenous women were often raped and forced into marriages with Spaniards) the daughter of Atahualpa, the Inka emperor, was asked by the viceroy of Peru (person appointed by the Spanish crown to rule Peru) to write the history of the Inkas, which he completed in 1557 (Davies, 1995). The volume produced by Bentazos was published under the title *Suma y Narracion de los Incas*. Unfortunately, given the devastation of the Inkas and its people during colonization, the information that remains to recount the richness of this glorious empire are the chronicles written by the very people who destroyed it. Thus in reading and trying to understand the history of the Inkas, it is important to keep in mind that much of what we know about their history, culture, and spirituality comes from the perspective of the colonizers (Davies, 1995; Ferguson, 2000; Jones, 2012).

Based on the available records, the Inka originate from a noble family, which ruled Cuzco and a small surrounding area around 1200 AD. The term Inka originally referred to the members of this royal family along with their approximately 40,000 descendants. Nonetheless, in contemporary times, the term has been applied to all people who eventually became part of the empire (Davies, 1995; Jones, 2012). The original Inka began to gain power in the early 13th century; however, their empire was not solidified until 1438 AD, when the ninth Inka emperor (known as Sapa) Pachacuti decided to conquer the regions around Cuzco and consolidate their cultures into one empire. He subsequently defeated the invasion of another tribe known as the Chancas. Following the defeat of the Chancas, Pachacuti expanded the Inka Empire by conquering other neighboring regions and tribes. The unification of the Inka into what became known as *The Four United Quarters* was continued by his son Topa Inka Yupanqui and his grandson Huayna Capac (Davies, 1995; Jones, 2012). The tribes conquered by the Inkas experienced forced labor and the appropriation of their resources. For instance, individuals from the conquered tribes were required to pay tribute (taxes) to the empire by working on a variety of construction projects (e.g., building of roads, terraces, irrigation canals, temples, and fortresses). Although gold and silver were plentiful, these metals were used for aesthetics (e.g., accessories) and had spiritual but no monetary value. Cuzco, the capital of the Inka Empire and home to the center of emperors, eventually became the richest city in the Americas (Davies, 1995; Jones, 2012).

Social Organization

In the Inka system of stratification, the Sapa Inka (emperor) and his wives occupied the privileged top. The emperor was regarded as the son of Inti (the Sun God) and as such was believed to be sacred. The Sapa Inka lived in Cuzco, the center of religious and social life. Second to the top in the system of stratification were the nobility. The nobles were highly educated, talented, and considered gifted members of the civilization; their skills were seen as pivotal to the success of the empire (Davies, 1995; Jones, 2012; Rostworowski de Diez Canseco, 1999). Third to the top were the high priest and the army commander in chief who were in charge of performing rituals and protecting the empire from invasion. Fourth to the top were the regional army commanders or the *Four Apus* who were then followed by the temple priests, architects, administrators, and army generals. At the next level in the system of stratification were the artisans, musicians, army captains, and the *quipucamayoc* (accountants). The sorcerers, farmers, herding families, and soldiers occupied the bottom of the system (Davies, 1995; Jones, 2012; Rostworowski de Diez Canseco, 1999).

Time

Although knowledge of the Inka calendar is limited, some scholars agree that they had two calendars based on their observations of the sun, the moon, and their relationship to the stars (Mason, 1988; Davies, 1995; Jones, 2012). The first was the sun or daytime calendar. This calendar had 365 days divided into 12 months with 30 days in each. Each month had its own festival, with a five-day celebration at the end of the year with each new year beginning in December. This calendar was used for activities related to economics, such as agriculture, mining, and construction. The second was the nighttime or lunar calendar, which had 328 days divided into 12 months with 27 1/3 nights each. This calendar was used to mark celebrations and festivals. The year began in June and ended on the first full moon after the June solstice (Davies, 1995; Jones, 2012; Rostworowski de Diez Canseco, 1999).

Education

In the Inka Empire, education was divided into two levels: a) education for the ruling class and b) education for the commoners. The nobility began their education at the age of 13, which was provided by *Amawtakuna* (philosopher-scholars). They were taught a number of subjects, including religion, history, government, moral norms, and military techniques. The nobility were also trained to develop an in-depth understanding of the *quipu*. Their education was formally complete after they passed formal examinations at the age of 19. During their formal graduation ceremony, they were given a *wara* (special kind of underwear), which symbolized their maturity. Members of the general population did not have access to formal education; instead, their elders taught them practical skills necessary for survival. These skills included agriculture, hunting, fishing, and stonework, as well as arts, religion, and morality. The Inka moral code of conduct included three mandates: do not steal, do not lie, and do not be lazy (Davies, 1995; Jones, 2012; Rostworowski de Diez Canseco, 1999).

Spirituality

The Inka were deeply religious people who practiced several different polytheistic religions that were unified by the worshiping of *Pachamama* and *Viracocha*. Faith permeated every aspect of their lives. For instance, they believed in reincarnation; thus, they saved their nail clippings, hair cuttings, and their teeth for use upon their return back to earth (Davies, 1995; Ferguson, 2000).

The Inka Gods were categorized into three groups. The first group included deities connected to the *Hannah Pacha* or to the sky such as *Inti* (the Sun God) and *Mama Quilla* (the Moon Goddess). The second group included Gods that occupied the *Uku Pacha* or inner world, which included *Supay* (the God of Death). The final group of Gods was composed of those that were connected to *Cay Pacha* or the center of the earth where humans resided. These Gods included *Pachamama* (the Earth Goddess), *Mamacocha* (the Sea Goddess), and *Kanopa* (the God of Pregnancy). The Inkas also believed natural places and some inanimate objects held divine energy, which they viewed as deities they called *Huacas*. Thus, besides their Gods and Goddesses, the Inka worshiped a number of *Huacas*, including mountaintops, battlefields, caves, springs, and the like. Through prayers and offerings, the Inka priests would pray to the *Huacas* for advice and assistance (Davies, 1995; de Diez Canseco, 1999; Ferguson, 2000; Jones, 2012).

Inti Raymi, the holiday dedicated to worshiping and celebrating *Inti* (the Sun God), was the most important, magnificent, and spectacular religious ceremony of the Inka Empire. *Inti Raymi* was celebrated on the winter solstice of the Southern Hemisphere (on the twenty-first of June of every year) in the main plaza of Cuzco. *Inti Raymi* consisted of a series of complex rituals that were performed to celebrate *Inti* and also to ask him for protection. The rituals typically began before dawn on June 21st and continued throughout the day. The day ended with a glorious celebration that included plenty of *chicha* (a drink derived from maize/corn), food, music, and entertainment. *Inti Raymi* is one of the few Inka holidays that survived colonization, and it continues to be celebrated every year in Cuzco, Peru. Actors wearing traditional Inka clothing and recreating traditional rituals of this holiday carry out the traditional festivities in contemporary times (Jones, 2012; Rostworowski de Diez Canseco, 1999).

Creation of the World

According to the Inka religion, the God *Con Ticci Viracocha Pachayachaic*, also known as "the teacher of the world" emerged from Lake Titicaca to bring life to the earth. In order to fill the empty world with creatures, *Viracocha* created a group of giants. These giants soon made *Viracocha* so angry that he turned them into stone and then sent an *unu Pachacuti* (great flood) to drown everything he had created. *Viracocha* then began working again, this time he called on the Sun, the Moon, and the Stars, who had been sleeping on the *Island of the Sun* on Lake Titicaca, and strategically gave each of them a particular place and time in the heavens (Ferguson, 2000).

However, according to the Inka's legend, the Sun became jealous of the Moon whose face was brighter than his. To dim her brilliance, the Sun then threw a handful of ashes onto the Moon's face. The Inka believe this is the reason why the Moon has a cloudy surface when viewed from earth. As *Viracocha* continued creating the new world, he went by the shores of Lake Titicaca, picked up some clay, and began to mold the first men and women out of the mud from the lake.

He then painted the first men and women with different dresses and styles as a way to mark their nations of origin. All the clay people were sent to earth by *Viracocha* to wait for the call to life with the exception of two individuals.

Imaymana Viracocha and *Tocapo Viracocha* were the names of the two clay individuals whom *Viracocha* kept. They helped him finish the creation of the world. Eventually, the three *Viracochas* (*Con Ticci, Imaymana*, and *Tocapo*) came to the earth and started calling the clay people waiting on earth. They named each waiting person after the nations to which they would belong. It is believed that at the command of the three *Viracochas*, people came to life by blinking into the light (Ferguson, 2000). Before returning to the oceans, the creator, *Con Ticci Viracocha Pachayachaic*, ordered a new group of people to rise from Cuzco, this new group would be the Inka (Ferguson, 2000; Jones, 2012).

Inka Legacy

The legacy of the Inka is alive today through their astonishing and spectacular engineering and architectural skills observed in the structures and road systems they built. Their advanced mastery of metallurgy, the beautiful and elegant works of art they produced, and their bewildering ability to adapt, live, and thrive at very high altitudes continue to impress historians in contemporary times. The Inka possessed advanced and innovative engineering and architectural skills. For instance, they built a 14,000-mile system of roads, which were used to create fast and reliable modes of transportation, which facilitated communication between people living in the mountains and those residing in the lowland desert areas. They paved the roads with flat stones and built stone walls around them as a way to prevent people from falling off the cliffs. Given the high altitudes at which these roads were built and the limitations posed by the lack of contemporary tools and technology, the construction of these roads is considered a significant accomplishment. Interestingly, these roads were so well-built that they continue to be used today. Thus it is clear that their design and construction required incredible levels of innovation, resourcefulness, and determination.

In addition to roads, the Inka built extravagant cities, fortresses, bridges, aqueducts, and irrigation channels. It is important that Latino/a students studying engineering in U.S. universities become knowledgeable of the many contributions of the Inka, given that most training programs describe engineering as originating in European countries. The Inka were also ingenious metalsmiths with sophisticated skills and knowledge of metallurgy. Their intricate metal work with gold, silver, and copper is often described as polished and elegant. Overall, the most important legacy provided by the Inka includes their incredible ability to imagine, design, and carry out impossible goals. Their contemporary descendants can be proud of carrying in their bloodline the legacy of a determined, ingenious, and talented group of people who developed the largest and wealthiest empire in the pre-Hispanic history of the Americas.

The Tainos and Caribs

Scholars posit that the Caribbean was home to fascinating ancestral civilizations whose history has shaped the identity of their descendants (Beckles & Shepherd, 2004). Most researchers discuss that by the time the Spaniards arrived, the Caribbean islands were home to approximately 5 to 13 million ethnically diverse groups (Beckles & Shepherd, 2004) that included the Ciboney, the Tainos, and the Caribs. Although each of these three ethnic groups were different to some extent, they have all been described as being ingenious, hardworking, and joyful people.

The history of the Indigenous people from the Caribbean is both intriguing and complex. The information available on this group of people predominantly comes from archaeological studies, accounts documented by the Spaniards, and, to a lesser extent, the oral tradition and written records of the Indigenous people themselves. Most of what is known about the Indigenous people from the Caribbean comes from the biased perspective of the same people who annihilated the Tainos and attempted to destroy their culture; thus their observations were likely misinterpreted. The limitations posed by the sources of information available regarding the Indigenous people from the Caribbean are important to consider as readers learn about the origin, social organization, spirituality, and overall legacy of these impressive people.

Origin

The cultural and historical origins of the Native Caribbean people are believed to date back to the times of other well-known civilizations, such as ancient Egypt and classic Greek. Considerable anthropological and archaeological research has sought to establish the precise origins and time of the Caribbean Indigenous people (Beckles & Shepherd, 2004). Nonetheless, most scholars agree today that the pillars of Caribbean culture were established by three distinct ethnic groups known as the Ciboney, Taino (also referred by some as the *Arawaks*), and the Carib (also referred at times as the *Kalinago*). Archaeological excavations suggest that the first human settlement found in the islands of the Caribbean dates as far back as 5000–3000 BC. Evidence suggests that people settled in the island of Cuba around 2050 BC, and community development in Santo Domingo was established around 5000 BC. (Beckles & Shepherd, 2004). Anthropologists and historians posit that the people who first settled in the Caribbean islands, known as the Ciboney, had traveled there from Central America and South America. The Ciboney had a simple social organization that did not use agriculture or farming and relied mainly on hunting, fishing, and gathering. Around 1000 BC, another group known as the Tainos, who spoke the Arawak language, joined the Ciboney. The Tainos, who had a more complex civilization that included innovative systems of agriculture and social organization, are believed to have traveled to the Caribbean from

Venezuela in South America. The third ethnic group of the Caribbean is the Caribs (*Kalinago*), speakers of the Cariban language who are known for being skilled warriors and seafarers. Of these three cultural groups, the Tainos were the largest and most complex, and they were the ones most studied by historians and archaeologists (Beckles & Shepherd, 2004). Thus the remainder of this section concentrates on this group. The term Taino in the Arawak language means "good" or "noble" (Hulme, 1986); this name certainly resembles the character of the Taino people who are described as peaceful and generous. They are believed to be descendants of the Saladoid people who traveled from the Orinoco drainage and river systems of South America to the Antilles and Puerto Rico.

Social Organization

The Tainos were a highly developed hierarchical civilization, organized by a complex matrilineal descent system (Hopper, 2008). Inheritance of *Zemis* (physical sculptural representation of Gods), ranks, and succession to the office of chief, were determined through female lineage (Keegan, 1997). Taino society was divided by different *caciquats* or kingdoms that were governed by a *cacique* (chief), a title held by both men and women. Within the Taino social structure, the *cacique* played numerous roles, such as that of the priest, healer, and administrator. Each *caciquat* was formed of approximately 2,000 residents, who lived in polygamous households. The *cacique* was permitted to have more wives than the other men of the chiefdom as long as he could provide for them (Keegan, 1997). Each chiefdom was further divided into *sub-caciquats* with *sub-caciques* who were not paid for her/his position, but held a position of high honor within the Tainos.

Following the birth of a baby, Tainos would perform a naming ritual where the child would be pronounced as a Taino and a human being (Keegan, 1997). In this system, new babies would automatically belong to the matriclan where they were socialized into the norms and customs of their *caciquats*. Various ritual ceremonies, such as haircutting were performed to mark the passage from childhood into adulthood. Ultimately, marriage was the ceremony that marked the entry into full adulthood. Male commoners in Taino culture were required to compensate the wife's lineage by providing what is referred to as "bride-service," where the man worked for several years for his in-laws. Typically, bride-service ended when the couple had their first child and contributed a new member to the *caciquat*. Males of the *nitaino* (elite class) would bypass bride-service by providing the wife's family with payments and goods.

Spirituality

Similar to other civilizations from the Americas, the Tainos were deeply religious people who practiced a polytheistic religion worshiping a number of Gods and Spirits. They had two main Gods, *Yucahu* (Lord of cassava and the sea) and *Atabey* (the Goddess of fresh water and human fertility). *Atabey* was considered the Supreme Goddess in the Taino faith and was celebrated at sumptuous annual festivals. The Gods were physically represented by sculptures made of wood, stone, bone, shell, clay, and cotton (*Zemis*). They were in charge of various functions of the universe and were worshiped in lavish ceremonies held by the *caciques*. In these elaborate ceremonies, people wore a special type of attire accompanied with feathers and shells, which they used to decorate their bodies from their knees to their feet. In addition, they used body paint to adorn their faces, arms, and torsos. While ceremonial beating of drums played in the background, carved figures were presented to the *Zemi* by the *cacique*. Attendees at these ceremonies would use a stick to induce vomiting as a way of purifying their bodies and spirits. Purification was followed by the consumption of sacred bread prepared by women, which the Taino people believed held special powers that would protect them. Finally, new generations would learn about their history through songs, with lyrics describing the collective heroic narrative of their village. In addition to these annual festivities, the Tainos also had complex rituals that were held to mark developmental stages and transitions (e.g., birth, death, marriage, harvest).

Similar to other Indigenous groups, the Tainos did not see death as the end, as extinction, or as punishment. Instead, according to their faith, death was a transitional period from one kind of existence to another. They believed that after death, the deceased would go to a place called *Coabay* (Pané, 1999) where they would be reunited with their dead relatives and friends while experiencing eternal joy and happiness. Tainos called the spirits of the dead *op'a*. They believed that the *op'a* would wait for dusk to go out, after which they would eat *guayabas* [guavas], have sex, participate in celebrations, perform dances, and accompany the living (Poviones-Bishop, 2001; Rodríguez, 1997). Interestingly, Tainos believed that the *op'a* could transform themselves into many things by taking the form of fruits, animals, and, at times, relatives who were still living. According to Taino faith, the living and the dead were in constant connection. Today, the beliefs of the Taino are alive and observed by their descendants, who often speak about feeling the presence of their deceased loved ones and at times report seeing them.

Taino & Carib Legacy — Carib

Despite centuries of European conquest and oppression, the Indigenous people of the Caribbean, the Tainos and the Caribs, are truly *sobrevivientes* (survivors). Their traditions and way of life have played a pivotal role in shaping contemporary Caribbean culture through advanced technologies, arts, language, cuisine, and survival skills. Overall, the Taino and Carib people are known for *ser trabajadore/as* or being hard working, a practice they valued and viewed not only as a means for surviving but as a way of prospering.

The Tainos' hard work can be observed in their skills, making crafts from different materials, as well as in their extensive nautical knowledge. For instance, the Tainos built efficient water transportation devices out of tree logs (e.g., canoes) that adapted well to the open sea with some having the capacity to accommodate up to 100 people (Rouse, 1992). They used their water transportation devices for traveling great distances, fishing, riding, and trading goods (Rouse, 1992). Their advanced nautical knowledge allowed them to develop an in-depth understanding of the formation and prediction of hurricanes and tsunamis in the region. With regard to other crafts, the Indigenous people of the Caribbean had advanced industrial technologies in the production of textiles, ceramics, and gold ornaments. They used wood, stone, shell, bone, clay, and cotton for personal adornment and offerings to their Gods and *Zemis*, as well as for trade (Hopper, 2008).

One of the areas where the spirit of the Tainos is vividly present today is in their language. A number of words used to describe items and places in modern-day Latin America can be traced back to the time of the Tainos. For instance, places such as *Bayamón, Jayuya*, and *Guánica* in Puerto Rico and *Quisqueya* (mother of all lands), another name used to refer to the Dominican Republic, still have Indigenous names (Dick, 1977; Jesse, 1966; Wilson, 1997). Other Indigenous names used in contemporary Latin American language include words such as *mofongos* (garlic-flavored semi-fried mashed plantains), *casabe* (cassava bread), *mazamorra* (*maize* based food), and *mamey* (sapote) to name a few (Wilson, 1997).

In closing, the legacy of the Indigenous people of the Caribbean plays a vital role in contemporary society. Their survival skills, perseverance, strengths, and abilities can serve as a source of inspiration to generations of their descendants (Dominicans, Puerto Ricans, Cubans, and other Latinos/as), who continue to face many of the same challenges and the oppression that their ancestors suffered at the hands of the Europeans. For survivorship in the 21st century, it is important for Dominicans, Puerto Ricans, and Cubans to know or be reminded that they come from a long legacy of strong-willed, determined, hardworking, and joyful people who celebrated life, invented concepts, generated ideas, and cultivated foods that continue to nourish and feed people around the world (e.g., Caribbean-based foods such as peanuts, cashew nuts, potatoes, tomatoes, pineapples, *manioc* [yucca roots, cassava], *maize*, and pumpkins, are now available in most parts of the world). Thus the Tainos are still alive today; they live through the words that we speak, the foods that nourish our souls, the songs that we sing and dance to, and the spirit of unbroken survival and hope.

Colonization: A Period of Destruction, Genocide, and Exploitation

The information reviewed in this chapter indicates that the flourishing civilizations of Mesoamerica, the Andean region, and the Caribbean rivaled those of ancient Egypt, Mesopotamia, and China. This is evidenced by the sophistication of their cities, buildings, and the extent and refinement of their intellectual accomplishments. By the time the Spaniards arrived in the Americas, the Tainos, Caribs, Incas, Mayas, and Aztecs had developed societies with high levels of technological and scientific advances. However, the future of these Indigenous groups was forever changed by the arrival of the Spanish conquistadors into what they arrogantly called the "new world." This period known as the "conquest" led to calamitous consequences for the Indigenous peoples of the Americas. For instance, they experienced widespread disease in the form of viral and bacterial infections that ultimately killed millions of natives. During the conquest, the Spaniards also invaded and appropriated Indigenous lands, burned and destroyed cities, and massacred, raped, and tortured Indigenous people. It is estimated that approximately eight million people died during the Indigenous genocide of the Americas. Following this period of chaos and destruction, the Spaniards focused their energies on reconstructing cities and converting natives to Catholicism. They also established an economic system designed to exploit the land, its natural resources, and the labor of Indigenous people known as the *encomiendas*. As the native population began to decline as a consequence of the inhumane labor conditions that they were subjected to, the Spaniards began to look for alternative ways to meet the labor demands of colonial Latin America (Garcia-Martinez, 2010). This demand was soon met by the labor of African people, who were forcibly kidnapped and transplanted into the Americas through large commercial slave trade (Soler-Castillo & Pardo-Abril, 2009). The challenges experienced by Afro-Latinos/as and the legacy of their values, ideals, and practices are described in the next section.

Third Ancestral Root: The African Presence in Latino/a America

The history of Africans in the Americas dates back to the period of colonization when they were forcibly taken from their homelands and brought to Latin America to work in the thriving Spanish colonies. Although more attention in the literature has been paid to the Africans who were brought to North America, scholars argue that the heart of the African diaspora in the Americas lies in Latin America and not in the U.S. (Andrews, 2004). In fact, it is estimated that over ten million African enslaved individuals were brought to Latin America. Given the degrading and cruel conditions that Africans endured, which tested their bodies, spirits, and hopes, they developed several strategies to survive, cope, and resist. One of the strategies frequently used among enslaved families was to maintain a close-knit community that provided emotional and economic support. Another strategy that served as a source of sustenance was music and dance, which they considered healing activities. They believed that

> rhythm was central to producing healing and energizing effects . . . one of the central messages of African music is that rhythm lifts us out of the daily grind by transforming consciousness, transforming time, transforming, and heightening our experience of the moment.
>
> (Andrews, 2004, p. 29)

Lastly, spirituality and faith helped enslaved people of African descent to survive their precarious conditions. They practiced *Santeria*, an earth-based religion that emphasizes the powerful role of one's ancestors (spirits of the dead), who are called on to help the living cope with life's difficulties. Overall, African people brought to the Americas their traditional cultural values, practices, and spiritual beliefs, which ultimately served to enrich the new Latino/a culture. Chapter 2 provides a more detailed account of Afro-descendants in Latin America.

Embracing and Living the Legacies of Survival and Resistance: A Strength-Based Latino/a Psychology

> It is because my roots are so strong that I can fly.
>
> (Nair, 2006, p. 49)

Today's Latinos/as are the descendants of remarkably advanced, fascinating, and resilient civilizations, rich in racial and cultural diversity. Their legacy is alive today in the strong traditional values that were an integral part of their cultures (e.g., collectivism, familism, *confianza* [trust], *lealtad* [loyalty], *responsabilidad* [responsibility], *ser trabajador* [hard-work ethic]) and continue to be practiced by their contemporary descendants. These cultural values and traditional practices, coupled with new strategies developed during the period of colonization, were instrumental in helping them to survive the cruel and brutal conditions they endured. From the combination of their cultural values, practices, and survival strategies, seven main psychological strengths emerged: 1) *Determination,* 2) *Esperanza (hope),* 3) *Adaptability,* 4) *Strong Work Ethic,* 5) *Connectedness to Others,* 6) *Collective Emotional Expression,* and 7) *Resistance* (see Table 1.1). These strengths continue to help Latinos/as survive and thrive despite the many challenges and barriers they face in the U.S. Mental health providers can use the *seven Latino/a psychological strengths* to aid in developing a strength-based Latino/a psychology, instead of the predominant deficit-based psychology that is often applied when studying and treating People of Color.

Table 1.1 The Seven Psychological Strengths of Latinos/as

Strengths	Descriptions
Determination	• The endless drive and courage to do what is necessary to meet goals despite the barriers encountered. For instance, Latinos/as will not rest until they have achieved their goals, whether that is coming to the U.S., buying a house, or earning an academic degree.
Esperanza	• Faith that even during the most difficult situations things will turn out to be okay. This strength is captured by the *dicho* (saying), *La esperanza es lo ultimo que muere* (Hope is the last thing that dies).
Adaptability	• The ability to adapt and thrive in a variety of different environments. Latino/a immigrants in the U.S. demonstrate an incredible capacity to adapt and thrive despite the vast differences in culture and language.
Strong Work Ethic	• Valuing the importance of working hard, producing quality, and taking pride in one's work endeavors regardless of social status or occupation. Overall, this value is guided by producing excellence for the betterment of self, family, and community.
Connectedness to Others	• Valuing the need and enjoyment of being emotionally, physically, and spiritually connected with others throughout the life span in order to witness and share in life's challenging and joyous times.
Collective Emotional Expression	• The ability, need, and desire to share strong emotions with others. All emotions ranging from sorrow and longing, to joy and gleefulness are freely expressed by Latinos/as through music, dance, spoken word, spiritual rituals, art, literature, and sporting events.
Resistance	• The willpower and courage to stand firmly for one's beliefs, ideals, and practices. This strength is also demonstrated in the determination of Latinos/as to defy the odds and limits placed on them by oppressive systems.

References

Akbar, N. (1998). *Know thyself*. Tallahassee, FL: Mind Productions & Associates.

Andrews, G. R. (2004). *Afro-Latin America 1800–2000*. New York, NY: Oxford University Press.

Becker, M. J. (2004). Maya hierarchy as inferred from classic-period plaza plans. *Ancient Mesoamerica, 15*, 127–138. doi:10.1017/S0956536104151079.

Beckles, H. McD., & Shepherd, V. A. (2004). *Liberties lost: The Indigenous Caribbean and slave systems*. Cambridge, England: Cambridge University Press.

Coe, M. D. (1999). *The Maya* (6th ed.). New York, NY: Thames & Hudson.

Cresson, H. T. (1883). Aztec music. *Proceedings of the Academy of Natural Sciences of Philadelphia, 35*, 86–94. Retrieved from http://www.jstor.org/stable/4060857

Davies, N. (1995). *The Incas*. Boulder, CO: The University Press of Colorado.

Davies, N. (2001). *The Aztecs.* London, England: Macmillan Publishers Ltd.

de Diez Canseco, R.M. (1999). *History of the Inca realm.* Cambridge, UK: Cambridge University Press.

Dick, K. C. (1977). Aboriginal and early Spanish names of some Caribbean, Circum-Caribbean Island and cays. *Journal of the Virgin Islands Archaeological Society,* 4, 17–41.

Duran, D. (1967). *Historia de las Indias de la Nueva España e Islas de la Tierra Firme.* Mexico, Mexico City: Porrua.

Escalante Gonzalbo, P. (2010). El posclásico en Mesoamérica. In El Colegio De México (Ed.), *Nueva historia general de México* (pp. 119–166). México, DF: El Colegio De México.

Ferguson, D. (2000). *Tales of the plumed serpent: Aztec, Inca, and Mayan myths.* New York, NY: Collins & Brown.

Foias, A. E. (2014). *Ancient Maya political dynamics.* Gainesville, FL: University Press of Florida.

Foster, L. (2002). *Handbook to life in the ancient Maya world.* New York, NY: Oxford University Press.

Furst, J. L. M. (1995). *The natural history of the soul in ancient Mexico.* New Haven, CT: Yale University Press.

Gallop, R. (1939). The music of Indian Mexico. *The Musical Quarterly,* 25(2), 210–225. Retrieved from http://www.jstor.org/stable/738909

Garcia-Martínez, B. (2010). Los años de la expansión. In El Colegio de México (Ed.), *Nueva historia general de México* (pp. 217–262). Mexico, DF: El Colegio de México.

Hammond, N. (2000). *The Maya.* New Brunswick, NJ: Rutgers University Press.

Hopper, R. (2008). Taino Indians: Settlements of the Caribbean. *Lambda Alpha Journal, 38,* 62–69.

Hulme, P. (1986). *Colonial encounters: Europe and the native Caribbean, 1492–1797.* New York, NY: Routledge.

Jesse, C. (1966). St. Lucia: The romance of its place names. In *St. Lucia miscellany,* Vol. 1. Castries, St. Lucia: St. Lucia Archaeological and Historical Society.

Jones, D. M. (2012). *The complete illustrated history of the Inca Empire.* London, UK: Lorenz Books.

Keegan, W. F. (1997). No man [or woman] is an island: Elements of Taíno social organization. In S. M. Wilson (Ed.), *The Indigenous people of the Caribbean* (pp. 109–117). Gainesville, FL: University Press of Florida.

Keoke, E. D., & Porterfield, K. M. (2001). Aztec botanical gardens. *Encyclopedia of American Indian Contributions to the World: 15,000 Years of Inventions and Innovations.* Retrieved from http://www.fofweb.com/activelink2.asp?ItemID=WE43&iPin=EIC185&SingleRecord=True

Long-Solis, J., & Vargas, L. A. (2005). *Food culture in Mexico.* Westport, CT: Greenwood Press.

López, A. A. (1980). *The human body and ideology: Concepts of the ancient Nahuas.* Salt Lake City, UT: University of Utah Press.

Marcus, J. (2004). Maya commoners: The stereotype and the reality. In J. C. Lohse & F. Valdez, Jr. (Eds.), *Ancient Maya commoners* (pp. 255–284). Austin, TX: University of Texas Press.

Martin, S., & Grube, N. (2000). *Chronicle of the Maya kings and queens: Deciphering the dynasties of the ancient Maya.* London and New York, NY: Thames & Hudson.

Mason, J. A. (1988). *The ancient civilizations of Peru.* New York, NY: Penguin Books.

Masson, M. A., & Lope, P. C. (2004). Commoners in post classic Maya society: Social versus economic class constructs. In J. C. Lohse & F. Valdez, Jr. (Eds.), *Ancient Maya commoners* (pp. 197–223). Austin, TX: University of Texas Press.

Meier, M. S., & Ribera, F. (1993). *Mexican Americans/American Mexicans: From conquistadors to Chicanos.* Canada: HarperCollins.

Mesoamerican Research Center. (2010). *Preclassic period.* Retrieved from http://www.marc.ucsb.edu/research/maya/ancient-maya-civilization/preclassic-period

Nair, M. (2006, June 26). Hooray for Bollywood. *Time, 167*(26), 49.

Nalda, E. (2010). El clásico en el México antiguo. In El Colegio De México (Ed.), *Nueva historia general de México* (pp. 71–116). México, DF: El Colegio De México.

Padilla, A. M. (1984). Synopsis of the history of Chicano psychology. In J. L. Martinez & R. H. Mendoza (Eds.), *Chicano psychology* (2nd ed., pp. 1–46). New York, NY: Academic Press.

Pané, F. R. (1999). *An account of the antiquities of the Indians: Chronicles of the New World encounter.* Durham, NC: Duke University Press Books.

Parham, T. A., Ajamu, A., & White, J. L. (2011). *The psychology of blacks: Centering our perspectives in the African consciousness* (4th ed.). Boston, MA: Prentice Hall.

Poviones-Bishop, M. (2001). The bat and the guava: Life and death in the Taíno worldview. *J.I. Kislak Foundation.* Retrieved from http://www.kislakfoundation.org/prize/200103.html

Rodríguez, M. (1997). Religious beliefs of the Saladoid people. In S. M. Wilson (Ed.), *The Indigenous people of the Caribbean* (pp. 80–87). Gainesville, FL: University Press of Florida.

Rouse, I. (1992). *The Taínos: Rise and decline of the people who greeted Columbus.* New Haven, CT: Yale University Press.

Saragoza, A. (2012). *The Aztecs' inheritance: The development of Mesoamerican technology.* Berkley, CA: ORIAS Summer Institute for K-12 Teachers.

Schendel, G. (1968). *Medicine in Mexico.* Austin, TX: University of Texas Press.

Sharer, R. J., & Traxler, L. P. (2006). *The ancient Maya* (6th ed., fully revised). Stanford, CA: Stanford University Press.

Soler-Castillo, S., & Pardo-Abril, N. G. (2009). Discourse and racism in Colombia: Five centuries of invisibility and exclusion. In T. A. Van Dijk (Ed.), *Racism and discourse in Latin America* (pp. 131–170). Lanham, MD: Lexington Books.

Stuart, E. G., & Swanson, W. (1992). *Ancient Mexico.* New Brunswick, NJ: Rutgers University Press.

Subcomandante Marcos. (2001). *Our word is our weapon: Selected writings.* New York, NY: Seven Stories Press.

Taube, K. (1993). *The legendary past: Aztec and Maya myths.* Austin, TX: University of Texas Press.

Thomas, H. (2004). *The conquest of Mexico* (2nd ed.). London, England: Pimlico.

White, J. L., & Cones, J. H. (1999). *Black man emerging: Facing the past and seizing a future in America.* New York, NY: Routledge.

White, J. L., & Parham, T. A. (1983). *The psychology of Blacks: An African-American perspective* (2nd ed.). Englewood Cliffs, NJ: Prentice Hall.

Wilson, S. M. (1997). The legacy of the Indigenous people of the Caribbean. In S. M. Wilson (Ed.), *The Indigenous people of the Caribbean* (pp. 206–213). Gainesville, FL: University Press of Florida.

Woodson, C. G. (1990). *The mis-education of the Negro.* Trenton, NJ: The Associated Publishers.

2 Skin-Color Differences Within Latinos/as

Historical and Contemporary Implications of Colorism

We are the end, the continuation, and the beginning . . . we are the stubborn history that repeats itself in order to no longer repeat itself, the looking back to be able to walk forward.

–Subcomandante Marcos (2001, p. 96)

Diversity within Latinos/as has received increasing attention in the literature over the last two decades. A number of foundational publications such as those by Bonilla-Silva (2010); Comas-Diaz (1996); Organista (2007a); and Santiago-Rivera, Arredondo, and Gallardo-Cooper (2002) coupled with the *Guidelines on Multicultural Education, Training, Research, Practice, and Organizational Change for Psychologists* (APA, 2003) provide a basis for facilitating professional dialogue about within-group stigma and discrimination. One such area is colorism or "a form of [racial] discrimination imposed upon Latino/as by members of their own ethnic group" (Organista, 2009, p. 291).

Although the psychological literature on colorism is sparse, the few studies available have found that darker skin-color prejudice negatively impacts Latino/a mental health (Montalvo, 2004; Montalvo & Codina, 2001, Ramos, Jaccard, & Guilamo-Ramos, 2003), education, and income (Arce, Murgia, & Frisbie, 1987). For example, in their seminal article examining the impact of skin color and phenotype on the life chances of Mexican Americans, Arce et al. (1987) found that as compared to their lighter-skinned and European-looking counterparts, darker and more Indigenous-looking participants reported less educational attainment (9.5 and 7.8 years, respectively), lower income ($12,721 and $10,450, respectively), and higher discrimination as assessed by self-report incidents of perceived discrimination with higher scores indicating more perceived discrimination (25.6 and 27.2). Additionally, a study conducted by Ramos, Jaccard, and Guilamo-Ramos (2003), compared the depressive symptoms between European American, African American, and Afro-Latino/a adolescents and found that Afro-Latinas reported the highest levels.

The purpose of this chapter is to 1) prime the reader for a historical appreciation of colorism and its current impact on Latinos/as, 2) provide questions to stimulate dialogue about this challenging topic, and 3) make recommendations for approaching research on colorism with Latinos/as. To accomplish these goals, a brief overview on the history of the conquest, the colonial period, and post-colonial era is provided to highlight the establishment of ethnic and racial stratification and its negative consequences for Latinos/as of Indigenous and African descent. The legacy of *mestizaje* is also outlined as a strategy to minimize and deny the racial privilege of lighter-skinned and European-featured Latinos/as. Furthermore, *mestizaje* is compared with more recent color-blind racial attitudes (CoBRA) in the United States (U.S.). We conclude with questions to stimulate reflection, recognition, and engagement in dialogue about colorism as a prelude to research recommendations.

The authors acknowledge that learning about within-group oppression or "family secrets" may elicit uneasy feelings such as discomfort or anxiety, as well as anger, pain, shame, and guilt within Latinos/as across the color continuum. However, such learning can also be stimulating, insightful, and motivating in extending our social justice efforts to include within-group efforts to reduce internalized oppression. We are also cognizant that inviting colorism dialogue may disturb the status quo within Latino/a relations, but hopefully in productive ways. By starting the colorism conversation, we do not minimize the history of oppression and discrimination that Latinos/as have and continue to experience due to cultural differences and immigration status, as well as gender, accentedness, socioeconomic status (SES), etc., which is all well documented in the literature (e.g., Dovidio, Gluszek, John, Ditlmann, & Lagunes, 2010; Lee & Ahn, 2012; Perez, 2012; C. Suarez-Orozco & Suarez-Orozco, 2001; Torres & Ong, 2010). Instead, this chapter is an invitation to learn more about colorism, its historical foundation, and current impact on Latinos/as and to stimulate further inquiry. Education through history is the "most powerful weapon we can use to change the world" (Nelson Mandela Centre of Memory, 2012, para 13).

Selective History of Racial Stratification in Latin America

The history of Latinos/as is a collective narrative of rich ancestral roots and traditions, conquest, colonization, slavery, and perseverance. If indeed we are committed to APA's (2003) Multicultural Guidelines and fostering a fairer society, the living legacy of history must be studied to avoid repeating its many pitfalls. In fact, the Multicultural Guidelines call upon us to understand the influence that social, political, historical, and economic context have on individual beliefs, attitudes, and behaviors.

The Conquest of Latin America: The Importation of Racist Ideologies

The conquest was one of the most violent periods in Latin American history, resulting in the massacre, domination, and oppression of Indigenous people

(Livi-Bacci, 2008; Soler-Castillo & Pardo-Abril, 2009). It began with the arrival of the Spanish conquistadors to the Caribbean islands that today are known as Cuba, the Dominican Republic, and Puerto Rico. There the conquistadors encountered the Tainos, the Caribs, and other smaller Indigenous groups. By 1518, the conquistadors had arrived at the coast of Veracruz, Mexico (Garcia-Martinez, 2010; Livi-Bacci, 2008). As they moved farther west into the coast of Mexico and South America, the conquistadors encountered the descendants of the Mayans, the Aztecs, and the Incas (Garcia-Martinez, 2010; Livi-Bacci, 2008; Nalda, 2010). During their settlements into what the Spaniards called the "new world," they encountered various groups of people with centuries of established traditions, beliefs, and customs (Garcia-Martinez, 2010; Livi-Bacci, 2008). They viewed Indigenous people as "heathens" who needed to be civilized (Livi-Bacci, 2008; Soler-Castillo & Pardo-Abril, 2009). Thus Spanish historical interpretations of Indigenous behaviors were rooted in a European perception of the world, and the foundation of social inequality between the White and non-White populations in Latin America took hold during this era (Soler-Castillo & Pardo-Abril, 2009).

Historians have described the encounter between the Spaniards and the Indigenous population as having a tremendous influence on the Spaniards' ability to survive and thrive in Latin America (Garcia-Martinez, 2010; Livi-Bacci, 2008). In fact, it has been postulated that while the Europeans found good conditions in the Americas (i.e., climate, food, epidemic disease at low levels), conditions for the Indigenous rapidly deteriorated (Livi-Bacci, 2008). For instance, the Indigenous people were faced with epidemic diseases for which they had no immunity and suffered dramatic economic and social "territorial dislocation" (Livi-Bacci, 2008, p. 7). Their traditions, religion, and even their names were lost. Overall, the Indigenous groups were forced to live by the expectations of the Spaniards, including their beliefs about racial superiority and practices, which transferred cross-generationally as Spaniards and Indigenous people inevitably mixed (Garcia-Martinez, 2010; Livi-Bacci, 2008; Soler-Castillo & Pardo-Abril, 2009).

The Colonial Period: A System Based on Inequality

During the colonial period, the Spaniards dominated Latin America and began using Indigenous laborers to exploit the natural resources of the "new world," which was rich in precious metals and agricultural lands (Casaus-Arzu, 2009; Tanck de Estrada & Marichal, 2010). Nevertheless, as the percentage of the Indigenous population declined, the Spaniards found themselves in need of additional laborers. Such need gave rise to the slave trade, and more than ten million African slaves were brought to Latin America. The survival and reproductive capacity of Afro-descendants in Latin America was severely compromised by the inhumane and brutal conditions that marked their loss of freedom (Andrews, 2004; Livi-Bacci, 2008). Moreover, African slaves experienced high rates of mortality due to the strenuous work performed in the burgeoning sugar cane plantations and silver mining industries. Even before such labor exploitation, large numbers of slaves died during their transplantation to the Americas with one-fifth to one-third dying within three years of arrival (Andrews, 2004; Engerman, 2000).

During the colonial period, Latin America was divided into a caste society, also referred to as a *system of stratification* (Organista, 2007b; Soler-Castillo & Pardo-Abril, 2009). This system was based on skin-color and phenotypical characteristics where White individuals predominated the top. Figure 2.1 illustrates the social stratification system of the colonial period, where the Spaniards and their descendants strategically occupied the top. Such a stratification system was designed to allow Spaniards to hold and control political, social, and economical power at the cost of impoverishing Indigenous and African groups (Ogbu, 1994; Organista, 2007b; Soler-Castillo & Pardo-Abril, 2009). Moreover, an individual's placement within the stratification system determined his or her power and privilege within the colonies, including noble titles, legal class divisions, censorship, and access to formal education and other life-enhancing resources (Livi-Bacci, 2008; Soler-Castillo & Pardo-Abril, 2009).

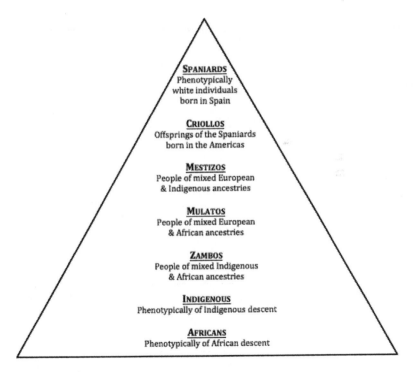

Figure 2.1 Latin American Social Caste Pyramid (LASCP)

The pyramid is informed by the 18th-century Latin American family caste paintings by Miguel Cabrera (Katzew, 1996). Racial mix determined hierarchy, social status, and economic privileges.

By the early 1800s, Spaniards composed about a quarter of the population, Africans a fifth, with the remainder a rapidly increasing racial blend of predominantly Indigenous and Spanish roots (Livi-Bacci, 2008). Although Spaniards were a shrinking minority, they possessed the power to discriminate on the basis of skin color and phenotype as one of the main strategies to maintain the stratification of race, ethnicity, and power (Casaus Arzu, 2009; Soler-Castillo & Pardo-Abril, 2009). The colonial period lasted for about three centuries, ending around 1830, with each Latin American country eventually gaining independence from Spain (Livi-Bacci, 2008).

Post-Colonial Era: Independence for Some and Continued Oppression for Others

During the post-colonial period, the foundation of White superiority, including the denial of inequality established by the Spanish conquistadors, flourished. These ideologies were built into the sociopolitical system. In fact, *mestizaje*, an ideology whereby everyone was deemed to be of mixed descent, was one of the main strategies the Spaniards used to de-emphasize privileges associated with phenotypically White characteristics (Gates, 2011; Soler-Castillo & Pardo-Abril, 2009). Consequently, even the descendants of the African slaves were socialized to buy into the idea of *mestizaje* connoting that all Latin Americans were of mixed Indigenous, African, and European heritage (Gates, 2011; Soler-Castillo & Pardo-Abril, 2009).

Afro-descendants and Indigenous people subscribed to *mestizaje*, albeit for different reasons than their White oppressors. *Mestizaje* was their feeble attempt to deny their racist ideologies and to "erase" the public discourse about their inferiority (Soler-Castillo & Pardo-Abril, 2009). To Afro-descendants, this ideology represented a forestalled acceptance of their humanity and a way to reject the stratification system established by the Spanish crown during the colonial period. In fact, one of the most well-known Mexican independence heroes, José Maria Morelos y Pavon, an Afro-descendant who fought to remove Mexico's class and race distinctions, stated "May slavery be banished forever together with the distinction between castes, all remaining equal, so Americans may only be known by their vice or virtue" (Morelos y Pavon, 1813).

Moreover, Vicente Guerrero, another Afro-descendant who became the second president of Mexico, made a decision that would have significant repercussions for future generations. He decided that race, as a demographic category, would no longer be part of Mexico's national census. His assumption was that if people were no longer categorized based on race, social inequality would cease to exist. Unfortunately, *mestizaje* rendered invisible Afro-descendants and Indigenous people throughout Latin America with minimal changes to social stratification (Soler-Castillo & Pardo-Abril, 2009).

The Legacy of *Mestizaje:* White Privilege in Contemporary Latin America

A related goal of *mestizaje* was the assimilation of Indigenous and African people into a culturally homogenous society. The direct descendants of the Spanish conquistadors or White elites believed that with time, *mestizaje* would lead to the disappearance of Indigenous and African cultures from Latin American society (Soler-Castillo & Pardo-Abril, 2009). Assimilation was further accomplished by the blending and mixing of races supported by the government or what were known as "whitening policies" in Latin America (Castellanos-Guerrero, Gomez-Izquierdo, & Pineda, 2009; Gates, 2011; Soler-Castillo & Pardo-Abril, 2009). These policies included two devious dimensions: 1) European immigration was encouraged, particularly to areas with high concentrations of Indigenous and African people (e.g., in Northern Mexico) (Castellanos-Guerrero, Gomez-Izquierdo, & Pineda, 2009), and 2) White prostitutes were sent to areas where high concentrations of Afro-descendants resided (e.g., in Colombia) (Soler-Castillo & Pardo-Abril, 2009). The White elites believed that through interracial breeding, they were going to "*mejorar la raza*" (improve the race) and dilute the African and Indigenous characteristics from Latin American (Castellanos-Guerrero, Gomez-Izquierdo, & Pineda, 2009; Soler-Castillo & Pardo-Abril, 2009). Interestingly, the phrase *mejorar la raza* is still used among U.S. Latinos/as today (Comas-Diaz, 1996).

Current Impacts of Colorism

> In the early 1990s, a group of people from Mata Clara was jailed in Mexico City. They were believed to be illegal immigrants from Central America. The police acted under the assumption that there are no blacks in Mexico and the fact that the detainees were not carrying any identification. Consequently, they were jailed. They were finally released after the intervention from the municipal president of Cuitlahuac, Veracruz, who confirmed to and convinced the Mexico City police that there were indeed black people in this territory.
>
> (Cruz-Carretero, 2006, p. 36)

The legacy of racism against non-White populations can be readily observed in today's Latin American society through rending them invisible by the devaluing of traditions rooted in Indigenous and African beliefs and framing these groups as exotic others (Gates, 2011; Soler- Castillo & Pardo-Abril, 2009). For instance, a national survey conducted in 2010 by the Mexican Consejo Nacional para Prevenir la Discriminación (National Council for the Prevention of Discrimination) (2012) identified discrimination as the main problem reported by the Indigenous community in Mexico. Further, traditional Indigenous clothing, accentedness, and behavioral mannerisms continue to be objects of everyday mockery and rejection in Mexico (Castellanos-Guerrero, Gomez-Izquierdo, & Pineda, 2009). Additionally, the Inter-American Commission

Table 2.1 Concealment Strategies: A Basis for Misinformation of Latinos/as

Strategies	Descriptions
Omission of social actors	• A deliberate and purposeful exclusion of the history, including past and current contributions of Afro-Latinos and Indigenous people.
Omission of racist practices	• References to racial and discriminatory practices disappear from history. There is denial that racist practices exist, and when discussed, it is acknowledged as occurring in foreign societies.
Naturalization	• Racism and discrimination are normalized as natural phenomena that occur as a result of how a society develops. In other words, racism and discrimination are expected occurrences.
Distortion	• Information on the history of Afro-Latinos/as and Indigenous people is not always portrayed accurately in textbooks and is often presented in a biased way.
Justification	• Excuses are made to justify racist practices: the White elite had the right to defend themselves and the Indigenous and Afro-descendants were blamed for the oppression they endured.

Note: Table informed by Soler-Castillo & Graciela Pardo-Abril, 2009.

on Human Rights (Comisión Interamericana de Derechos Humanos, 2011) reports that Afro-Latinos/as in the Americas continue to be negatively stereotyped, described in a pejorative manner, and exoticized when represented in the media.

It is worth noting, however, that racism pervades a variety of other variables such as SES and gender (Montalvo & Codina, 2001). Although current SES is a direct result of centuries of marginalization, oppression, and exclusion, Indigenous and Afro-descendants are often blamed for their struggles and are repeatedly perceived to be lazy, incompetent, and unable to improve their conditions (Castellanos-Guerrero, Gomez-Izquierdo, & Pineda, 2009; Soler-Castillo & Pardo-Abril, 2009). Furthermore, concealment strategies were systematically used by White elites to provide misinformation to Latinos/as relative to persons of Indigenous and Afro ancestry. For example, Table 2.1 describes four major concealment strategies used to misinform Latinos/as about the historical and current implications of skin-color privilege. Despite such pervasive concealment strategies, Indigenous and Afro-descendant people throughout Latin America have staged various forms of resistance and protest against racism and discrimination.

The Struggle for Equality: Indigenous and Black Uprisings

Racism has limited opportunities for Indigenous and Afro-descendant communities for centuries. These two groups have historically been the poorest segments of Latin American societies (Casaus-Arzu, 2009; Castellanos-Guerrero, Gomez-Izquierdo, & Pineda, 2009; Soler-Castillo & Pardo-Abril, 2009). Unfortunately, such realities hold true today. For instance, epidemiological studies reveal high rates of health problems, low literacy and formal education, and high poverty (Hall & Patrinos, 2006; Ñopo, 2012). However, numerous social movements have shed light on such SES and health disparities.

The following section briefly discusses the Zapatista movement in Mexico, the Mayan movement in Guatemala, and the Afro-descendants movement in Colombia as vibrant illustrations of resistance to social stratification on the basis of ethnicity, race, and color. Although a more comprehensive historical analysis is beyond the scope of this manuscript, these movements (e.g., Casaus-Arzu, 2009; Marquez & Meyer, 2010; Soler-Castillo & Pardo-Abril, 2009) were selected because they provide concrete examples of contemporary organized social movements by Indigenous and Afro-Latinos/as against colorism.

The Zapatistas: An Indigenous Movement in Mexico

The rebellion of the Mayan Zapatistas in 1994 illustrated the racist discourse and practices that the Mexican government and phenotypically White citizens have engaged in for centuries (Castellanos-Guerrero, Gomez-Izquierdo, & Pineda, 2009). In 1996, the movement reached a major milestone with the passage of the San Andres Treaty, which judicially recognized Indigenous groups as part of Mexico's population and also recognized their autonomy. However, the treaty was never implemented because it reportedly threatened national unity (Marquez & Meyer, 2010). Such maintenance of national unity sounds similar to maintenance of the status quo and is perhaps yet a current version of *mestizaje* in effect today. Sadly, the Indigenous of Mexico continue to have the highest indices of poverty (Castellanos-Guerrero, Gomez-Izquierdo, & Pineda, 2009; Subcomandante Marcos, 2001).

The Mayan Movement in Guatemala

Guatemala is home to the largest number of Indigenous inhabitants in all of Latin America, with one of the highest inequality indices in the entire world (Hall & Patrinos, 2006; Minority Rights Group International, 2011). For example, the World Bank reports that Indigenous people make up 58% of the poor and 72% of the extreme poor in Guatemala (Ñopo, 2012).

In the late 1970s, Guatemala experienced an unprecedented rise of Indigenous individuals moving from the mountains of Guatemala into the cities. They also began to occupy high ranks in various armed organizations (e.g., La Organización del Pueblo en Armas [ORPA], El Ejército Guerrillero de los Pobres [EGP]). "This irruption of indigenous people into public life caused a commotion among the power [White] elites and the fantasy of the 'unredeemed' Indian reappeared" (Casaus-Arzu, 2009, p. 194). Between 1980 and 1985, a number of individuals who considered themselves White descendants of Europeans reached political power and committed one of the largest genocides in the history of Guatemala with approximately 200,000 killings and 100,000 disappearances (Casaus-Arzu, 2009).

Similar to Mexico's Zapatista movement in the mid-1990s, the Guatemalan Mayan social movement was propelled to the fore by socioeconomic disparities and brutality. Although the movement was successful at occupying new public spaces and having Indigenous representation at local and regional governmental agencies, such progress did little to decrease marginalization and poverty. Moreover, public opinion about non-Whites in Guatemala continues to be negative (Casaus-Arzu, 2009). Reports conducted by the Human Rights Office and the CEDIM Foundation in Guatemala document that racism and discrimination against Indigenous groups have not decreased in today's Guatemala (Cojti & Edda, 2005; Diene, 2005; Human Rights Office & Morales-Alvarado, 2004).

An Afro-Descendant Movement in Colombia

Colombia is home to the second largest Afro-descendant population in Latin America (Asher, 2009), which is estimated at 10.6% by the Colombian government (Minority Rights Group International, 2008). However, the United Nations estimates the total population of Afro-Colombians to be at 26% (Minority Rights Group International, 2008). For centuries, Afro-Colombians have been the victims of oppression and invisibility. Although the Catholic Church condemned the brutality experienced by the Indigenous community in Colombia during the colonial era, similar condemnation has not been expressed toward experiences relative to Afro-Colombians. In fact, the church has remained silent about the atrocities experienced by Afro-Colombians during the time of slavery and beyond (Soler-Castillo & Pardo-Abril, 2009).

By the early 1990s, Afro-Colombians sought formal recognition as an autonomous ethnic group. They reached some degree of success in 1993 with the passage of Law 70 facilitated by the new Colombian constitution of 1991 (Asher, 2009; Soler-Castillo & Pardo-Abril, 2009). Law 70 recognized the multiethnic/multiracial diversity of the country, especially Indigenous and African descendants. Until that time, Afro-Colombians had not been fully recognized as ethnic groups because they were perceived not to possess "native characteristics." Moreover, Law 70 granted Afro-Colombians the right to the land that their ancestors occupied and developed (Asher, 2009; Soler-Castillo & Pardo-Abril, 2009). Nevertheless, such rights were restricted. That is, the property titles were given to the collective Afro-Colombian group rather than individuals (Asher, 2009, p. 6). Moreover, the regions occupied by Afro-Colombians are the lands most ignored and neglected by the government and also impacted by high rates of violence resulting from wars between the government and the paramilitary groups.

Finally, despite the legislative accomplishments of the Afro-descendant communities, they continue to face forced displacement, high levels of poverty, and low levels of literacy (Asher, 2009; Bernard & Audre Rapoport Center for Human Rights, n.d.).

Throughout Colombian history, Afro-Colombians have attempted to define themselves in their own terms and raise awareness about their rich ancestral heritage, which was central to the development of today's Colombian culture (e.g., music, dance, spiritual beliefs, and food). The Afro-Colombian movement has also achieved new forms of participation within Colombia and continues to fight negative stereotypes (Asher, 2009). As in the U.S., black skin color in Colombia has traditionally been associated with "laziness, backwardness, lethargy and neglect" (Soler-Castillo & Pardo-Abril, 2009, p. 135). In fact, José María Samper, an influential 19th-century politician, described the Black man as "primitive, coarse, brutal, indolent, semi-savage and dark brown" (Soler-Castillo & Pardo-Abril, 2009, p. 136), which is reminiscent of U.S. stereotypes of African Americans during this period and still today.

From *Mestizaje* in Latin America to Color-Blind Racial Attitudes in the U.S.

Words such as "post-racial" and "post-racial era" are becoming more en vogue in today's U.S. lexicon (Bonilla-Silva, 2010; Schorr, 2008) particularly after the election of Barack *Hussein* Obama. Such post-racial ideology or attitudes suggest that we have transcended race; that in today's society race no longer matters and that our judgments are race-free (Bonilla-Silva, 2010).

Post-racial ideologies or modern racism are not new. In fact, they were introduced and have been studied since the early '60s under different frameworks, including color-blind racism in the '60s (Bonilla-Silva, 2010), modern racism in the '80s (McConahay, 1983, 1986), new racism in the '90s (Bonilla-Silva, 2010; Cones & White, 1999), Racism 2.0 (Wise, 2008), color-blind racial attitudes (CoBRA), and color-blind racial ideology (CoBRI) at the turn of the century (Neville, Lilly, Duran, Lee, & Browne, 2000). While these terms vary, all connote and describe the same phenomenon: one that "denies or pretends to deny" (Helms, 2008, p. 12) the power of structural racism that leads individuals to believe that race/skin color is inconsequential in people's daily existence (Helms, 2008; Neville, Worthington, & Spanierman, 2001). In fact, Sue (2003), a pioneering leader in multicultural psychology, points out that "white Americans, however, have distorted or conveniently used colorblindness as means of color denial" (p. 149). Table 2.2 provides examples of the four main tenets of CoBRA, which are reminiscent of *mestizaje*.

As a society, we need to make an informed and conscious effort toward seeing skin color and accepting that it is an "integral part of who we are" (Helms, 2008, p. 12) and a signifier of inequality that must be challenged. By acknowledging our differences and engaging in honest dialogues about privilege within our communities, we can begin to progress as a society that is not color-blind

Table 2.2 Four Dimensions of Color-Blind Racial Attitudes (CoBRA)

Dimensions	Tenets	Descriptions	Examples
Definition	1. CoBRA are new forms of racial attitude expressions related to racial prejudice.	1. A modern form of racism that is more covert compared to old Jim Crow racism.	1. Persistent negative stereotyping and blaming People of Color for racial disparities.
Cognitions	2. CoBRA are a cognitive schema, reflecting a conceptual framework and corresponding affect.	2. Skin color is unimportant in terms of social and economic experiences. Affect is associated with this idea and corresponding beliefs.	2. For Whites, the fear of being called a racist and belief in a just world. For People of Color, the fear of using the "race card."
Multi-dimensionality	3. CoBRA are multidimensional.	3. CoBRA are complex and reflect multiple beliefs.	3. Color-evasion, referring to all people as being the same, evades the notion of White racial superiority.
			3a. Power-evasion, referring to belief that everyone has the same opportunities to succeed regardless of skin color, refers to the myth of meritocracy.
Expression	4. CoBRA are differentially expressed in White and People of Color populations.	4. Anyone can adopt a color-blind racial perspective, irrespective of skin color. However, the degree and implication of adopting CoBRA vary depending on one's skin color.	4. Whites on average adopt significantly higher CoBRA than racial and ethnic minorities.
			4a. Whites experience discomfort about their own thoughts about race.

Dimensions	Tenets	Descriptions	Examples
			4b. Discomfort for People of Color stems from feeling different and being associated with inferiority.

but racially conscious in a social justice–oriented manner. The next section unpacks the fallacy of using Latinos/as as a pan-ethnic label because it may lead to the perception of a homogenous group where everyone is of mixed racial makeup, thus promoting a CoBRI within the Latino/a population.

The Fallacy of Latino/a as a Pan-ethnic Label

Latinos/as in the U.S. now comprise 50.5 million or 16% of the total U.S. population (U.S. Census Bureau, 2011). Latinos/as are described as an ethnic group of individuals who can trace their descendants back to the Spanish-speaking countries of Latin America and the Caribbean (M. M. Suarez-Orozco & Paez, 2008). Due to historical racial mixing, Latinos/as exhibit a broad range of physical characteristics, including wide variations in skin color and phenotype (Lopez, 2008), making it difficult for the government to categorize Latinos/as with regard to race. But Latinos/as also experience the challenge of racial self-identification with 36% identifying as White, 3% as Black, and 51% as some other race (U.S. Census, 2011).

In the U.S., social stratification has served to maintain a color gradient with European descendants at the top of the hierarchy and non-Whites at the bottom. The literature defines the advantages automatically conferred to those of European phenotype as White privilege. In fact, Helms (2008) states "regardless of what socioeconomic level one observes, whites are more advantaged" (p. 19) than their People of Color counterparts. She affirms that "white privilege is the benefit of being white and is the foundation of racism" (p. 19). It is no surprise that previous studies have found that Latinos/as who are darker or who self-identify as Black experience worse mental health outcomes (Ramos, Jaccard, & Guilamo-Ramos, 2003), higher prevalence of hypertension, poorer self-rated health, lower incomes (Borrell, 2005, 2006; Borell & Crawford, 2006; Denton & Massey, 1989), and lower occupational prestige (Espino & Franz, 2002; Organista, 2007b) than lighter Latinos/as who do not identify as Black.

We posit that the use of a pan-ethnic label, such as Latinos/as, obscures the realities of darker-skinned Latinos/as and those who have less European-looking phenotypes. It also renders invisible the privilege conferred to lighter-skinned

Latinos/as. In other words, light-skinned Latinos/as also benefit from White privilege to varying degrees, but this mostly "is an unacknowledged secret that is overtly and covertly denied and protected through the use of self-deception" (Sue, 2003, p. 137). Light-skinned Latino/a privilege is reflected in their higher SES relative to darker Latinos/as (Espino & Franz, 2002; Frank, Akresh, & Lu, 2010; Organista 2007b).

For Latinos/as, the *mestizaje*/color-blind racial perspective has facilitated denial and self-deception. This socialization is congruent with

> the racial reality of white [U.S.] America [which] is a biased and bigoted one, [and has been] transmitted through our educational system and the informal but powerful stream of socialization practices of families, peers, groups, neighborhoods, churches, mass media, and other organizations.
>
> (Sue, 2003, p. 74)

So how do Latinos/as begin to talk about colorism?

Colorism: Can We Talk About It?

The socialization of Latinos/as through the ideology of *mestizaje*, as well as race privilege in the U.S., has resulted in a number of revealing statements frequently heard within the Latino/a experience:

- We are all *mestizos* (racially mixed).
- In Latin America, social class "matters more" than skin color.
- We have had an Indigenous president in Latin America.
- There is no racism in Latin America.
- That's how things are.

Interestingly, other frequent comments seemingly connote a clear understanding of a skin-color hierarchy but with a persistent preference for whiteness:

- *Hay que mejorar la raza o cásate con un blanco* (We need to better the race by marrying a White individual).
- *¡Ahi que bonita es su niña, es tan güerita/blanquita* (Oh! How pretty your daughter is, she's so beautifully white!)*!
- *Vete por la sombrita* (Go into the shade [to avoid getting darker]).
- *Oh, nació negrito/prietito pero aun asi lo queremos* (Oh, he was born black/dark, but we still love him all the same).
- *Pobrecita, tiene el cabello tan malo* (Poor little thing, her hair is so bad [coarse]).
- *Eres tan Indio* (You are so Indian [connoting negative stereotypes about Indigenous people]).

Table 2.3 Four Main Strategies to Justify or Deny Contemporary Racial Inequality

Main Strategies	Latinos/as Usage of Strategies
1. **Minimization:** Suggests discrimination is no longer a central factor affecting the lives of minorities; CoBRA	1a. There is no racism in Latin America 1b. We are all *mestizos* (racially mixed)
2. **Rationalization:** Racial phenomena are explained as natural occurrences	2a. That is life 2b. That's how things are
3. **Deflection:** Ignoring evidence of widespread systematic racism in health, criminal justice, education, and employment	3a. We have had an Indigenous or a Black president 3b. In Latin America, social class matters more than skin color 3c. I came to this country with nothing but my dreams
4. **Competing Victimization:** The myth of reverse discrimination	4a. I have been discriminated against for being poor

Note: This work builds upon the work of Bonilla-Silva (2010) and Wise (2008) by providing Latino/a illustrations of their strategies (Adames, Chavez-Dueñas, & Comas-Díaz, 2012).

The discrepancy between what Latinos/as say about the insignificance of skin color and their preference for whiteness is not unique. Many groups use similar tactics to avoid experiencing the unpleasant effect and thoughts associated with discussions related to privilege. Historically, people have developed reasons to justify inequality, avoided focusing on their privilege, and denied responsibility for the status of non-White individuals (Bonilla-Silva, 2010; Johnson, 2005; Wise, 2008). Table 2.3 describes four main strategies used to justify or deny contemporary racial inequality with Latino/a illustrations.

Latinos/as use language that suggests understanding of the racial hierarchy, yet they implement strategies to deny and justify the role of racism. We posit that the denial of how skin-color privilege has benefited light-skinned Latinos/as, often at the expense of darker-skin Latinos/as, contributes to the old practice of divide and conquer devised by those at the top of the stratification system. Current practices of denial, coupled with the legacy of our collective history, make it difficult for Latinos/as to engage in honest and self-critical dialogue regarding colorism needed to subvert this entrenched legacy.

Despite any unpleasant insights and feelings that learning about our past may engender, we must lean into our discomfort, integrate all parts of our past, and take collective responsibility for the privileges of whiteness. We believe that many Latinos/as are committed to eradicating the oppression of People of Color. However, such efforts may be undermined if we underestimate the role that skin-color privilege plays in our richly racially diverse families and communities. The next section offers a call for increasing awareness by stimulating dialogue as a prelude to increasing research on colorism.

A Call for Dialogue and Research on Colorism With Latino/a Populations

Stimulating Dialogue About Colorism

The majority of us are not socialized to reflect and deliberate on our areas of privilege, which can lead to difficulties seeing, acknowledging, discussing, and studying the consequences of within-group stigma and discrimination. During occasions when skin-color privilege becomes part of the discourse, it is often done in a superficial manner, leading to a shallow and fragmented understanding. This is furthered exacerbated by feelings of discomfort, guilt, shame, and the like, which serve to promote silence, avoid inquiry, and maintain the status quo.

In this chapter, we invite readers to deliberately reflect and engage in dialogue about within-group differences that lead to privilege for some at the expense of others. Our aim is to render more visible the experience of individuals of Indigenous and African descent who are still ignored within our communities.

In an effort to facilitate the reader's continued recognition, reflection, and understanding of colorism and its unique and current impacts on Latinos/as, we offer five key questions:

1. How and where can you learn more about the historical foundations of racial differences within Latinos/as?
2. What are the implications of your own skin color and phenotypic features with regard to differential treatment within one's own family as well as the greater society?
3. How can you use your areas of privilege (e.g., skin-color privilege) to mindfully open access routes for those with less privilege?
4. What are some ways in which you may have benefited from the system of oppression and what are you doing to end it?
5. Have you ever used your minority status to your advantage without thinking of how to give something back to the community?

Research Recommendations

Dialogue stemming from the aforementioned questions can serve as a prelude for stimulating colorism research. Given the underresearched state of colorism, exploratory and qualitative methods of inquiry are warranted to begin to deepen our understanding of such complex phenomena in the lives of Latinos/as today. Researchers currently conducting studies with Latino/a populations are encouraged to pay closer attention to how skin color may serve as a mediating and moderating variable. To facilitate such research directions, the following research recommendations are offered:

1. Future studies should elicit the narratives of Afro-Latinos/as and Indigenous Latinos/as to explore both within-group (i.e., within the family or

among peers in school and community) and between-group (i.e., with mainstream or non-Hispanic White society) experiences of colorism and related attitudes, beliefs, and feelings.

2. An exploration of how colorism impacts Latino/a racial and ethnic identity development could expand our understanding of how such models apply to Latinos/as across the color and phenotype gradient.

3. Studies regarding how Latino/immigrants viewed the concept of race prior to their immigration to the U.S. can advance the literature on colorism, especially longitudinal studies to explore the impact of exposure to race-conscious U.S. society and how this may compound colorism in complex ways.

4. It is important to explore how colorism impacts family dynamics, such as parenting practices and sibling relations, in order to inform family interventions.

5. It would be fruitful for psychologists to collaborate with colleagues from across the social sciences (i.e., history, anthropology, sociology) to develop more complex conceptions of colorism and impacts on individuals and communities in contemporary race-conscious U.S. society.

6. Organista (2009) recommends developing and validating multidimensional scales of colorism to advance such psychological assessment research. Specifically he states:

> Because Latinos can be both the targets and agents of phenotyping and colorism, both such experiences should be assessed as well. Further, because phenotyping and colorism can be experienced as positive

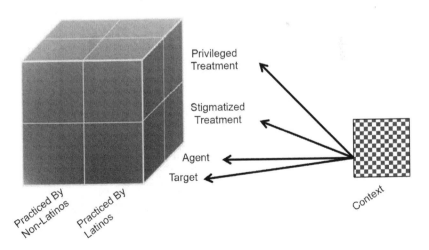

Figure 2.2 Dimensions of Latino/a Phenotyping and Colorism

Adapted from Organista (2009). The role of context has been added to the figure. Context will determine if an individual is the target or agent of phenotyping and colorism and whether privileged or stigmatized treatment is experienced.

treatment related to lighter skin privilege or negative treatment related to darker skin stigma, the resulting scale domains form two types of discrimination (phenotyping, colorism) by 2 directions of discrimination (target, agent) by 2 types of treatment (privilege, stigma) (p. 5).

His multidimensional matrix is depicted in Figure 2.2 with a slight modification to convey the ever-present role of context in Latino/a phenotyping and colorism.

Conclusions

In closing, we affirm that Latino/a psychology and its culture-centered perspective has made great strides toward creating a deeper and more complex understanding of Latino/a behavior and mental processes as influenced by culture and ethnic minority status in America. However, similar to other disciplines and fields of study, there continues to be under studied yet important areas of inquiry in need of our attention, such as colorism. In an effort to stimulate more dialogue and research in this area, a brief overview of the history of colorism in Latin America was offered. This historical account helps to ground our individual and collective efforts to better the lives of our Latino/a brothers and sisters through theory, research, and practice. "We must set apart a place for memory, for history, for that mirror which reminds us of who we were, shows us who we are, and promises what we may become" (Subcomandante Marcos, 2001, p. 93).

References

Adames, H. Y., Chavez-Dueñas, N. Y., & Comas-Díaz, L. (2012). *On race and privilege in Latina/o Psychology: Unmasking unearned advantages.* Paper presented at the biennial meeting of the National Latina/o Psychological Association. New Brunswick, NJ.

American Psychological Association. (2003). Guidelines on multicultural education, training, research, practice, and organizational change for psychologists. *American Psychologist, 58*(5), 377–402.

Andrews, G. R. (2004). *Afro-Latin America 1800–2000.* New York, NY: Oxford University Press.

Arce, C. H., Murgia, E., & Frisbie, W. P. (1987). Phenotype and life chances among Chicanos. *Hispanic Journal of Behavioral Sciences, 9,* 19–22.

Asher, K. (2009). *Black and green: Afro-Colombians, development, and nature in pacific lowlands.* Durham, NC: Duke University Press.

Bernard and Audre Rapoport Center for Human Rights. (n.d.). In *Afro-Colombian human rights: The implications for U.S.-Colombia Free Trade Agreement.* Retrieved from http://www.utexas.edu/law/centers/humanrights/projects_and_publications/colombia-memo.pdf

Bonilla-Silva, E. (2010). *Racism without racists: Color-blind racism and racial inequality in contemporary America.* New York, NY: Rowan & Littlefield Publishers.

Borrell, L. N. (2005). Racial identity among Hispanics: Implications for health and well-being. *American Journal of Public Health*, 95(3), 379–381. doi:10.2105/AJPH.2004.058172

Borrell, L. N. (2006). Self-reported hypertension and race among Hispanics in the National Health Interview Survey. *Ethnicity and Disease*, 16(1), 71–77.

Borell, L. N., & Crawford, N. D. (2006). Race, ethnicity, and self-rated health status in the Behavioral Risk Factor Surveillance System Survey. *Hispanic Journal of Behavioral Sciences*, 28(3), 387–403. doi:10.1177/0739986306290368

Casaus Arzu, M. (2009). Social practices and racist discourse of the Guatemalan power elites. In T. A. Van Dijk (Ed.), *Racism and discourse in Latin America* (pp. 171–216). Lanham, MD: Lexington Books.

Castellanos-Guerrero, A., Gomez-Izqueirdo, J., & Pineda, F. (2009). Racist discourse in Mexico. In T. A. Van Dijk (Ed.), *Racism and discourse in Latin America* (pp. 217–258). Lanham, MD: Lexington Books.

Cojti, D. C., & Edda, F. (2005). *Resultado de Decenio Internacional de los Pueblos Indígenas 1994–2004: Caso Guatemala*. Guatemala, CEDIM.

Comas-Díaz, L. (1996). LatiNegra: Mental health issues of African Latinas. In M. P. Root (Ed.), *The multiracial experience: Racial borders as the new frontier* (pp. 167–190). Thousand Oaks, CA: Sage Publications.

Comisión Interamericana de Derechos Humanos. (2011). *La situación de las personas Afrodescendientes en Las Americas [The situation of people of African descent in the Americas]*. Retrieved from http://www.oas.org/es/cidh/afrodescendientes/docs/pdf/AFROS_2011_ESP.pdf

Cones, J. H., & White, J. L. (1999). *Black man emerging: Facing the past and seizing a future in America*. New York, NY: Routledge.

Consejo Nacional para Prevenir la Discriminación. (2012). Encuesta nacional sobre discriminación en Mexico: Resultados sobre diversidad cultural [National survey of discrimination in Mexico: Results about cultural diversity]. Retrieved from http://www.conapred.org.mx/userfiles/files/Enadis-DC-INACCSS.pdf

Cruz-Carretero, S. (2006). *The African presence in Mexico: From Yanga to the present*. Chicago, IL: Mexican Fine Arts Center Museum.

de Estrada, T. D., & Marichal, D. (2010). ¿Reino o colonia? Nueva España, 1750–1804. In El Colegio De México (Eds.), *Nueva historia general de México* (pp. 307–353). México, DF: El Colegio De México.

Denton, N. A., & Massey, D. S. (1989). Racial identity among Caribbean Hispanics: The effect of double minority status on residential segregation. *American Sociological Review*, 54, 790–808.

Diene, D. (2005). *El racismo, la discriminacion racial, la xenophobia y todas las formas de discriminacion*. Special report, Adicion, Mision a Guatemala.

Dovidio, J. F., Gluszek, A., John, M., Ditlmann, R., & Lagunes, P. (2010). Understanding bias toward Latinos: Discrimination, dimensions of difference, and experience of exclusion. *Journal of Social Issues*, 66(1), 59–78. doi:10.1111/j.1540–4560.2009.01633.x

Engerman, S. L. (2000). A population history of the Caribbean. In M. R. Haines & R. H. Steckel (Eds.), *A population history* (pp. 506–509). Malden, MA: Polity Press.

Espino, R., & Franz, M. M. (2002). Latino phenotypic discrimination revisited: The impact of skin color on occupational status. *Social Science Quarterly*, 83(2), 612–623.

Frank, R., Akresh, I. R., & Lu, B. (2010). Latino immigrants and the U.S. racial order: How and where do they fit in? *American Sociological Review*, 75(3), 378–401. doi:10.1177/0003122410372216

Garcia-Martínez, B. (2010). Los años de la expansión. In El Colegio De México (Eds.), *Nueva historia general de México* (pp. 217–262). Mexico, DF: El Colegio De Mexico.

Gates, H. L. (2011). *Black in Latin America.* New York, NY: New York University Press.

Hall, G., & Patrinos, H. A. (2006). *Indigenous peoples, poverty and human development in Latin America.* London, England: Palgrave.

Helms, J. E. (2008). *A race is a nice thing to have: A guide to being a white person or understanding the white persons in your life* (2nd ed.). Alexandria, VA: Microtraining Associates.

Human Rights Office & Morales-Alvarado, S. F. (2004). *Resolución del procurador de los derechos humanos, en protección y defensa de los pueblos indígenas.* Guatemala: Procuraduría de los Derechos Humanos de Guatemala, Defensoría de Pueblos Indígenas.

Johnson, A. G. (2005). *Privilege, power, difference* (2nd ed.). Boston, MA: McGraw-Hill.

Katzew, I. (1996). Casta painting: Identity, and social stratification in colonial Mexico. In I. Katzew (Ed.), *New world orders: Casta painting and colonial Latin America* (pp. 17–29). New York, NY: Americas Society.

Lee, D. L., & Ahn, S. (2012). Discrimination against Latinas/os: A meta-analysis of individual-level resources and outcomes. *The Counseling Psychologist, 40*(1), 28–65. doi:10.1177/0011000011403326

Livi-Bacci, M. (2008). *Conquest: The destruction of the American Indios.* Malden, MA: Polity Press.

Lopez, I. (2008). But you don't look Puerto Rican: The moderating effect of ethnic identity on the relation between skin color and self-esteem among Puerto Rican women. *Cultural Diversity and Ethnic Minority Psychology, 14*(2), 102–108.

Marquez, G., & Meyer, L. (2010). Del autoritarismo a la democracia frágil, 1985–2010. In El Colegio De México (Eds.), *Nueva historia general de México* (pp. 747–792). México, DF: El Colegio De México.

McConahay, J. B. (1983). Modern racism and modern discrimination: The effects of race, racial attitudes, and context on simulated hiring decisions. *Personality and Social Psychology Bulletin, 9*(4), 551–558. doi:10.1177/0146167283094004

McConahay, J. B. (1986). Modern racism, ambivalence, and the modern racism scale. In J. F. Dovidio & S. L. Gaertner (Eds.), *Prejudice, discrimination, and racism* (pp. 91–125). San Diego, CA: Academic Press.

Minority Rights Group International. (2008). World Directory of Minorities and Indigenous Peoples-Colombia: Afro-Colombians. *United Nations High Commissioner for Refugees (UNHCR).* Retrieved from http://www.refworld.org/docid/49749d3cc.html

Minority Rights Group International. (2011). State of the world's minorities and indigenous peoples. *United Nations High Commissioner for Refugees (UNHCR).* Retrieved from http://www.unhcr.org/refworld/docid/4e16d37246.html

Montalvo, F. F. (2004). Surviving race: Skin color and the socialization and acculturation of Latinas. *Journal of Ethnic and Cultural Diversity in Social Work, 13*(3), 25–43.

Montalvo, F. F., & Codina, G. E. (2001). Skin color and Latinos in the United States. *Ethnicities, 1*(3), 321–341. doi:10.1177/146879680100100303

Morelos y Pavon, J. M. (1813). *Sentimientos de la Nación.* In Secretaria de Gobernación de Mexico. Retrieved from http://www.bicentenarios.es/doc/img/8130914.pdf

Nalda, E. (2010). El clásico en el Mexico antiguo. In El Colegio De Mexico (Eds.), *Nueva historia general de Mexico* (pp. 71–117). Mexico, DF: El Colegio De Mexico.

Nelson Mandela Centre of Memory. (2012). *Lighting your way to a better future: Speech delivered by Nelson R. Mandela at launch of Mindset Network*. Retrieved from http://db.nelsonmandela.org/speeches/pub_view.asp?pg=item&ItemID=NM S909&txts

Neville, H. A., Lilly, R. L., Duran, G., Lee, R. M., & Browne, L. (2000). Construction and initial validation of the Color-Blind Racial Attitudes Scale (CoBRAS). *Journal of Counseling Psychology*, 47(1), 59–70. doi:10.1037/0022-0167.47.1.59

Neville, H. A., Worthington, R. L., & Spanierman, L. B. (2001). Race, power, and multicultural counseling psychology: Understanding white privilege and color-blind racial attitudes. In J. G. Ponterotto, J. M. Casas, L. A. Suzuki, & C. M. Alexander (Eds.), *Handbook of multicultural counseling* (2nd ed., pp. 257–288). Thousand Oaks, CA: Sage Publications.

Ñopo, H. (2012). *New century, old disparities: Gender and ethnic earnings gaps in Latin America and the Caribbean*. Washington, DC: The Inter-American Development Bank.

Ogbu, J. U. (1994). Racial stratification and education in the United States: Why inequality exists. *Teachers College Record*, 98(2), 264–298.

Organista, K. C. (2007a). *Solving Latino psychosocial and health problems: Theory, practice, and populations*. Hoboken, NJ: John Wiley & Sons.

Organista, K. C. (2007b). The social stratification of Latino ethnicity, power, and social welfare in the United States. In K. C. Organista (Ed.), *Solving Latino psychosocial and health problems: Theory, practice, and populations* (pp. 39–63). Hoboken, NJ: John Wiley & Sons.

Organista, K. C. (2009). Latino clinical perspective on Montalvo's ethnoracial gap in clinical practice with Latinos. *Clinical Social Work Journal*, 37, 287–293. doi:10.1007/s10615- 009–0231-3

Perez, W. (2012). *Undocumented Latino students and the promise of higher education*. New York, NY: Teachers College Press.

Ramos, B., Jaccard, J., & Guilamo-Ramos, V. (2003). Dual ethnicity and depressive symptoms: Implications of being Black and Latino/a in the United States. *Hispanic Journal of Behavioral Sciences*, 25(2), 147–173. doi:10.1177/0739986303025002002

Santiago-Rivera, A. L., Arredondo, P., & Gallardo-Cooper, M. (2002). *Counseling Latinos and la familia: A practical guide*. Thousand Oaks, CA: Sage Publications.

Schorr, D. (2008). *A new, "post-racial" political era in America*. Retrieved from http://www.npr.org/templates/story/story.php?storyId=18489466

Soler-Castillo, S., & Pardo-Abril, N. G. (2009). Discourse and racism in Colombia: Five centuries of invisibility and exclusion. In T. A. Van Dijk (Ed.), *Racism and discourse in Latin America* (pp. 131–170). Lanham, MD: Lexington Books.

Suarez-Orozco, C., & Suarez-Orozco, M. M. (2001). *Children of Immigration*. Cambridge, MA: Harvard University Press.

Suarez-Orozco, M. M., & Paez, M. (2008). Introduction: The research agenda. In M. M. Suarez-Orozco & M. M. Paez (Eds.), *Latinos remaking America* (pp. 1–37). Berkeley, CA: University of California Press.

Subcomandante Marcos. (2001). *Our word is our weapon: Selected writings*. New York, NY: Seven Stories Press.

Sue, D. W. (2003). *Overcoming our racism: The journey to liberation*. San Francisco, CA: Jossey Bass.

Torres, L., & Ong, A. D. (2010). A daily diary investigation of Latino ethnic identity, discrimination, and depression. *Cultural Diversity and Ethnic Minority Psychology*, 16(4), 561–568. doi:10.1037/a0020652

U.S. Census Bureau. (2011). *The Hispanic population: Census 2011 brief*. Retrieved from http://www.census.gov/compendia/statab/brief.html

Wise, T. (2008). *Speaking treason fluently: Anti-racism reflections from an angry white male*. Berkeley, CA: Soft Skull Press.

3   The History of Latinos/as in the United States
Journeys of Hope, Struggle, and Resilience

Once social change begins, it cannot be reversed.

–Cesar Chavez, 1984, para. 85

As we entered into the new millennium, the United States (U.S.) had become one of the most multiracial, multiethnic, and multilingual societies in the world. Latinos/as, one of the groups contributing to the racial, ethnic, and linguistic diversity of the U.S., are currently the largest ethnic minority group with approximately 55 million individuals and growing. Consequently, the future of this country will largely be tied to the destiny of this community, including both U.S.-born citizens of Latino/a descent (e.g., second generation and beyond), and Latino/a immigrants (legal permanent residents, unauthorized immigrants). Thus in an effort to assist mental health professionals gain the conceptual knowledge necessary to become culturally and racially responsive providers for Latinos/as, an account of their history in the U.S. and immigration patterns is necessary. This chapter offers a critical look at the history of Latinos/as in the U.S. and their immigration. The chapter begins with a brief review of Mexicans, Puerto Ricans, Cubans, and Dominicans, four groups that account for a significant percentage of U.S. Latinos/as. The chapter also includes a section that describes the unauthorized Latino/a population and the myriad of challenges they experience, which impact their mental health. The chapter concludes with the ways in which Latinos/as have mobilized locally and nationally to advocate for their right to live and work in the country they call home.

Mexicans in the U.S.

Invasion and Colonization of Mexican Territory by the U.S.

The history of Mexicans in the U.S. is a story of struggle, survival, resistance, pride, and resilience in the face of insurmountable challenges. People of Mexican descent have deep roots in the U.S. dating back to pre-Columbian times when groups of Indigenous people lived in what is known today as the Southwest U.S. (Casaus & Andrade, 1983). The Spaniards are believed to be the first European group to reach the Appalachian Mountains, the Mississippi River, the Grand Canyon, and the Great Plains. They explored, claimed, and settled Spanish colonies in about half of today's lower 50 U.S. states. In this regional area, they founded what would later become the first U.S. American cities, where ironically Spanish was the official language. When Mexico gained its independence from Spain in 1821, this geographical area became part of the newly formed country called the United States of Mexico. However, in the late 1830s, British individuals began migrating west into the states of California and Texas. Many of them arrived and settled without the approval of the Mexican government, living there illegally until 1836 when the U.S. declared war on Mexico (Casaus & Andrade, 1983; Marin & Marin, 1991; Meier & Ribera, 1993). The Mexican–American War ended in 1848 with the Treaty of Guadalupe Hidalgo, resulting in Mexico being forced to give up the states known today as Arizona, California, Colorado, Kansas, Nevada, New Mexico, Oklahoma, Utah, and Wyoming (Meier & Ribera, 1993; Santiago-Rivera, Arredondo, & Gallardo-Cooper, 2002). Approximately 80,000 Mexican people who lived in these nine states in the years following the Mexican–American War were given the choice of staying and becoming U.S. citizens or moving south to the newly established U.S. Mexican border (Casaus & Andrade, 1983; Meier & Ribera, 1993). Unfortunately, the "Mexican families (who stayed) became disenfranchised in their own homeland. Farms or ranchos were lost, and the White immigrants gained the right to rule and suppress the original landowners" (Santiago-Rivera et al., 2002, p. 24). In addition to becoming a minority in their own lands, Mexicans in the U.S. experienced overwhelming levels of oppression and discrimination.

Mexican Immigration to the U.S.

In addition to the original U.S. citizens of Mexican descent who lived in the southwest prior to the invasion of White undocumented British immigrants, the largest increase in the population of Mexican origin has been due to immigration. Historically, Mexican immigrants have traveled to the U.S. in search of employment opportunities and better life conditions (Meier & Ribera, 1993; Santiago-Rivera et al., 2002). However, employment opportunities available to Mexican immigrants have fluctuated depending on the economic circumstances and sociopolitical climate of the U.S., as well as its need for cheap labor. For instance, when the U.S. was building its railroads in the 1880s, large numbers of Mexican citizens were invited to immigrate north of the border to fill available job positions (Marin & Marin, 1991). Yet the new Mexican immigrants did not fare any better than the Mexican American population. In fact, as Ogbu (1987) pointed out, "those who later emigrated from Mexico were accorded the subordinate status of the conquered group" (p. 259). It has been documented that immigration laws become more flexible when a need for cheap labor arises and is not fulfilled by U.S. citizens (Buriel, 1984; Santiago-Rivera et al., 2002). For instance, approximately one-eighth of the Mexican population immigrated to the U.S. during the early 1900s when the demand for cheap labor was very high (Mirande, 1985). Additionally, during World War II, when factory and agricultural jobs needed to be filled, the U.S. government created "special" programs such as the Bracero Program, which allowed Mexican immigrants to work in the U.S. (Rodriguez, 1999). During this period, "thousands of Mexicans were recruited and hired to serve as seasonal, farm, and industrial laborers throughout the U.S." (Santiago-Rivera et al., 2002, p. 23). On the other hand, when the U.S. experiences economic hardships, such as in the 1930s, immigrant laws become stricter and immigrants are used as scapegoats and blamed for the economic downturn of the country (Santiago-Rivera et al., 2002). For instance, in the 1930s, Mexicans living in the country were attacked and approximately 290,000 were deported for arguably violating immigration laws (Meier & Ribera, 1993; Rodriguez, 1999). Sadly, many of those deported were U.S. citizens with families and property on U.S. soil (Meier & Ribera, 1993). A similar episode occurred in 1954 when the U.S. Attorney General Herbert Brownell Jr. put the Operation Wetback Program into effect. Under this program, 1,075,000 Mexican immigrants were "rounded up and sent back to Mexico . . . the civil liberties and human rights of deportees and their families were often callously ignored, and physical treatment of deportees was sometimes marked by intimidation, harshness, and contempt" (Meier & Ribera, 1993, p. 189).

Mexicans Are the Past, Present, and Future of the U.S.

As of 2013, there were approximately 34 million people of Mexican descent living in the U.S. (Gonzalez-Barrera & Lopez, 2013). Of the 34 million, 34% or 11.7 million are immigrants (both documented and undocumented). Interestingly, due to the current sociopolitical climate in the U.S., the net migration flow of Mexicans between the U.S. and Mexico has declined. Recent reports indicate that between 2009 and 2014, more Mexicans were leaving than coming to the U.S., with an estimated net loss of 140,000 Mexican individuals (Gonzalez-Barrera, 2015). In total, about a million Mexicans and their families (including U.S. American children) left the U.S. in that same time period (Passel, Cohn, & Gonzalez-Barrera, 2012; Rosenblum & Meissner, 2014). These numbers suggest that the enchantment of the "American Dream" has dissipated for many Mexicans who often viewed the U.S. as the land of opportunity. The idea behind the "American Dream" has been replaced by a more realistic view of the U.S. as a country where Mexicans continue to endure inequities in every sector of society.

The contributions of Mexicans to the U.S. are undeniable. Most people are familiar with how the U.S. has been influenced by Mexican food (e.g., tacos, guacamole, enchiladas, tortas) and music (e.g., banda, ranchera, mariachi); however, few know about the incredible contributions of Mexicans to science, medicine, and psychology. For instance, many U.S. Americans are not familiar with Mario Molina (scientist awarded the Nobel Prize in chemistry), Albert Vinicio Baez (physicist who contributed to the development of the X-ray microscope), Ellen Ochoa (former astronaut and director of the Johnson Space Center), or Alfredo Quiñones-Hinojosa (neurosurgeon and oncologist who directs the Neurosurgery Brain Tumor Stem Cell Laboratory at Johns Hopkins University). Within the field of mental health, Mexicans have also contributed tremendously. For instance, Martha E. Bernal was the first woman of Latina/o descent to successfully complete a Ph.D. in clinical psychology and was a pioneer in ethnic identity who helped establish the Committee on Ethnic Minority Affairs of the APA. Also, Dr. Melba J. T. Vasquez is the first Latina/o president of the APA. Although it is likely that Mexicans in the U.S. will continue to experience challenges, their history of resiliency, hard work, and persistence also suggests that they will continue breaking barriers and making paths for new generations of proud Mexicans.

Puerto Ricans in the U.S.

The history of Puerto Rico is marked by double colonization: first during the conquest when the island was named Borinquen and the Spanish conquistadors invaded its native inhabitants, the Tainos. Soon after this first invasion, the island's name was changed to Puerto Rico, which means "Rich Port." The Tainos suffered greatly from diseases brought by the Spaniards, forced labor, and violence. African slaves were brought to the island as the result of the high number of Tainos dying from the conditions created by the Spaniards. Puerto Rico claimed its independence from Spain in 1868 with the *Grito de Lares*; however, it was not until 1897 that Puerto Ricans were granted political autonomy by the Spanish crown. Although Puerto Ricans had the autonomy to elect their own government, this freedom was unfortunately short lived.

Following the Spanish–American War of 1898, the second colonization took place, wherein the U.S. government invaded the island. The island's strategic military location, as well as its rich natural soil, prime for the production of sugar, was of particular interest to the U.S. Soon thereafter, the U.S. took control of the economic production of the island (Acosta-Belen & Santiago, 2006). Through the Foraker Act, Puerto Rico was incorporated into the U.S. trade network and became part of the economic system. This act also instituted civilian rule that limited the participation of Puerto Ricans in political affairs. For instance, with the approval of the Senate, the U.S. president appointed a governor of Puerto Rico and heads of other departments. The new instituted laws forced Puerto Ricans to live under the U.S. regime without being granted U.S. citizenship or voting representation in any branch of the U.S. government. From 1898 to 1917, Puerto Ricans were citizens of no country. However, right before World War I, the Jones Act of Puerto Rico (also referred by some as the Puerto Rican Federal Relations Act of 1917) was enacted, granting U.S. citizenship to Puerto Ricans (Acosta-Belen & Santiago, 2006). Many have asserted that the impetus to the act was to draft Puerto Ricans to fight in World War I. Puerto Ricans were allowed to pick their own governor for the first time in 1948, and they elected Luis Muñoz Marín. Four years later, Puerto Rico officially became an *estado libre associado* (commonwealth) of the U.S., which many posit is a politically correct way to say that Puerto Rico remains a colony. In fact, Puerto Ricans still have no representation in the U.S. Congress, they do not have the right to vote in any presidential or congressional elections, and they are not afforded the same social programs (e.g., social security, Medicare/Medicaid, unemployment compensation) as non-Puerto Rican U.S. citizens (Acosta-Belen & Santiago, 2006).

The Puerto Rican Diaspora

The immigration of Puerto Ricans to the U.S. is unique and complex given that it has been marked by a history of colonization and exploitation, forcing them to escape the poverty of the island. Given their legal status with the U.S., Puerto Ricans are able to travel freely to and from the mainland. Thus as a group they are often described as a *commuter nation* (Rivera-Batiz & Santiago, 1994) with a circular migration pattern (Melendez, 1993). However, there have been two big exoduses of people from Puerto Rico to the mainland U.S. The first exodus is known as the Great Migration, which took place in the 1950s and 1960s (Rodriguez Ayuso, Santana, & Santiago, 2013). The second exodus is taking place now in the new millennium. The economic crisis that began in 2006 and is currently contributing to high levels of unemployment and poverty in Puerto Rico has propelled people out of the island in search of job opportunities on the mainland. Interestingly, the gap between the number of people who leave the island and those who go back has widened in recent times. Today, approximately 4.9 million Puerto Ricans reside in the U.S. mainland, which is slightly higher than the 3.7 million Puerto Ricans living on the island (Brown & Patten, 2013). These figures account for about 9.5% of the total U.S. Latino/a population, making Puerto Ricans the second-largest Latino/a group in the country. Most Puerto Ricans in the U.S. have settled in the northeast (53%) and in the south (30%), mostly in Florida (Brown & Patten, 2013). This pattern, coupled with low birth rates, has led to a decline in the total population of Puerto Ricans on the island. Despite leaving their land in search of better opportunities, most Puerto Ricans tend to be worse off than other ethnic groups in several indicators of well-being. For instance, they have lower median household incomes, lower homeownership rates, and are more likely to live below the poverty line (Acosta-Belen & Santiago, 2006; Brown & Patten, 2013).

Despite the long history of colonization, oppression, and poverty, Puerto Ricans have persisted and showed resiliency in the face of incredible adversity. Their strength can be observed in the many contributions they made to different areas of U.S. society. For instance, Carlos Albizu Miranda was one of the first Puerto Ricans to earn a Ph.D. in psychology. He is the first Latino/a educator to have a North American university renamed in his honor. Puerto Ricans have also held high offices in the U.S. government, including Antonia Coello Novello, who served as the first Latina woman to be named U.S. Surgeon General, and Jose F. Cordero, who is the founding director of the National Center on Birth Defects and Developmental Disabilities at the Centers for Disease Control and Prevention (CDC). More recently, Justice Sonia Sotomayor was nominated and confirmed to serve in the highest court of the U.S. She is the first Latina woman in history to have a seat at the U.S. Supreme Court. As can be ascertained from this brief section, Puerto Ricans are a clear example of resiliency, adaptability, and hope. We hear the echoes of their zest for life and passion for their country and people in the beats of Tito Puente (Latin jazz composer), the voice of Marc Anthony (renowned and beautiful salsa singer), and the art of Rita Moreno (performer who has won all four major entertainment awards: the Oscar, Emmy, Grammy, and Tony).

Dominican Immigration

To understand the history of migration for people of the Dominican Republic (D.R.), it is important to review the long and contentious history shared between the two countries. After concerns from the U.S. government, who feared that the Germans would use the D.R. as a military base to attack the U.S. mainland during World War I, the U.S. occupied the D.R. (U.S. Department of State, 2001). The presence and dominance of the U.S., which lasted for eight years, propelled the D.R. into the global economic system (Torres-Saillant & Hernandez, 1998) as it became one of the main agricultural exports of sugar, *cacao* (cocoa bean), and coffee.

El Trujillato and the Butterflies

In 1930, Rafael Leónidas Trujillo, nicknamed *"El Jefe"* (the boss), began a dictatorial regime in the D.R. Today, historians and scholars often describe Trujillo as one of the most ruthless dictators of Latin America (Diaz, 2007; Torres-Saillant & Hernandez, 1998). To maintain power, Trujillo resorted to imprisoning, torturing, and killing anyone who opposed his views or spoke ill of him and his government. By the 1960s, the D.R. was experiencing "mysterious" daily disappearances of people who were later found either dead or as political prisoners, where they eventually were murdered by Trujillo's government. During this time, Patria Mercedes Mirabal, Minerva Mirabal, and Maria Teresa Mirabal, collectively known as *Las Hermanas*

Mirabal (The Mirabal Sisters) were assassinated by the government for courageously leading the rebellion in opposition of Trujillo's regime. The murder of *Las Hermanas Mirabal* received criticism from the international community with the Organization of American States imposing sanctions on the D.R. government following their deaths (Levitt, 2007; Lopez, 2015). In addition, President John F. Kennedy criticized and withdrew his support of Trujillo's government (Levitt, 2007). In 1961, Trujillo was assassinated (Encyclopedia of World Biography, 2004). The Mirabal Sisters, who by this time were known as *Las Mariposas* (The Butterflies) are often credited for sacrificing their lives and playing a key role in bringing an end to *El Trujillato* (era of Trujillo; Alvarez, 1994). In honor of their political activism, the United Nations General Assembly designated November 25 (anniversary of the day of the murder of the Mirabal Sisters) as the annual International Day for the Elimination of Violence Against Women (NLPA, 2015; United Nations, n.d.). To learn more about the Mirabal Sisters, we encourage you to read the historical novel, *In the Time of the Butterflies* by Julia Alvarez (1994).

Three Waves of Dominican Migration

Before and during *El Trujillato*, there was sporadic migration of people from the D.R. to the U.S (approximately 1,000 people during the 1950s; Levitt, 2007). Prior to *El Trujillato*, the majority of Dominican immigrants were from the upper class (e.g., highly educated, government officials, business people). During *El Trujillato*, the D.R. government allowed fewer Dominicans to leave the country due to fear that they would organize overseas to overthrow Trujillo's regime (Alvarez, 1994; Torres-Saillant & Hernandez, 1998). By the 1960s, approximately 10,000 Dominicans were migrating annually to the U.S. The first wave of immigrants from the D.R. were *Trujillistas* (followers and supporters of Trujillo) who feared for their safety following the approval and adoption of a democratic constitution signaling an end to *El Trujillato*. Their motivation to leave the country was also fueled by the election of Professor Juan Bosch in 1963, who was considered a reformist and progressive president. The U.S. was displeased with Bosch's ideologies and feared that he would turn the country into another communist country like Cuba. As a result, the D.R. was re-occupied by the U.S. in 1965 following civil unrest resulting from the overthrow of Bosch's government (Lawler & Yee, 2005). During this time, political unrest contributed to what would become the second wave of Dominican migration to the U.S., which began in 1968. That year, approximately 9,250 people arrived, and by 1973, around 14,000 Dominicans had settled in the U.S. (Graziano, 2006; Lawler & Yee, 2005; Levitt, 2007). The third wave of migration took place during the Dominican economic crisis of the 1980s and 1990s following the 2.2 billion dollar embezzlement by Banco Intercontinental. Consequently, there was widespread deterioration of incomes and high levels of poverty in the country, propelling people to migrate to the U.S. in search of better economic opportunities (Baerga & Thompson, 1990).

Dominicans in the U.S.: Profound Optimism and Hard Work

By 1990, there were approximately half a million Dominicans living in the States with over 65% residing in the New York City metropolitan area (Hernandez, 2004). The number of Dominicans had risen to over one million by the turn of the millennium; currently, there are approximately 1.8 million Dominicans in the U.S., accounting for 3.3% of the total U.S. Latino/a population (Lopez & Patten, 2015). Approximately 80% of individuals of Dominican descent in the U.S. are concentrated in the northeast, specifically in the New York, New Jersey, Rhode Island, and Eastern Massachusetts metropolitan areas, with another large Dominican community in the state of Florida (Lopez, 2015; Nwosu & Batalova, 2014).

Despite the multiple cultural strengths and zest for life that is often part of the Dominican DNA, they are faced with numerous challenges in the U.S., which are wisely captured by the Dominican saying, *no es facil en los paises* ("It is not easy in the states," connoting the struggles in the U.S.). For instance, the percentage of Dominicans who live in poverty is higher compared to the average U.S. (28% vs. 16% respectively) and Latino/a (25%) populations (Lopez, 2015). Similar patterns are seen with regard to their income, homeownership, and health insurance. With regard to education attainment, Dominicans have higher levels of education when compared to other U.S. Latinos/as (17% vs. 14% respectively); however, their level is significantly lower than the general U.S. population (30%; Lopez, 2015). Lastly, nearly half of Dominicans are bilingual (43%), about half are Spanish-dominant (48%) with 88% speaking Spanish at home, which is significantly higher compared to other Latinos/as (73%) in the U.S. (Lopez, 2015). A very dismal number of Dominicans are English-dominant (3%).

Dominicans have contributed to different areas of U.S. society. Although Dominicans are well known for their *merengue, bachata,* and the many great players in Major League Baseball, many have also contributed to academia, science, literature, and fashion. For instance, Dr. Elsa Gomez of Dominican descent was the first Latina woman to be president of a major U.S. public university (i.e., Kean University; Telgen & Kamp, 1993). Other notable Dominicans include Julia Alvarez, a scholar, novelist, and poet; Junot Diaz, a Pulitzer Prize winner and a 2012 MacArthur "genius grant" Fellow; Oscar de la Renta, a world-renowned fashion designer; and Victor Carreño, one of the few Latino/a aerospace engineers in NASA (National Aeronautics Space Administration), who invented the Single Frequency Multitransmitter Telemetry System. Dominicans, similar to other Latinos/as, are profoundly optimistic and hardworking as they continue to believe in making a difference in an imperfect place such as the U.S.

Cubans in the U.S.

Much attention has been paid to the exodus of immigrants that resulted from the Cuban Revolution of the late 1950s; however, the presence of Cubans in the U.S. dates back to the 19th century, when the island was still a Spanish colony (Perez, 2007). The earliest settlements of Cubans in the U.S. can be traced to three main geographical areas of the country: Florida, New Orleans, and New York (Perez, 2007). During the 1870s and 1880s, a large number of Cuban immigrants who were artists, writers, intellectuals, and those who worked in the tobacco industry settled in the U.S. (Perez, 2007). In 1898, the U.S. declared war on Spain with the alleged intent of helping to liberate Cuba from Spain. However, the U.S. maintained military occupation of the island and intervened in Cuban affairs for three years following Cuba's independence (i.e., Platt Amendment). For instance, the U.S. government called for amendments to the Cuban constitution giving the U.S. a military base (Guantanamo Bay) on that island.

In the early 20th century, immigration of Cubans into the U.S. continued, often as a result of employment opportunities. However, by the 1950s, Cubans were leaving the island primarily due to political unrest resulting from the dictatorship of Fulgencio Batista. The largest exodus of Cubans to the U.S. took place after the Cuban Revolution of 1959. This period has been divided into four distinct migration waves, which are briefly described in the following subsections.

First Wave: The Golden Exiles

The first large wave of Cuban migration to the U.S. took place between 1959 and 1962, following the Cuban Revolution. During this period, approximately 200,000 people were granted automatic refugee status in the U.S. This first wave of Cubans was composed of members from the privileged society (e.g., White, middle- and upper-class entrepreneurs, professionals) who had the most to lose from the socialist revolution (Stepick & Stepick, 2009). Cubans from the first wave settled in Miami Dade County in Florida, where they established what was ultimately called the Miami enclave. An important aspect of Cuban American history is the positive reception experienced by the first wave of Cuban immigrants, which was unlike that given to any other group throughout U.S. history. This initial encounter helped Cubans become the most economically and politically successful Latinos/as in the U.S. Their success was assured by the many resources and programs developed for them to prosper. Such resources were offered in both direct and indirect forms of assistance. A form of assistance from the U.S. government that directly benefited this community was the Cuban Refugee Program, which spent approximately one billion dollars between 1965 and 1976 (Pedraza-Bailey, 1985). The Cuban Refugee Program sponsored the transportation costs from Cuba to the U.S. and provided financial assistance to newly arrived refugees, as well as to states and agencies that served them. Cubans also benefited from programs that were not specifically created for them. For instance, between 1968 and 1980, 46.9% of all Small Business Administration grants in Miami Dade County were given to Latinos (almost all of whom were Cubans). In addition, Cuban immigrants were supported through indirect forms of assistance, such as by employment opportunities (e.g., University of Miami employing approximately 12,000 Cubans, laws passed to facilitate the process of recertification of Cuban professionals; Didion, 1987; Stepick & Stepick, 2009).

Second Wave: The Freedom Flights

The second wave of Cuban migration, which started in 1965, is considered the largest of all waves and brought approximately 260,500 individuals to the U.S. During this period, the Cuban government allowed people residing in the U.S. to pick up their relatives first by boat and then, upon the agreement of the U.S. government, by air. These flights were known as the freedom flights. The second wave of Cuban immigrants consisted primarily of women and elders. These individuals were also automatically granted refugee status similar to the first wave of Cubans (Perez, 2007).

Third Wave: The Marielitos

In 1980, the Cuban government allowed unrestricted immigration to the U.S. for the second time. During a span of six months, approximately 125,000 individuals left the island from Cuba's Mariel Harbor on small boats. Cubans who migrated during this wave are often referred to as the *Marielitos*. The demographic profile of this later wave of Cuban exiles was very different than the first two and included individuals from racially diverse backgrounds (Afro-Cubans in particular) and from lower socioeconomic status. Rumors indicated that the Cuban government had purposefully placed convicted felons and individuals suffering from mental health conditions in the boats. Media attention placed on these individuals led to public rejection, and those who had no relatives in the U.S. were placed in refugee camps until sponsors were found for them (Perez, 2007).

Fourth Wave: The Drafter Crisis

In the summer of 1994, the Cuban government announced that it would not stop or detain anyone who tried to leave the island by sea. However, unlike previous eras, the U.S. government was unwilling to welcome Cubans into the country. As a result, the U.S. Coast Guard sent Cubans rescued at sea to Guantanamo Bay (U.S. naval base in Cuba). The approximate 37,000 people who were detained were eventually admitted into the U.S. (Perez, 2007). These events became known as the "drafter crisis," which was finally stopped when the U.S. agreed to give visas to at least 20,000 Cubans each year. In turn, the Cuban government agreed to accept the return of any unauthorized Cubans captured at sea before reaching U.S. soil. The agreement is known as the "wet foot, dry foot policy"; that is, Cubans caught at sea (wet foot) are returned to Cuba, but if they are found in the U.S. (dry foot), they are allowed to stay.

The future of U.S.–Cuban relations is uncertain; however, a new chapter in Cuban America history began in 2014 when the U.S. government announced the renewal of political ties with the Cuban government. Since then there has been an increase of 78% in the migration of Cubans to the U.S. The future of this new group of Cuban immigrants will likely be shaped by the current sociopolitical climate as well as by the strong and loyal Cuban American community residing in this country.

Cuban Americans in the U.S.

Currently, there are two million Cubans living in the U.S. (Lopez & Patten, 2015). Several factors characterize the contemporary Cuban population, including low-fertility rates and older median age (40 years of age) when compared to other Latino/a groups, high levels of education, and economic success (Lopez & Patten, 2015). In general, Cubans tended to be political conservatives who often endorsed anticommunist policies and economic sanctions against the Cuban regime. However, these characteristics are more likely to hold true for Cubans who were part of the first wave of immigrants than for those of later generations. In fact, the overall Cuban population has become more politically diverse, especially across generational lines (Perez, 2007).

Overall, Cubans have benefited from the many programs designed to assist them in adapting and succeeding in the U.S.; however, they have also demonstrated many strengths (e.g., strong work ethic, adaptability) that have helped them to translate such benefits into political and economic capital that has benefited their community as a whole. Cuban Americans have also made significant contributions to many areas of U.S. society. For instance, in the arts, many may be familiar with the music of Celia Cruz, and Gloria and Emilio Estefan. However, Cubans have also made important advances in science. In fact, Luis Walter Alvarez was awarded the Nobel Prize in physics for his work in resonance particles. In addition, Isabel Pérez Farfante was the first Cuban woman to receive a doctoral degree from an Ivy League institution, and she is one of the most renowned zoologists for her study of prawns. In the area of business, Cuban Americans have proven to be brilliant entrepreneurs as well as innovative, creative leaders. Jeff Bezos, raised by a Cuban immigrant, founded and currently owns Amazon.com and developed one of the most successful and innovative business concepts.

Latino/a Immigrants in the U.S.

The commonly used phrase, "The U.S. is a land of immigrants" has never been more true than it is today. The latest available data from the U.S. Census Bureau indicates that as of 2013, the foreign-born population consisted of 41.3 million people (13% of the total U.S. population), of which 19.3 million (46% of total immigrants in the U.S.) reported being of Latino/a descent (Migration Policy Institute, 2013). Contrary to popular misconception, the majority (65% or 36 million) of Latinos/as in the U.S. are native born and 35% or 19.2 million are immigrants. Within the Latino/a immigrant population, 46% (8.8 million) are undocumented (Migration Policy Institute, 2013). Given the unique experiences of unauthorized Latinos/as in the U.S., this section provides an overview of the challenges and immigration laws that impact the mental health of undocumented individuals.

Undocumented Immigrants in the U.S.

Unauthorized Immigrants Defined

An undocumented or unauthorized immigrant is "a person who *resides* in the United States but who is *not* a U.S. citizen, has *not* been admitted for permanent residence, and is *not* in a set of specific authorized temporary statuses permitting longer-term residence and work" (Pew Hispanic Center, 2005, p. i). Hence, undocumented immigrants either enter the country without authorization or they come with a visa and stay after it has expired. Immigrants who enter the U.S. without authorization may be smuggled across the border by *coyotes* (people smugglers) for a fee, or they cross the border on their own, risking their lives across the desert or the Río Grande in order to reach U.S. territory (Ramos, 2005). Crossing the border has become increasingly more difficult in recent decades due to the multitude of measures that have been used by the Department of Homeland Security (DHS) to prevent people from crossing the southern U.S. border and deport those who have reached U.S. territory (see Figure 3.1). Even after they enter into the U.S., unauthorized immigrants are often subject to arrest and deportation. Table 3.1 provides a list of U.S. border control measures used to deter unauthorized migration. As a result, immigrants experience many difficulties finding a stable job and often live in fear of deportation.

Unaccompanied Minors

Typically, discussions on undocumented immigration center on the experiences of adults (Suárez-Orozco & Suárez-Orozco, 2001). However, some attention has recently been paid to the unaccompanied minors crossing the U.S.–Mexico border without authorization and with no adult family member or guardian (Chavez-Dueñas, Adames, & Goertz, 2014; Women's Refugee Commission, 2012). These children, known as *unaccompanied minors*, significantly increased in number between 2011 and 2014. During those three years, immigration officials at the U.S.–Mexico border apprehended approximately 6,800 unaccompanied minors (NIJC, 2014). Moreover, during the 2012 and 2013 fiscal years, the number of unaccompanied minors

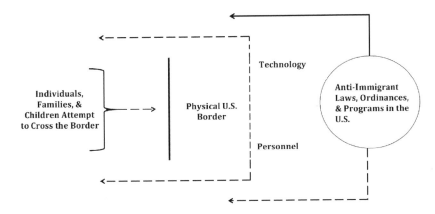

Figure 3.1 Border Control Measures Encountered by Unauthorized Immigrants

Dotted arrows depict deportation. The solid arrow represents immigrants who return to their homeland by choice for various reasons (e.g., family reunification, anti-immigrant sentiment in the U.S., lack of economic opportunities).

Table 3.1 Measures Used to Deter Unauthorized Migration

Measures	Type	Description
Border Patrol Agents	*Personnel*	• The DHS has increased the number of border patrol officers on the Mexico-U.S. border from 9,100 to approximately 17,700. A quarter of all Immigration and Customs Enforcement (ICE) personnel have been deployed to the southwest border region of the U.S. Dual purpose canine teams are used to detect humans, narcotics, and explosives crossing the border.
1993 Operation Hold the Line	*Governmental Strategic Plan*	• Purpose: To decrease the number of unauthorized people crossing the southern border in the area of Arizona and El Paso, Texas. Resulted in an increased number of immigrants who died attempting to cross the border.
1994 Operation Gatekeeper	*Governmental Strategic Plan*	• An expansion of Operation Hold the Line. Purpose: To decrease the number of unauthorized people crossing the border in San Diego, California. Goal: To have the traffic of people move eastward where the U.S. border patrol had a strategic advantage, allowing them to arrest and deport those crossing the border without authorization.

(Continued)

Table 3.1 Continued

Measures	Type	Description
2005 Operation Streamline	*Governmental Strategic Plan*	• Enforces criminal penalty (6 months in prison for first attempt and up to 20 years for second attempt) for undocumented immigrants caught trying to cross the southern U.S. border.
Unmanned Aerial Vehicles (UAVs)	*Technology*	• Pilotless planes designed to survey different areas in an attempt to locate individuals trying to cross the border; also referred to as drones.
Integrated Automated Fingerprint Identification System (IAFIS)	*Technology*	• Biometric database with over 47 million records. Fingerprints of individuals apprehended at the border or in other locations are entered into the system, which is also connected to the Federal Bureau of Investigation (FBI) criminal records.
Radiation Detectors	*Technology*	• Small devices (size of a pen or cell phone) that sense material, hidden people, and the like. Border patrol agents are equipped with these devices.
Tethered Aerostat Radar Systems (TARS)	*Technology*	• Blimp-like surveillance devices/radars that provide data on unauthorized movement into U.S. air and land space.

detained doubled to 13,000 and 24,000 children, respectively. By 2014, the number of minors held in custody by immigration officials was over 67,000 (U.S. Department of Homeland Security, 2016). Unfortunately, U.S. government officials were not adequately prepared to handle the arrival of unaccompanied minors, and many of these children experienced dehumanizing treatment (Chavez-Dueñas et al., 2014). The children are detained and housed in warehouses without access to basic necessities (e.g., food, water, showers). Although the numbers dropped to 39,000 by fiscal year 2015, experts posit that as long as the circumstances that propel children to leave their home countries do not change, they will continue to make the treacherous journey to the U.S. in search of safety, family reunification, and an overall better quality of life (Chavez-Dueñas et al., 2014; Kennedy, 2014; NIJC, 2014). This is also true of adult unauthorized immigrants and their families who are also faced with a myriad of challenges and remain at risk of being deported if the DHS finds them.

The Myriad of Challenges Faced by Unauthorized Immigrants

As a result of their legal status and their fear of deportation, undocumented immigrants are vulnerable to exploitation and abuse from their employers, who often deny them even the most basic labor rights (e.g., breaks, access to water, restroom facilities) and expose them to dangerous working conditions (Kronick & Hargis, 1998; National Council of La Raza, 1990; 2008; C. Suárez-Orozco & Suárez-Orozco, 2001; Velásquez, 1993). In addition, children of undocumented immigrants live with the constant fear that their parents might be deported. In fact, C. Suárez-Orozco and Suárez-Orozco (2001) reported that "a common terror many undocumented children experience is that they will never be reunited with their parents" (p. 35). Children who are undocumented immigrants themselves, confront additional challenges as their parents may significantly restrict their activities outside the home for fear they will be arrested and deported.

Fear of deportation experienced by families often leads to distrust of people in positions of authority, such as school officials, police officers, and medical doctors (C. Suárez-Orozco & Suárez-Orozco, 1995, 2001). Additionally, undocumented immigrants confront a host of struggles not experienced by most authorized individuals. For example, the opportunities available to immigrants, as well as their ultimate adjustment, depend on their legal status, job stability, and social support (Chavez, 1992; C. Suarez-Orozco & Suárez-Orozco, 1995). Unfortunately, given their legal status, it is often difficult for undocumented immigrants to find good paying jobs; hence a large proportion work in service, domestic, seasonal farming, fishing, and the construction and repair industries (Migration Policy Institute, 2013; Passel & Cohn, 2015).

Deportation and Its Devastating Impact on Latino/a Families

The impact of aggressive and excessive enforcement of immigration policies has a devastating effect on Latino/a communities, which often experience and perceive the "federal and local law enforcement as a threat and a predator, rather than a public servant" (Magaña-Salgado, 2014, p. 3). Aggressive immigration enforcement has a negative impact not only on the individual who may be apprehended and deported but also on families. In the U.S., there are approximately 5.5 million children with at least one undocumented parent, 80% (4.5 million) of whom are U.S. citizens (Wessler, 2011). Families that include members who are both documented (e.g., U.S. citizens, legal permanent residents) and undocumented are referred to as *mixed status*. Mixed-status families experience a multitude of challenges, including the fear of separation. Such fear, coupled with aggressive and excessive enforcement of immigration policies, often forces mixed status families to grapple with the possibility of deportation. Thus families could make one of three decisions: 1) the entire family may leave the U.S., 2) the undocumented parent may choose to leave the country, or 3) the family may decide to stay in the U.S. indefinitely (Fix & Zimmerman, 2001). Regardless of what may happen, all members of mixed-status families are likely to live with the fear of separation from their loved ones. This fear may lead to symptoms of anxiety and feelings of isolation (Yoshikawa, Godfrey, & Rivera, 2008). For instance, a study by Brabeck and Xu (2010) examining the impact of deportation policies on mixed-status Latino/a families, found that having a family member at high risk of deportation negatively impacted the mental health of the rest of the family. It also disrupted intrafamilial relationships and negatively affected the emotional well-being and academic performance of children. Moreover, for families that have experienced the process of deportation, symptoms related to abandonment, trauma, and financial problems were common (Capps, Castañeda, Chaudry, & Santos, 2007; Yoshikawa et al., 2008). The deportation of a parent may exacerbate the already precarious economic conditions experienced by many Latino/a families by removing a source of income. The consequences of deportation may be more devastating when both parents are arrested and children are left in the care of relatives or taken into the custody of the Department of Children and Family Services (e.g., the foster care system; Wessler, 2011). Even when there is no family separation, children are likely to be negatively impacted. For instance, when children leave the U.S. with their parents, they face the consequences of being uprooted from their social, familiar, and linguistic environments. Lamentably, family separation through deportation has become a very profitable business.

The Business of Deporting Dreams

Latinos/as are overrepresented in the total number of individuals deported (Magaña-Salgado, 2014). For instance, in 2013, 78% of undocumented immigrants were of Latino/a origin; however, 97.7% of individuals deported were Latinos/as (Zong & Batalova, 2015). Consequently, some civil rights organizations (e.g., Mexican American Legal Defense and Educational Fund (MALDEF), National Council of La Raza (NCLR)) have suggested that the overrepresentation of Latinos/as in deportations is "the direct result of discriminatory policies at the federal, state, and local level and not just due to the large proportion of undocumented immigrants who are of Latino/a descent" (Magaña-Salgado, 2014, p.1). Table 3.2 provides examples of laws, local ordinances, and tactics that disproportionately target Latinos/as. Some of these laws "criminalize the mere presence of undocumented immigrants" (Magaña-Salgado, 2014, p.2), while others either exclude or make immigrants afraid to seek critical services (e.g., medical care, police assistance).

The federal enforcement of immigration policies is aided by the unprecedented allocation of funds in the form of resources and personnel. Studies demonstrate that the federal government spends more money on the enforcement of immigration policies than any other form of enforcement combined (Meissner, Kerwin, Chishti, & Bergeron, 2013). For example, during fiscal year 2012, the U.S. government spent approximately $18 billion on the enforcement of immigration laws, which was 24% more than what it spent

Table 3.2 Anti-Immigrant Laws, Ordinances, Programs, and Tactics

Year	Title (Location)	Description
1996	*287g (National)*	• An ICE program allowing state and local law enforcement agencies to partner with ICE to perform the functions of federal immigration agents.
2006–2007	*Ordinance Hazelton (Pennsylvania)*	• Legislation seeking to punish landlords and employers accused of renting to and hiring undocumented immigrants.
2007	*Save Manassas Prince William County (Virginia)*	• Local ordinance targeting undocumented immigrants. The ordinance attempted to curb undocumented immigrants' access to public services and increased immigration enforcement by local law authorities/police.
2007–present	*E-Verify (National)*	• A program run by the DHS and the Social Security Administration that confirms an employee's legal status to work in the U.S. As of 2015, 18 states required the use of the program, as well as public agencies and contractors.
2008–2014	*Secure Communities (National)*	• A program of the DHS designed to identify undocumented immigrants in U.S. jails and prisons. Participating facilities submit fingerprints of individuals arrested to criminal and immigration databases.
2010	*SB 1070 (Arizona)*	• Law passed in Arizona in 2010 and upheld by the Supreme Court in 2012 allowing police officers, under the authority of state law, to inquire about an individual's immigration status during a routine traffic stop.
2010	*Utah Letter (Utah)*	• Anonymous letter that included the names, addresses, and other confidential information of over 1,300 Latino/a residents of Utah believed to be undocumented. The letter was sent to the media, law enforcement agencies, various state agencies and officials, and the DHS.
2015–present	*Priority Enforcement Program, PEP (National)*	• Program enabling the DHS to work with state and local law enforcement to take custody of individuals who they determine pose a "danger" to public safety.

(Continued)

Table 3.2 Continued

Year	Title (Location)	Description
2015	*HB 318 (North Carolina)*	• Law prohibiting local governments from adopting "sanctuary" ordinances that limit the enforcement of federal immigration law and prohibits some government officials from accepting various forms of identification and E-Verify. The governor of North Carolina signed this law into effect on October 2015.

on the FBI, Drug Enforcement Administration (DEA), U.S. Secret Service, and U.S. Marshals Service and Bureau of Alcohol, Tobacco, Firearms, and Explosives combined. Overall, since 1986, nearly $187 billion have been used for immigration enforcement (Magaña-Salgado, 2014; Meissner et al., 2013).

State laws and local ordinances serve to funnel undocumented immigrants arrested for minor violations into jails and privately owned detention centers. These laws and ordinances have produced a surge of lobbyists who spent $45 million over the past decade (2002–2012) in efforts to influence the U.S. Congress to increase the number of immigrants who are detained to keep their businesses profitable (Fang, 2013). Lobbying has contributed to an increase in the amount of resources allocated to the enforcement of immigration laws (Fang, 2013). According to a report from the *Nation Magazine*, in fiscal year 2012, two publicly traded prison companies (i.e., Corrections Corporation of America, Geo Group) made over $441.9 million in federal contracts from the detention of undocumented immigrants. That same year, the two companies' combined netted $296.9 million in revenues from ICE contracts. The report also states that between the years 2011 to 2013, these companies contributed over $380,000 to Republican candidates and committees, which is almost six times the amount they have contributed to politicians from the Democratic Party. Thus it is clear that the enforcement of immigration policies has become a profitable business, where wealthy corporations determine the destiny of undocumented immigrants, and politicians seek to benefit from the dreams and hopes of one of the most vulnerable segments of the U.S. population. Despite these reprehensible actions, undocumented immigrants continue to contribute tremendously to the country.

Contributions of Undocumented Immigrants to the U.S.

Undocumented immigrants bear the stigma associated with living in the U.S. without permission of the government, which makes them ineligible for many social services (e.g., social security benefits, Medicare, the Affordable

Care Act, the Link program). However, all immigrants pay taxes in various forms, regardless of their legal status. For instance, undocumented immigrants pay sales and property taxes, just like all people residing in the U.S. In addition, undocumented immigrants who use false social security numbers have income taxes deducted from their paychecks just like anyone else. To complete their annual income tax returns, immigrants use an Individual Taxpayer Identification Number, which is provided by the IRS. The money collected from the taxes paid by undocumented immigrants helps to fund federal programs for which they are ineligible. In fact, it is estimated that individuals who use incorrect or false social security numbers contribute approximately $7 billion annually to the Social Security Administration and about $1.5 million to Medicare (Porter, 2005). Overall, all immigrants will pay $80,000 more in taxes per capita than they use in government benefits over their lifetimes (Smith & Edmonston, 1997). These statistics markedly contradict anti-immigrant groups and the media's portrayals of undocumented immigrants as people who overuse social services and make no contributions to the U.S. economy.

The Immigration Movement

> "You cannot oppress the people who are not afraid anymore."
> –Cesar Chavez, 1984, para, 85

On December 16, 2005, the U.S. House of Representatives passed the Border Protection, Anti-terrorism, and Illegal Immigration Control Act (H.R. 4437). Among other provisions, this bill intended to address undocumented immigration in four ways: 1) building a 700-mile fence along the U.S.–Mexico border, 2) increasing penalties for hiring undocumented immigrants, 3) making it a felony to house undocumented immigrants, and 4) criminalizing the presence of undocumented immigrants in the U.S. by expanding the definition of "aggravated felony" to include unauthorized entrance into the U.S. Although the bill did not pass the Senate, the fear it created among the Latino/a community served as a catalyst for a grassroots social action that we (Adames & Chavez-Dueñas) are calling *The Immigration Movement*.

The Immigration Movement contained three pillars with the first one focusing on grassroots community activism. This pillar was built by coalitions of different sectors across the community, including the Catholic Church, labor union leaders, local immigrant rights organizations, student groups, Latinos/as, and members of other ethnic communities with large percentages of immigrants (e.g., Koreans, Filipinos). Organized activism was evident in the massive marches that took place in 2006 across the U.S. to protest H.R. 4437 and advocate for immigration reform. An estimated 3.5 to 5 million immigrants and their advocates marched across 160 cities (Bada, Fox, & Selee, 2006). In addition to the marches, protesters also called on the community to boycott the government by not attending school or work on May 1, 2006. The goal of the national day of boycott, known as a *Day Without Immigrants*, was to demonstrate the vital contributions that Latino/a immigrants make to the U.S. with their labor and economic power.

The second pillar of *The Immigration Movement* involved the work of civil rights organizations, including those of the MALDEF, NCLR, and the League of United Latin American Citizens (LULAC) among many others. These organizations helped plan the marches and publicly expressed their strong opposition and condemnation of H.R. 4437. For instance, in 2006, over 88 social service and civil rights organizations jointly wrote a letter to then president George W. Bush in which they stated,

> As organizations that advocate on behalf of and provide assistance to millions of Latinos, we are astonished that the White House supported such a bill. This proposal would be extremely harmful to Americans while doing absolutely nothing to solve our real immigration problems.
> (NCLR, 2006, para. 2)

Many of these organizations also published landmark documents in which they challenged common stereotypes about undocumented immigrants given the rampant amount of misinformation circulating about this group. One of the better-known fact sheets was published by the NCLR in 2006 was titled "Common Myths About Undocumented Immigrants." The document outlines and refutes five specific misconceptions about undocumented immigrants and provides accurate information about the various contributions they make.

The third pillar of the movement includes the undocumented youth or the *DREAMers*. These youth organized themselves to protest the aggressive enforcement of immigration policies and to advocate for immigration reform in general. Moreover, they sought to obtain support for the passage of the Development, Relief, and Education for Alien Minors (DREAM) Act. This bill, first introduced to the U.S. Congress in 2001, aimed to provide undocumented youth who immigrated to the U.S. before the age of 16 with a path toward legalization on the condition that they attend college or serve in the U.S. military for a minimum of two years (Batalova & McHugh, 2010). Although the U.S. Congress has not passed the DREAM Act, DREAMers have shown incredible social and political advocacy skills and determination. For instance, the social movement they created ultimately led to the Deferred Action for Childhood Arrivals (DACA) an executive order announced in 2012 by the secretary of Homeland Security and signed by the U.S. president, Barack Hussein Obama. DACA gave DREAMers the possibility of obtaining a two-year relief from immigration enforcement. Although DACA does not provide lawful immigration status or a path to a green/resident card or citizenship, it allows DREAMers to be lawfully employed, apply for social security numbers, and obtain a driver's license (depending on their state of residence; Passel & Lopez, 2012). In 2014, President Obama

announced Deferred Action for Parents of Americans and Lawful Permanent Residents (DAPA), a second executive order. Unfortunately, a federal
district court in Texas issued an order that temporarily blocked DAPA from
being implemented. In 2016, the U.S. Supreme Court announced that they
would take on this case and make a decision about whether to allow this
order to go forward.

The *Immigration Movement* continues even as this book goes into press
(circa, 2016). In fact, 2016 began with a news article published in the *Washington Post* announcing that the DHS had begun a new operation consisting
of a series of raids targeting hundreds of undocumented immigrant families
for deportation (Rein, 2016). As the news about 121 undocumented immigrants who were arrested during the first weekend of 2016 began to circu-
late, fears swept across the Latino/a community. However, unlike previous
events, this time it only took a couple of days for community organizations
to disseminate information about ways for people to protect themselves
and safeguard their rights. Although the future of immigration reform is
uncertain, current developments (e.g., immigration raids), coupled with
recent anti-immigrant rhetoric spewed by a significant number of U.S. 2016
presidential candidates (e.g., Donald J. Trump, Rafael Edward "Ted" Cruz,
Marco A. Rubio), indicate that undocumented immigrants are once again
being used as scapegoats for the problems the U.S. is facing. Nevertheless,
The Immigration Movement is a reminder to Latinos/as that a strong sense
of solidarity, the belief in the power of resistance, and profound *esperanza*
(hope) unifies this community. Thus Latinos/as will likely continue advocat-
ing for their right to live and work in the country they call home.

References

Acosta-Belen, E., & Santiago, C. E. (2006). *Puerto Ricans in the United States:
A contemporary portrait.* Boulder, CO: Lynne Rienner Publishers.
Alvarez, J. (1994). *In the time of the butterflies.* Chapel Hill, NC: Algonquin Books.
Ayuso, R. I., Santana, G. K., & Santiago, M. M. (2013). *Perfil del migrante 2011* (p. 28).
San Juan, PR: Instituto de Estadísticas. Retrieved from http://www.estadisticas.gobi
erno.pr/iepr/LinkClick.aspx?fileticket=9qCLtkwFQnc%3D& ta bid=165
Bada, X., Fox, J., & Selee, A. (2006). *Invisible no more: Mexican migrant civic par-
ticipation in the United States.* Washington, DC: Wilson Center. Retrieved from
https://www.wilsoncenter.org/sites/default/files/Invisible%20No%20More_0.pdf
Baerga, M. del C., & Thompson, L. (1990). Migration in a small semi-periphery:
The movement of Puerto Ricans and Dominicans. *International Migration Review,*
14(4), 656–683.
Batalova, J., & McHugh, M. (2010). *DREAM vs. Reality: An analysis of potential
DREAM Act beneficiaries.* Washington, DC: Migration Policy Institute, National
Center on Immigrant Integration Policy.
Brabeck, K., & Xu, Q. (2010). The impact of detention and deportation on Latino
immigrant children and families: A quantitative exploration. *Hispanic Journal of
Behavioral Sciences,* 32(3), 341–361. doi:10.1177/0739986310374053

Brown, A., & Patten, E. (2013). *Hispanics of Puerto Rican origin in the United States, 2011.* Retrieved from www.pewhispanic.org/2013/06/19/hispanics-of-puerto-rican-origin-in-the-united-states-2011/

Buriel, R. (1984). Integration with traditional Mexican American culture and sociocultural adjustment. In J. L. Martinez, & R. Mendoza (Eds.), *Chicano psychology* (2nd ed., pp. 95–130). New York: Academic Press.

Capps, R., Castañeda, R. M., Chaudry, A., & Santos, R. (2007). *Paying the price: The impact of immigration raids on America's children.* Washington, DC: National Council of La Raza & Urban Institute. Retrieved from www.urban.org/sites/default/files/alfresco/publication-pdfs/411566-Paying-the-Price-The-Impact-of-Immigration-Raids-on-America-s-Children.PDF

Casaus, L., & Andrade, S. (1983). A description of Latinos in the United States: Demographic and sociocultural factors of the past and the future. In S. J. Andrade (Ed.), *Latino families in the United States: A Resource Book for Family Life Education* (pp. 19–34). New York, NY: Planned Parenthood Federation of America Education Department.

Chavez, C. (1984). *Cesar Chavez address to the Commonwealth Club of California.* Retrieved from http://www.chavezfoundation.org/_cms.php?mode=view&b_code=001008000000000&b_no=16&page=1&field=&key=&n=7

Chavez, L. (1992). *Out of the barrio: Toward a new politics of Hispanic assimilation.* New York: NY: Basic Books.

Chavez-Dueñas, N. Y., Adames, H. Y., & Goertz, M. T. (2014). Esperanza sin fronteras: Understanding the complexities surrounding the unaccompanied refugee children from Central America. *Latina/o Psychology Today, 1*(1), 10–14.

Díaz, J. (2007). *The brief and wondrous life of Oscar Wao.* New York, NY: Riverhead Trade.

Didion, J. (1987). *Miami.* New York, NY: Random House.

Encyclopedia of World Biography. (2004). *Rafael Leónidas Trujillo Molina.* Retrieved from http://www.encyclopedia.com/doc/1G2–3404706463.html

Fang, L. (2013, February 27). How private prisons game the immigration system. *The Nation.* Retrieved from http://www.thenation.com/article/how-private-prisons-game-immigration-system/

Fix, M., & Zimmerman, W. (2001). All under one roof: Mixed-status families in an era of reform. *International Migration Review, 35*(2), 397–419.

Gonzalez-Barrera, A. (2015). *More Mexicans leaving than coming to the U.S.* Retrieved from http://www.pewhispanic.org/2015/11/19/more-mexicans-leaving-than-coming-to-the-u-s/

Gonzalez-Barrera, A., & Lopez, M. H. (2013). *A demographic portrait of Mexican-origin Hispanics in the United States.* Retrieved from http://www.pewhispanic.org/2013/05/01/a-demographic-portrait-of-mexican-origin-hispanics-in-the-united-states/

Graziano, F. (2006). Why Dominicans migrate: The complex of factors conducive to undocumented maritime migration. *Diaspora, 15*(1), 1–33.

Hernandez, R. (2004). On the age against the poor: Dominican migration to the United States. *Journal of Immigrant & Refugee Services, 2*(2), 87–107. doi:10.1300/J191v02n01_06

Kennedy, E. (2014). *No children here: Why Central American children are feeling their homes.* American Immigration Council (AIC). Retrieved from http://www.immigrationpolicy.org/sites/adefault/files/docs/no_childhood_here_why_central_american_children_are_fleeing_their_homes_final.pdf

Kronick, R. F., & Hargis, C. H. (1998). *Dropouts: Who drops out and why—and the recommended action.* Springfield, IL: Charles C. Thomas Publishing.

Lawler, D., & Yee, C. (2005). *Foreign Relations of the United States, 1964–1968: Dominican Republic, Cuba, Haiti, Guyana.* Washington, DC: United States Government Printing Office. Retrieved from http://static.history.state.gov/frus/frus1964-68v32/pdf/frus1964-68v32.pdf

Levitt, P. (2007). Dominican Republic. In M. C. Waters & R. Ueda (Eds.), *New Americans: A guide to immigration since 1965* (pp. 399–411). Cambridge, MA: Harvard University Press.

Lopez, B. (2015). *The Mirabel Sisters: Heroes, not victims.* Retrieved from www.huffingtonpost.com/belkys-lopez/the-mirabal-sisters-heroe_b_8647552.html

Lopez, G. (2015). *Hispanics of Dominican Origin in the United States, 2013.* Washington, DC: Pew Research Center. Retrieved from www.pewhispanic.org/2015/09/15/hispanics-of-dominican-origin-in-the-united-states-2013/

Lopez, G., & Patten, E. (2015). *The impact of slowing immigration: Foreign-born share falls among 14 largest U.S. Hispanic Origin Groups.* Washington, DC: Pew Research Center. Retrieved from www.pewhispanic.org/2015/09/15/the-impact-of-slowing-immigration-foreign-born-share-falls-among-14-largest-us-hispanic-origin-groups/#diverse-origins

Magaña-Salgado, J. (2014). *Detention, deportation, & devastation: The disproportionate effect of deportations on the Latino community.* Los Angeles, CA: The Mexican American Legal Defense and Educational Fund; The National Day Laborer Organizing Network; & The National Hispanic Leadership Agenda. Retrieved from http://www.maldef.org/assets/pdf/Deportation_Brief_MALDEF-NHLA-NDLON.pdf

Marin, G., & Marin, B. (1991). *Research with Hispanic populations.* Thousand Oaks, CA: Sage Publishing.

Meier, M. S., & Ribera, F. (1993). *Mexican Americans/American Mexicans: From conquistadors to Chicanos.* Canada: HarperCollins.

Meissner, D., Kerwin, D. M., Chishti, M., & Bergeron, C. (2013). *Immigration enforcement in the United States: The rise of a formidable machinery.* Washington, DC: Migration Policy Institute.

Melendez, E. (1993). The unsettled relationship between Puerto Rico poverty and migration. *Latino Studies Journal, 4*(3), 45–55.

Migration Policy Institute. (2013). *Profile of the unauthorized population: United States.* Washington, DC: Migration Policy Institute. Retrieved from http://www.migrationpolicy.org/data/unauthorized-immigrant-population/state/US

Mirandé, A. (1985). *The Chicano experience: An alternative perspective.* Notre Dame, IN: University of Notre Dame Press.

National Council of La Raza. (1990). *Immigration reform.* Retrieved from http://www.nclr.org/content/topics/detail/500/

National Council of La Raza. (2006). *Letter to the White House from Latino organizations in support of comprehensive immigration reform.* Retrieved from http://publications.nclr.org/bitstream/handle/123456789/180/36910_file_Affiliate_letter_to_WH_2_06_FINAL.pdf?sequence=1&isAllowed=y

National Immigrant Justice Center. (2014). *Unaccompanied immigrant children: A policy brief from Heartland Alliance's National Immigrant Justice Center.* Retrieved from https://immigrantjustice.org/sites/immigrantjustice.org/files/NIJC%20Policy%20Brief%20%20Unaccompanied%20Immigrant%20Children%20FINAL%20Winter%202014.pdf

National Latina/o Psychological Association. (2015). Knowing nuestra herstory: Las Hermanas Mirabal. *Latina/o Psychology Today, 2*(1), 40.

Nwosu, C., & Batalova, J. (2014). *Immigrants from the Dominican Republic in the United States.* Washington, DC: Migration Policy Institute. Retrieved from http://www.migrationpolicy.org/article/foreign-born-dominican-republic-united-states

Ogbu, J. U. (1987). *Variability in minority responses to schooling: Nonimmigrant vs. immigrants.* Mahwah, NJ: Lawrence Erlbaum Associates.

Passel, J. S., & Cohn, D. (2015). *Share of unauthorized immigrant workers in production, construction jobs falls since 2007.* Washington, DC: Pew Research Center. Retrieved from http://www.pewhispanic.org/2015/03/26/share-of-unauthorized-immigrant-workers-inproduction-construction-jobs-falls-since-2007/

Passel, J. S., Cohn, D., & Gonzalez-Barrera, G. (2012). *Net migration from Mexico falls to zero- and perhaps less.* Washington, DC: Pew Research Center. Retrieved from http://www.pewhispanic.org/2012/04/23/net-migration-from-mexico-falls-to-zero-and-perhaps-less/

Passel, J. S., & Lopez, M. H. (2012). *Up to 1.7 million unauthorized immigrants may benefit from new deportation rules.* Retrieved from http://consulmex.sre.gob.mx/boise/images/stories/2012/medios12/phunauthorized-immigrant-deportation.pdf

Pedraza-Bailey, S. (1985). *Political and economic migrants in America: Cubans and Mexicans.* Austin, TX: University of Texas Press.

Perez, L. A. (2007). *Cuba between empires, 1878–1902.* Pittsburgh, PA: University of Pittsburgh Press.

Pew Hispanic Center. (2005). *Unauthorized migrants: Numbers and characteristics.* Retrieved from http://www.pewhispanic.org/2005/06/14/unauthorized-migrants/

Porter, E. (2005, April 5). Illegal immigrants are bolstering social security with billions. *The New York Times.* Retrieved from http://www.nytimes.com/2005/04/05/business/illegal-immigrants-are-bolstering-social-security-with-billions.html?_r=0

Ramos, J. (2005). *Dying to cross: The worst immigrant tragedy in American history.* New York, NY: Harper Collins.

Rein, L. (2016, January 4). U.S. authorities begin raids, taking 121 illegal immigrants into custody over the weekend. *The Washington Post.* Retrieved from https://www.washingtonpost.com/news/federal-eye/wp/2016/01/04/u-s-authorities-begin-raids-taking-121-illegal-immigrants-into-custody-over-the-weekend/

Rivera-Batiz, F., & Santiago, C. E. (1994). *Island paradox: Puerto Rico in the 1990s.* New York, NY: Russell Sage Foundation.

Rodriguez, G. G. (1999). *Raising nuestro niños: Bringing up Latino children in a bicultural world.* New York, NY: Fireside Books.

Rosenblum, M., & Meissner, M. (2014). *The deportation dilemma: Reconciling tough and humane enforcement.* Washington, DC: Migration Policy Institute. Retrieved from http://www.migrationpolicy.org/research/deportation-dilemma-though-humane-enforcement

Santiago-Rivera, A. L., Arredondo, P., & Gallardo-Cooper, M. (2002). *Counseling Latinos and la familia: A practical guide.* Thousand Oaks, CA: Sage Publications.

Smith, J. P., & Edmonston, B. (1997). *The new Americans: Economic, demographic, and fiscal effects of immigration.* Washington, DC: National Academy Press.

Stepick, A., & Stepick, C.D. (2009). Power and identity: Miami Cubans. In M. M. Suarez- Orozco & M. M. Paez (Eds.), *Latinos remaking America* (pp. 75–92). Berkeley, CA: University of California Press.

Suarez-Orozco, C., & Suarez-Orozco, M. M. (1995). *Transformations: Immigration, family life, and achievement motivation among Latino adolescents.* Stanford, CA: Stanford University Press.

Suarez-Orozco, C., & Suarez-Orozco, M. (2001). *Children of immigration.* Cambridge, MA: Harvard University Press.

Telgen, D., & Kamp, J. (1993). *Notable Hispanic American women.* Washington, DC: Gale Research.

Torres-Saillant, S., & Hernandez, R. (1998). *The Dominican Americans.* Westport, CT: Greenwood Press.

United Nations. (n.d.). *International day for the elimination of violence against women.* Retrieved from www.un.org/en/events/endviolenceday/

U.S. Department of Homeland Security. (2016). *Southwest border unaccompanied alien children statistics FY 2016.* Retrieved from www.cbp.gov/newsroom/stats/southwest-border-unaccompanied-children/fy-2016

U.S. Department of State. (2001). *Dominican Republic, 1916–1924.* Retrieved from 2001-2009.state.gov/r/pa/ho/time/wwi/108649.htm

Velasquez, L.C. (1993). *Migrant adults' perceptions of schooling, learning, and education.* Doctoral dissertation College of Education, University of Tennessee, Knoxville, TN.

Wessler, S. F. (2011). *Shattered families: The perilous intersection of immigration enforcement and the child welfare system.* Washington, DC: Applied Research Center. Retrieved from http://act.colorlines.com/acton/attachment/1069/f-0079/0/-/-/l-sf-cl-70140000000T6DHAA0–000f/l-sf-cl-70140000000T6DHAA0–000f:11446/file.pdf

Women's Refugee Commission. (2012). *Forced from home: The lost boys and girls of Central America.* Retrieved from http://www.womensrefugeecommission.org

Yoshikawa, H., Godfrey, E. B., & Rivera, A. C. (2008). Access to institutional resources as a measure of social exclusion: Relations with family process and cognitive development in the context of Immigration. *New Directions for Child and Adolescent Development, 121,* 63–86. doi:10.1002/cd

Zong, J., & Batalova, J. (2015). *Frequently requested statistics on immigrants and immigration in the United States.* Washington, DC: Migration Policy Institute. Retrieved from http://www.migrationpolicy.org/print/15209#.VqEQZFH38t

Part II

Understanding Within-Group Latino/a Differences

4 Sociohistorical Construction of Latina/o Gender Ideologies

Integrating Indigenous and Contemporary Perspectives into Treatment

It is not our differences that divide us. It is our inability to recognize, accept, and celebrate those differences.

–Audre Lorde, n.d., para. 6

In this chapter, we focus our attention on the social construction of gender and the role that it has played in the lives of Latinos/as throughout the centuries. We begin by providing a brief overview on how gender was introduced into the lexicon of academia as a prelude to reviewing various constructs that communicate gendered identities and expression. The chapter continues with a review of the historical development on *machismo* and *marianismo*, the two culturally gendered ideologies associated with traditional Latino/a culture. Although there is a plethora of literature focusing on gender, this chapter integrates information from various disciplines to provide a richly historical and contemporary contextual account on the effects of *marianismo* and *machismo* on the lives of Latinos, Latinas, Latin@s, and Latinxs. The chapter concludes with recommendations for Latin@s across the gender spectrum.

Sex, Gender, and Language

Sex differences, the biological distinctions between women and men, have been the focus of much research in the social sciences. Interestingly, much of the earlier work comparing the sexes was not the primary focus of most investigators. In her seminal article, Rhoda K. Unger (1979), a social psychologist and pioneer in Women's Studies Research, explains that when analyses of research studies revealed significant differences between the sexes, investigators provided brief and surface interpretations, often based on biological differences. However, when differences were not found, researchers often neglected to theorize or discuss their findings. The message connoted from this practice was that differences between the sexes were based on biological distinctions. A number of pitfalls and assumptions accompany this epistemology.

Unger (1979) posits,

> A major problem in this area appears to be the too inclusive use of the term sex. In various contexts, sex can be used to describe the chromosomal composition of individuals, the reproductive apparatus and secondary characteristics that are usually associated with these chromosomal differences, the intrapsychic characteristics presumed to be possessed by males and females, and in the case of sex roles, any and all behaviors differentially expected for and appropriate to people on the basis of membership in these various sexual categories.
>
> (p. 1085–1086)

Instead of sex differences, Unger proposed that scholars and practitioners use the term *gender*, a socially constructed label used to describe sets of behaviors, traits, and expectations that a given culture assigns as male or female. Other scholars disagreed with Unger's assertions and argued that it is not feasible to extrapolate the differences between sex and gender, since biology and social aspects of the construct at hand are not mutually exclusive (e.g., Maccoby, 1988).

Today, many scholars use the term *sex* to refer to biological differences (e.g., chromosomes composition, internal reproductive organs, external genitalia) and *gender* to refer to the cultural norms and expectations that are socially constructed based on an individual's biological sex (mainly the individual's reproductive apparatus and secondary characteristics). However, some scholars continue to use both terms interchangeably. These practices are often influenced by the scholar's discipline. For instance, the APA *Guidelines for Psychological Practice with Lesbian, Gay, and Bisexual Clients* adopted a definition of gender similar to the one Unger proposed as an alternative to sex differences. The guidelines describe gender as, "the attitudes, feelings, and behaviors that a given culture associates with a person's biological sex" (APA, 2012, p. 11). Thus behavior that is congruent with cultural expectations is referred to as *gender normative*, while incongruence between cultural expectations and gender is often labeled *gender nonconformity*. Both Unger and APA's definition are complimentary; however, they tend to favor behavioral aspects of gender without explicitly centering on a person's subjective sense of what gender means to him or her. Hence, *gender identity* refers to an individual's sense of him or herself as male, female, or transgender. In concert with this line of thinking, an individual may choose to identify as transgender or another gender variant term, such as transsexual, when his or her gender identity and biological sex are not congruent (Gainor, 2000). For individuals whose gender identity is the same label as their biological sex or birth assigned category, the term *cisgender* is used (Tate, Youssef, & Bettergarcia, 2014). Lastly, the term *gender expression* is used to distinguish between gender identity and gendered behavior. Gender expression refers to the

> way in which a person acts to communicate gender within a given culture; for example, in terms of clothing, communication patterns [e.g., nonverbal communication, voice intonation], and interests. A person's gender expression may or may not be consistent with socially prescribed gender roles, and may or may not reflect his or her gender identity.
>
> (APA, 2008, p. 28)

In writing this chapter, we have come to appreciate the limits of verbal language. Yet the use of language is necessary to communicate ideas, thoughts, and subjectivities with others. Language can liberate us, but it can also bind us to express ourselves in ways that are not freeing. When we write about socially created concepts such as gender, we acknowledge that words are limited and bound by history, politics, religion, context, and epistemology. Thus it is important to center and ground all discussion on gender within a historical, political, and contextual framework. To help clinicians understand how gender has evolved in Latin America, and how it has shaped the consciousness of groups and individuals, the next section provides a brief overview on the historical origins of the two Latino/a gender ideologies, *machismo* and *marianismo*.

Machismo

Machismo, a "socially constructed, learned, and reinforced set of behaviors comprising the content of [the] male gender role in Latino/a society" (De La Cancela, 1986, p. 291) has influenced the lives of Latino men throughout history. The interdisciplinary literature on *machismo* is extensive, where an array of scholars from the fields of history, cultural anthropology, sociology, gender studies, and psychology have contributed to the rich academic discourse on Latino masculinity (Baca-Zinn, 1982; De La Cancela, 1981; Mirande, 1988; Ramírez, 1993; Torres, 1998; Torres, Solberg, & Carlstrom, 2002). Examining *machismo* from the different fields of study provides a layered perspective of the historical and contemporary underpinnings of Latino/a masculinity and its implications for mental health.

Historical Perspective

Although different perspectives exist regarding the origin of behaviors associated with *machismo*, one of the classic conceptualizations suggests that the ideology "evolved from specific historical processes and from social and cultural transformations" (Torres et al., 2002, p. 166). This historical perspective describes the term *machismo* as originating in the pre-Columbian era. According to this view, the root of the word *macho* comes from the Nahuatl word *matti*. Nahuatl was the language spoken by the Mexica people, who are also known as the Aztecs. *Matti* means "to know" or "to be known." In the Aztec Empire, men showed how much they "knew" by exhibiting a set of virtues that included courage, vigor, fortitude in adversity, public achievement, order, discipline, happiness, strength, and justice (Rodriguez, 1999). In Taino/Carib culture, masculinity was achieved through men participating in leadership roles and through marriage. As a matrilineal culture (rule of descent affiliated with mothers), Taino/Carib men were socialized and raised by their mothers' uncles, which is how many of the male virtues, similar to the Aztec's conception of masculinity, were taught to Taino/Carib boys (Keegan, 1997). This set of virtues allowed men to achieve prominence and be recognized within their communities; hence "to be known, to be a *Matti*." Overall, the characteristics associated with a *Matti* man, according to the Aztec and Taino/Carib concept of *machismo/macho*, were predominately positive.

Machismo has also been associated with negative behaviors. Some scholars posit that these behaviors stem from maladaptive manifestations of male behavior rooted in the oppression and the loss of identity, dignity, family, and material possessions experienced by Indigenous men during the period of colonization (Mirande, 1988; Rodriguez, 1999). Mirande (1988), a pioneer in the study of Latino masculinity, refers to this conceptualization of *machismo* as the Compensatory Model.

Compensatory Model

The Compensatory Model of *machismo* posits that during colonization, Indigenous men lost everything that this group valued. For instance, their native Indigenous names were replaced with Spanish ones (e.g., Achcauhtli replaced with Jose). They were forbidden from practicing their religion and spirituality; instead, they were forced to convert to Catholicism. In addition, they were not allowed to speak their native language nor engage in the practice of cultural traditions (e.g., their month-long celebration of the dead was forbidden). Lastly, women and children became the property of the Spaniards; as a result, the women were raped, and the children were sold (Rodriguez, 1999). Overall, during colonization, Indigenous men lost their identities, their self-respect, and the ability to control their own destinies. As noted in Chapter 2, African men began arriving in the Americas as a result of the slave trade during the period of colonization. These men also experienced a pattern of oppression and marginalization at the hands of Spaniards.

Due to the struggles Indigenous and African men faced as a consequence of racism and oppression, during colonization, they were unable to fulfill their gender-role expectations. In other words, they could neither provide nor protect their families and communities. The inability to fulfill their gender-role expectations resulted in Indigenous and African men experiencing a deep sense of shame, hopelessness, and resentment. According to the Compensatory Model, the complete loss of power and agency led to the negative behaviors typically associated with *machismo* today (Rodriguez, 1999). Thus "when a man cannot even provide basic needs for the family or knows who he is, he hides under the mask of shame and diverts his control onto the people he loves (Rodriguez, 1999, p. 299)." During the colonial period, the home was the only setting where Indigenous and African men maintained their status. Consequently, according to this model, men focused on exerting power over those they could control, which ended up being their wives and children (Rodriguez, 1999). Furthermore, other scholars argue that the historical and anthropological roots of some of the characteristics of *machismo*, such as the repression of the public display of emotion and bravado, are also a direct consequence of the Latin American conquest by the Spaniards and the humiliation suffered by Indigenous and African men (Mirande, 1988; Riding, 1985).

The Ethical View

The second conceptualization of *machismo* is referred to as the Ethical View and focuses on the evolution of "a code of ethics that stresses honor, respect, and courage" (Mirande, 1988, p. 65). This perspective highlights the positive aspects of Latino/a masculinity or what Mirande (1988) calls *hombria*. Based on the Ethical View, a *macho* is not

> cold and insensitive, but warm and emotional . . . his behavior is motivated by the desire to uphold his own honor and integrity of the group. [Thus] the essential components of *machismo* are not violence, aggressiveness, or virility, but honor, respect, dignity, and bravery.
>
> (p. 68)

Although the behaviors described by the Ethical View are consistent with those rooted in the Aztec and Taino/Carib cultures, such historical dimension is not an integral part of this theory. Instead, the Ethical View argues that a positive and idealized conception of *machismo* "has always coexisted" alongside the negative one. Although the Ethical View is known among many Latino/a scholars, a main criticism is that it lacks the conceptual, contextual, and historical anchors offered in the Compensatory Model. However, others argue that the Ethical View offers a nonpathological framework of Latino masculinity (De la Cancela, 1986; Mirande, 1988).

Contemporary Perspectives on Machismo

Despite the positive characteristics historically associated with *machismo*, contemporary United States (U.S.) society often describes and views *machismo* as a monolithic concept consisting primarily of negative, stereotypic characteristics, including male dominance, aggression, promiscuity, alcoholism, sexism, and authoritarianism. Until recently, frameworks mirroring society's negative views of *machismo* have dominated the literature in the U.S. For instance, some early works on *machismo* (i.e., Anders, 1993; Ingoldsby, 1991; Penalosa, 1968) generalized characteristics of sexism and hypermasculinity (e.g., aggression, fearlessness, excessive alcohol use, stoicism, restricted emotional range, controlling behaviors, and aloofness) to all Latino males. Fortunately, the overly simplistic view of *machismo* has received considerable criticism over the years, leading to scholars developing more complex and bidimensional paradigms of *machismo*. Today, the concept of *machismo* has been described as having both positive and negative aspects.

The positive aspects of *machismo* described by contemporary scholars are very similar to those rooted in Indigenous cultures. For instance, Morales (1996) defined *machismo* as "a man's responsibility to protect, defend, and provide for his family" (p. 274). He further argued that a man's "loyalty and sense of responsibility to family, friends, and community make him a good man" (p. 274). Santiago-Rivera, Arredondo, and Gallardo-Cooper (2002) agreed with the positive aspects of *machismo* espoused by Morales. They state that within the Latino culture, males are raised to develop a sense of loyalty and responsibility for their families, friends, and the communities in which they live. More recently, the view of *machismo* as a multidimensional construct has received empirical support. A study conducted by Arciniega, Anderson, Tovar-Blank, and Tracey (2008) found two independent factors that together comprise *machismo*, which are labeled in their study as 1) traditional *machismo* and 2) *caballerismo*. Traditional *machismo* includes what has been described thus far in this chapter, as the negative stereotypic characteristics of the construct. *Caballerismo* is composed of the behaviors rooted in the Indigenous definitions of masculinity, including emotional connectedness, honor, and nurturance.

In another study, Torres et al., (2002) hypothesized that a low number of Latino men subscribe to traditional definitions of *machismo* (e.g., negative aspects) and investigated whether *machismo* can be conceived of as a multidimensional construct. In their study, 184 participants of Mexican and Puerto Rican descent (N = 184) were asked to complete a number of measures of *machismo*, masculinity, and gender-role identity in order to assess whether Latino adult males subscribe to different aspects of *machismo* (e.g., positive, negative). As hypothesized, their cluster analysis provided evidence in support of the multidimensionality of *machismo*, which included five clusters: contemporary masculinity, *machismo*, traditional *machismo*, conflicted/compassionate *machismo*, and contemporary *machismo*. Although these differences support the construct of *machismo* as having multiple dimensions, the study failed to clearly differentiate between the various clusters, suggesting the need for more research in this area to understand the nuances among the different dimensions of *machismo*.

Chicano/Latino Perspective

Contemporary views of *machismo* in the U.S. continue to be negative. Latino/a scholars posit that, "Anglo-American interpretations [*of machismo*], reduce it to self-aggrandizing male bravado that flirts with physical harm to be sexual, like some rutting for the right to pass on genes" (Rodriguez, 1996, p. 37). Moreover, many Latino/a scholars argue against how White Americans define and associate *machismo* with sexism and violence (Espada, 1996; Gonzalez, 1996). They further postulate that the use of the Spanish word *machismo* and its connection to Latino men has served to justify the constant oppression and systemic violence experienced by many males of Latino descent in the U.S. (Espada, 1996; Gonzalez, 1996).

Latino/a authors have also commented on how Latino men's communication style is often pathologized and characterized as overly aggressive. Instead, many Latino/a scholars see the *macho* communication style in a more positive light. "*Macho* oratory lays out belief in full view, with a sweep of the hand, perhaps, as if to say: *There I am, right or wrong, and now it is your turn*" (Castañeda, 1996, p. 46). This bravado assumes the listener is equipped to listen to the message directly and is free to provide any rebuttal. In other words, *macho* ways of communicating note, "I [as a man] take my right to speak and assume your power to do the same" (Castañeda, 1996, p. 45). Castañeda further posits that if the way Latinos communicate is perceived as being aggressive, the "aggression" is then considered to be

> against the status quo that belittles people and makes them ashamed of strong will and presence; in comparison, Anglo-American discourse seeks to maintain the status quo by shaming noncomplacent individuality and making differences of opinion an egotism or aggression. Such shame can only result in more easily controlled people.
>
> (Castañeda, 1996, p. 45)

A Chicano/Latino Definition of Machismo

From a Chicano perspective, *machismo* is complex and multifaceted, encompassing both positive and negative aspects. Chicano scholars state that being a *macho* man "does not mean the bully, the jock, the knucklehead. He is the warrior, protector, defender, and lover. He is the artist, hero, father, and elder" (Rodriguez, 1996, p. 201). Interestingly, the definition of *machismo* that is offered by Chicano writers mirrors the concept used to describe masculinity (i.e., *matti*) during the pre-Columbian time. Unfortunately, many scholars in the U.S. have often neglected these positive aspects of *machismo*.

How Racism Contributes to Negative Aspects of Machismo

The literature on Latino masculinity and *machismo* is extensive. One of the classic texts entitled *Soy Muy Macho* edited by Gonzalez (1996) describes the perceptions of *machismo* among Latino men in the U.S. In the volume, the authors describe the struggles they face, including violence, racism, and poverty, along with how these factors impact their lives. From a Chicano perspective, *machismo's* negative aspects are directly connected to the experiences of oppression and discrimination that most Latino men face in the U.S. Due to such experiences, Latino men often internalize the rage they feel as a result of the bigotry and injustices they face in U.S. society. To illustrate how racism shapes the experience of many Latino men in the U.S., we turn to an essay entitled "The Puerto Rican Dummy and Merciful Son" by Martin Espada (1996), a well-known Puerto Rican author, poet, and lawyer, who describes how racism has shaped his experience:

> To defend myself against a few people would have been feasible, to defend myself against dozens and dozens of people deeply in love with their own racism was a practical impossibility. So I told no one, no parent or counselor or teacher or friend, about the constant racial hostility. Instead, I punched a lamp, not once but twice, and watched the blood ooze between my knuckles as if somehow I could leech the poison from my body. My evolving manhood was defined by how well I could take punishment, and paradoxically, I punished myself for not being man enough to end my own humiliation.
>
> (Espada, 1996, p. 79)

Rudolfo Anaya, another prominent Latino author of Mexican descent (best known for his novel *Bless Me Ultima*), eloquently describes how feelings of powerlessness affect him and leave him with very few options to experience and express vulnerability.

> In a community that is poor and often oppressed there is so much suffering, [that] he is taught *aguantar*: to grin and bear it. "*Aguantate*," the men around him say. A macho man does not cry in front of men. A *macho* doesn't show weakness. Grit your teeth, take the pain, bear it alone, and be tough. You feel like letting it out? Well, then let's get drunk with our *compadres* [close friends], and with the *grito* [scream] that comes within we can express our emotions.
>
> (Anaya, 1996, p. 63)

When examining how the negative aspects of *machismo* developed among Latino men in the U.S., it becomes apparent how their experiences are similar to those of Indigenous and African men during colonization. Experiences of systemic oppression, discrimination, and racism have had a detrimental impact on the positive aspects of *machismo*. The Chicano perspective described in this section underscores the complexity of *machismo* and the urgent need for mental health professionals to expand their definition of the term to include Latino narratives. Latino men can be empowered by helping them reconnect with their ancestral roots of masculinity and engaging them in critical dialogue regarding how colonization and systemic oppression have impacted the way *machismo* is defined and expressed.

Research on Machismo in the U.S.

Machismo has received some research attention within the last three decades and has been associated with a host of variables. Unfortunately, most of the available research has used deficit frameworks to study *machismo*, with a heavy focus on the negative aspects of the construct. Thus it is not surprising that much of the research on *machismo* has found that it is associated with negative outcomes.

A study conducted by Arciniega et al. (2008) with a sample of a educationally and socioeconomically diverse group of 477 men from the U.S. who identified as Latinos, found that higher traditional *machismo* (i.e., negative aspects of *machismo*) was associated with more arrests and fights, as well as higher alcohol consumption, greater emotional restriction, and greater use of wishful thinking as a coping style. *Machismo* has also been linked to the mental health of Latinos. For instance, research has revealed that the negative aspects of *machismo* are associated with higher levels of depression and stress (Fragoso & Kashubeck, 2000), but with lower levels of help-seeking behaviors (Sobralske, 2006).

In addition, traditional aspects of *machismo* are negatively correlated with nurturing practices among Latino parents (Ferrari, 2002). For instance, Glass and Owen (2010) analyzed Latino fathers' perceptions about their parental involvement and both aspects of *machismo* (i.e., traditional *machismo* and *caballerismo*, or positive aspects of *machismo*). Their study suggests that Latino fathers who endorsed traditional *machista* attitudes were associated with lower levels of parental involvement. The authors discuss that traditional *machista* attitudes may be associated with underlying anger and frustration resulting from oppression, which is expressed through negative behaviors and serves as a source of disconnect with their children. No associations were found between *caballerismo* and parenting involvement in this study. Interestingly, these results are not consistent with other studies, suggesting that *caballerismo* can serve as a protective factor among Latino men in the U.S. For instance, *caballerismo* has been related to positive outcomes such as affiliation, emotional connectedness, greater problem-solving styles, and psychological well-being (Arciniega et al., 2008). *Caballerismo* has also been associated with higher levels of self-esteem (Ojeda & Piña-Watson, 2014).

Machismo has also been examined among men who identify as being gay. Conclusions from studies with gay Latino men suggest that traditional cultural expectations associated with *machismo* are not different for gay Latinos. In fact, a study conducted by Estrada, Rigali-Oiler, Arciniega, and Tracey (2011), showed that gay Latino men did not "dispose of their *machismo* by simply identifying as gay, and that most embody masculinity in a structural fashion similar to their heterosexual counterparts" (p. 362). This study also suggests that the negative aspects of *machismo* predicts internalized homophobia and is associated with high-risk sexual behavior.

Closing Remarks About Machismo

This section situates the ideology of *machismo* within a sociohistorical framework. Awareness about the various historical and current narratives of Latino masculinity can assist clinicians in expanding their views of the Latino male experience beyond the stereotypic images depicted in U.S. society. It is promising to see how the pre-Columbian conception of *machismo*, focusing on prosocial and adaptive behaviors used to protect the family and the community, is supported by the voices of contemporary Chicano and Latino authors. Moreover, the recent shift in the empirical literature has moved away from a unidimensional and simplistic definition of *machismo* to a bidimensional and multinarrative perspective. This shift is providing a more nuanced understanding of masculinity and better captures the experience of Latino men in the U.S.

Marianismo

Marianismo is defined as socially constructed, learned, and reinforced behaviors comprising the content of the female gender role in traditional Latino/a society. Although the literature on *marianismo* is sparse, work from history, cultural anthropology, and archaeology help to provide a sociohistorical perspective of the contemporary underpinnings of gender-role expectations for women in Latino/a societies. In the following sections, we provide an account of how women have been viewed, treated, and portrayed throughout different historical periods in Latin America to contextualize contemporary notions of *marianismo*.

Pre-Columbian History

Among pre-Columbian Indigenous cultures of Latin America, women held important roles. They were creators of change and served as social transformative agents within their societies. Anthropological and archaeological research suggests that a wide range of gender socialization and role expectations existed among the different Indigenous groups of women. In many of these groups, women played key roles in the spiritual lives of their communities. Women in some Indigenous groups (e.g., Mexica, Mixtec, Inka, Tainos) carried out a variety of political, productive, and social activities, in addition to horticultural and agricultural labor.

Mesoamerican Women

The Mexica/Aztec and Mixtec civilizations of Mesoamerica (complex Indigenous cultures that developed in the area that is today considered from Mexico to Central America) had two of the most seemingly egalitarian cultures of any other Mesoamerican cultural group with regard to gender. However, work patterns were highly gendered with predominately women being responsible for domestic labor. Nonetheless, women fought alongside their male counterparts in military battles, had parallel roles in the job world, performed vital labors, and negotiated in market exchange (engaged in business trade). With regard to gender roles, the Mexica civilization was more flexible than many other Indigenous cultures. They associated sexual activity with pleasure for both sexes and viewed sexual activity as a natural part of human life and not inherently sinful. Moreover, Mexica women "were not the subordinate, passive, and silent beings dominated by patriarchal fathers and husbands. The gender parallelism of Mexica thought and social institution formed, expressed, and reinforced the integration of complementary oppositions" (Kellogg, 2005, p. 30)." Among the Mexica culture, "good mothers" were described as those who were "energetic workers, careful and thrifty, who would teach and serve others" (Kellogg, 2005, p. 25). Women had a great level of authority, and good grandmothers and great-grandmothers were respected and praised by others. They were valued as founders of kin groups either by themselves or with their husbands. Mexica nobility followed from female as well as male sources. In everyday life, a child was seen as connected to ancestors by the mother's blood and father's semen. Contrary to the Mexica, the Maya of southern Mesoamerica developed cultural patterns that were characterized by more strict gender dichotomies that adhered to a more patriarchal structure.

Andean Women

In the Andean region (what today is considered the Andes regions in South America), pre-Hispanic groups displayed various degrees of gender egalitarianism. In contrast to Mesoamerica, Andean women and men's divisions of labor overlapped. The pattern became more asymmetrical with the rise of the Inka Empire, a group that enforced more strict divisions of labor and patriarchy than other Andean groups. Although the Inka had a hierarchical society with a male as the supreme ruler, the Quya (Inka queen) presided over female centered rituals (e.g., birth of a child). Moreover, in the absence of the Inka king, the Quya had the power to make decisions. Lastly, the majority of Andean cosmologies featured prominent female deities, including goddesses and creators of the world and universe.

Taino Women

Similar to the Mexica, the Tainos also had a matrilineal society in which access to land and succession to offices of power, such as chiefdoms (power behind the throne) were determined by maternal line. Women were the producers and the distributors of goods such as wooden furniture, household objects, cotton, and other agricultural goods (Wilson, 1990). Control of these agricultural and household goods were of significant benefit for women in Taino society since this was one way that social power was determined. Interestingly, land ownership did not determine Taino social power, unlike other societies in history in which the possession of land is highly valued.

With regard to political organization, there is not much known about the ways in which most Taino groups were organized. However, within the elite Tainos (also known as the *nitaino*), their *caciques* (individuals who ruled over large territories) were predominantly males despite some records suggesting that women also held such positions. However, women predominantly held chiefdoms. In their observations, the Spaniards reported that the eldest son, in some instances inherited the chiefdom from the father, which would contradict the matrilineal system. However, some scholars discuss that the influence of the Spaniards contributed to Indigenous groups not fully adhering to their original matrilineal way of life (Keegan, 1997; Wilson, 1990). As the Spaniards succeeded in their conquest of Taino land and culture, patrilineal dogmas began to influence and change Taino society.

The Conquest

As discussed in Chapter 2, the conquest was one of the most violent periods in Latin American history, resulting in the massacre, domination, and oppression of Indigenous people. During their settlements into what the Spaniards called "the new world," they encountered various groups of people in what today is known as Hispaniola, Cuba, Puerto Rico, and Mexico. In this "new land," the Spanish conquistadors encountered Indigenous individuals of Taino, Mayan, Aztec, and Inca descent and viewed them as heathens who needed to be civilized. Indigenous women were pivotal in the survival of their ancestral cultural traditions. Thus the oppression and massive rape of Indigenous women during the conquest has been described as one of the most brutal forms of colonization used by the Spaniards to dominate and control the Americas. During this period, Indigenous women were accused of "falling in love" with the Spanish conquistadors and consequently blamed for betraying the Americas and their people.

The story of La Malinche, an Indigenous Mayan woman, who upon the arrival of the Spaniards to Mexico reportedly fell in love Hernán Cortés, has two common versions. One accounts La Malinche as a person gifted with the ability to speak multiple languages (i.e., Maya, Nahuatl, Spanish). Given her language skills, she became Cortés's personal translator. Upon the Spaniards arrival at Tenochtitlan (what is considered Mexico City today), La Malinche was instrumental in facilitating communication between the Aztec Emperors and the Spaniards. She is often blamed for disclosing the secrets of the Indigenous people to the Spaniards and playing a crucial role in contributing to the success of the conquistadors in winning the war. The other version describes La Malinche as a 14-year-old Indigenous woman who had lost both of her parents and lived within a Mayan community near the coast of Veracruz, Mexico. During this time, Hernán Cortés took her by force and used her exceptional language skills to his benefit. This story also explains that La Malinche became Cortés's translator and that they had a child together. The narrative concludes with Cortés becoming tired of La Malinche, resulting in having her passed down to other men. Similar narratives of Indigenous women and their reported relationships with Spaniards exist for Taino and Andean women, including Anacaona and Quispe Sisa, respectively.

Historic documents and letters written by the Spaniards from the period of the conquest indicate that relationships between the conquistadors and Indigenous women were by no means romantic in nature. Some of these documents describe how Indigenous women were treated as objects to be passed along from one Spaniard to another. "European men treated coercion as a normal part of the range of sexual relations, and everywhere Iberians [from the Iberian Peninsula] went, from the Caribbean to California to Peru, sexual violation occurred" (Kellogg, 2005, p. 59). A famous passage written by Michele de Cuneo, a Spanish conquistador exemplifies the brutality experienced by Indigenous women as well as the disregard that these men had for Indigenous women's humanity and dignity, which was so common during the conquest:

> While I was in the boat I captured a very beautiful Carib woman, whom the said Lord Admiral gave to me, and with whom, having taken her into my cabin, she being naked according to their custom, I conceived desire to take pleasure. I wanted to put my desire into execution but she did not want it and treated me with her fingernails in such a manner that I wished I had never begun. But seeing that (to tell you the end of it all), I took a rope and thrashed her well, for which she raised such unheard of screams that you would not have believed your ears. Finally we came to an arrangement in such a manner that I can tell you that she seemed to have been brought up in a school of harlots.
>
> (Sale, 1990, as cited in Kellogg, 2005, p. 59)

The Colonial Period

The colonization period was a time of profound transformation and trauma in the lives of Indigenous women from Latin America. During this time, African women were transplanted into the Americas to fill many labor needs in the plantations and Spanish households. Both groups of women experienced extreme and chronic forms of violence and exploitation. Moreover, the role of Indigenous women within the political, economic, and spiritual affairs of their communities was diminished due to the new expectations set forth by the conquistadors. The Spaniards brought with them a religious faith that expected and enforced women's passivity, enclosure, purity, and honor, which ultimately led to the loss of power and authority that many Indigenous women had enjoyed in pre-Columbian times (Kellogg, 2005). In fact, "The Spaniards reproduced the medieval hierarchy of the sexes that prevailed in Europe: man as lord and master, woman as servant and reproductive machine" (Stavans, 1996, p. 147). Despite the unimaginable challenges faced by Indigenous and African women in this historical period, they "demonstrated an admirable capacity to survive, adjust to, or resist myriad of challenges, barriers, and problems" (Kellogg, 2005, p. 53).

Indigenous Women

During the colonial period, Indigenous women experienced many forms of violence at the hands of the Spaniards, ranging from exploitative labor to physical and sexual abuse. Additionally, the role of Indigenous women in society during the colonial period underwent significant changes, with the Spaniards taking complete control over the lives of Indigenous women. The Spaniards controlled every aspect of women's lives, including the type of activities women engaged in on a day-to-day basis, the way they dressed, and even their bodies (e.g., rape). For instance, women were forced to provide household services to the Spaniards that consisted of domestic labor (e.g., cooking, cleaning, child care). In exchange for their labor, women were sometimes paid in wages, goods, or room and board. At times they were also required to perform nontraditional and arduous labor, such as being *tlamemes* (human carriers of a variety of goods).

Daily Life of Women in Colonial Times

Regarding everyday activities, Indigenous women continued to be in charge of the traditional tasks of the home. However, as the native population began to dramatically decline as a result of infectious diseases, abuse, and warfare, the demand for women's labor increased, and women were called to provide additional services in the colonies. In fact, Europeans assigned new types of work to women, and as the population declined, the demand for women's labor intensified. Indigenous women were needed to develop textiles for clothing and bedding for the Spaniards and the growing population of enslaved African men and women, who by then had been transplanted to the Americas. Thus Latinas had additional demands placed on their time, especially since many women had lost their husbands during the war and were raising children as single mothers. Under the Spanish rule, not only did women have to participate in forced labor, but they also had to make tribute payments (i.e., taxes) to the Spanish crown. This rule increased the vulnerability for labor exploitation among women, as they had the additional burden of making money to pay taxes. According to the Spanish rules, payments were expected from all women regardless of their marital status (e.g., married, single, widow) beginning as early as the age of 14.

Labor, Sexual Exploitation, and Violence

Indigenous women also experienced sexual exploitation. For instance, documents from this time period demonstrate that

> *encomenderos* (holders of encomienda grants of tribute and labor) rented out women for several months at a time to sailors traveling from Central America to Peru. These women provided both domestic and sexual services and received rental payments based on their attractiveness. (Kellogg, 2005, p. 67)

While slavery of Indigenous women might have been rare, it did take place. Enslaved women were forced to work in the textile industry, perform manual and domestic labor, and work in the mining industries. Moreover, it can be argued that Indigenous women who were not "enslaved" were not actually free, as the Spaniards not only coerced them but also kidnapped widows to provide domestic service and other types of labor that suited their personal needs. In some countries, such as Mexico and Peru, there is evidence that girls as young as six years of age worked as domestic servants in Spanish households.

The treatment experienced by Indigenous women during the colonial period included violence, enslavement, and compulsory labor, which had detrimental and disruptive effects on the family and gender relations. In fact, it was not uncommon for Indigenous women who had new babies to be "drafted" (taken by force) to become wet nurses for Spanish children, where the women were required to breastfeed and care for the children. This often led to Indigenous women not having enough breast milk to feed their own children. Such disruption of the development of the mother-child attachment process "carried severe consequences including marital breakup and even mothers killing their newborns or themselves or both" (Kellogg, 2005, p. 72). Violence was also experienced by Indigenous women at the hands of their husbands who were coping with their own sense of powerlessness and hopelessness. Unfortunately, despite the insurmountable amount of challenges experienced by Indigenous women, they were expected to bear the trauma silently. Although women sought help from the Spanish authorities (i.e., the Catholic Church), little changed since the dissolution of marriage was not permitted by the Catholic Church. Hence women remained in abusive relationships. Women were expected to suffer in silence during the colonial period, which laid the foundation for many of the behaviors observed today among traditional Latina women.

African Women

African women were first brought to Latin America in the 16th century as part of the transatlantic slave trade. African women played an important role in the development of Latin American societies despite their lack of freedom and access to even the most basic human rights. Their experiences during the colonial period are in many ways similar to those of Indigenous women. For instance, they experienced the exploitation of their labor, as well as physical and sexual violence at the hands of the Spaniards. Their forced labor included working under the harsh conditions of the sugar cane and coffee plantations. They also performed domestic labor in Spanish households, including being housekeepers, cooks, personal servants to Spanish women, and wet nurses. Many African women were also involved in the care of Spanish children, serving as their nannies. Similar to Indigenous women, they were frequently raped and forced to engage in nonconsensual sexual activities with their masters. Lastly, their traditions and cultural practices came under the scrutiny of the Catholic Church. For instance, the way that African women dressed, communicated (e.g., tone of voice, use of gestures), danced, and even their posture were viewed with disdain and suspicion, as they were accused of being provocative and attracting the attention of the Spaniards (Andrews, 2004).

Female Role in Spirituality During Colonial Times

Women's spiritual lives underwent a profound transformation during the colonial period. For instance, female deities, which were often worshiped by Indigenous groups, were replaced with a male God. Examples include Coyolxauhqui (Aztec Goddess), Pachamama (Inka Goddess), Ixchel (Maya Goddess), and Atabey (Supreme Goddess of the Tainos). Moreover, the Spaniards portrayed female deities as sinful and evil. Women's roles in the newly introduced Catholic faith were secondary and required them to be subservient to the rules of the Spanish and to the expectations of the men in their lives (i.e., fathers, husbands, sons). Despite the new limits placed on the expression of their spirituality by the Catholic Church, Indigenous women continued to serve their communities in the roles of *curanderas* (healers), midwives, and matchmakers. Lastly, despite the exploitative and often brutal nature of the relationships of Indigenous and African women with Spanish men, Spaniards placed a strong emphasis on females being pure, chaste, and reserved.

The Virgin Mary came to symbolize the Spaniards ideology of women. Although the Virgin became one of the Catholic Church's most important images of womanhood representing the gender-role expectations, her depiction as a White woman made it difficult for Indigenous and African women in the Americas to connect with her. However, during the colonial period, individuals throughout the Americas reported a number of apparitions of the Virgin Mary. In each reported appearance of the Virgin, she took a different form. For instance, in Mexico, *La Virgen de Guadalupe* (Virgin of Guadalupe) appeared as an Indigenous woman with Brown skin speaking in Nahuatl. In Colombia, she appeared as a Black Madonna and was named

La Virgen Morena de Monserrat (The Brown Virgin of Monserrat), in Paraguay as the *Virgen de Caacupe*, and *Nuestra Señora de la Altagracia* (Our Lady of Altagracia) in the Dominican Republic. The Virgin Mary in her many forms continues to be a central figure of Latino/a spirituality and influences the lives of many Latinas today.

Marianismo in Contemporary Latino/a Culture

In traditional Latin American culture, the Virgin Mary is one of the most significant and powerful figures in Catholicism (Baldwin & DeSouza, 2001). Consequently, the importance of the Virgin Mary is the direct result of the influence of the Catholic religion. The Virgin Mary is often described as "the worker in the home, the self-sacrificing woman, the balance of motherhood, and purity" (Baldwin & DeSouza, 2001, p. 10). This ideology of the Virgin Mary constitutes an ideal Latina, a "good woman" defined as pious, dedicated, and sexless (Del Priore, 1993). Latinas who conform to this ideal of women are expected to be pure, long-suffering, nurturing, humble, and spiritually stronger than men (Gil & Vazquez, 1996; Santiago-Rivera et al., 2002). Furthermore, women who subscribe to the ideology of the Virgin Mary are expected to avoid engaging in any sexual activity until marriage (Santiago-Rivera et al., 2002).

These ascribed traditional roles of women in Latin American society are often referred to as *marianismo* by contemporary anthropologists, sociologists, and psychologists. Overall, *marianismo* exerts a powerful influence on the socialization of gender identity among some Latina women. Although no empirical data was found that explores the characteristics that illustrate *marianismo*, *The Maria Paradox*, a book by Gil and Vazquez (1996), lists the "ten commandments" that identify characteristics of *marianismo*. These characteristics include 1) do not forget a woman's place; 2) do not forsake tradition; 3) do not be single, self-supporting, or independent minded; 4) do not put your own needs first; 5) do not wish for more in life than being a housewife; 6) do not forget that sex is for making babies, not for pleasure; 7) do not be unhappy with your man or criticize him for infidelity, gambling, verbal and physical abuse, alcohol or drug abuse; 8) do not ask for help; 9) do not discuss personal problems outside the home; 10) do not change those things that make you unhappy that you can realistically change (Gil & Vazquez, 1996). These ten commandments provide the roadmap to being a "good woman" and are implicitly and explicitly taught to young Latinas in traditional Latin American culture.

According to Gil and Vazquez (1996), commitment to the ten commandments may have both positive and negative consequences for Latin-American women who subscribe to these ideologies. For instance, following these commandments may afford Latin American women "a level of protection as a wife and mother, [it] gives her certain power and much *respeto* [respect] as well as a life free from loneliness and want" (Gil & Vazquez, 1996, p.7).

Alternatively, following these very strict rules may lead to feelings of inadequacy and depression, as *"marianismo* insists that [women] live in a world which no longer exists and which perpetuates a value system equating perfection with submission [which leads to] feeling more like a servant than a subject of adoration" (Gil & Vazquez, 1996, p. 8). As with *machismo*, some scholars have contested the negative views held of a *marianismo* ideology (Ruiz, 1981; Valdés, Barón, & Ponce, 1987). For instance, Chaney (1979) argues that Latina women are raised to develop dual characteristics, some that may seem consistent with *marianismo* such as being dependent, subordinate, and self-sacrificing in the home. At the same time though, she asserts that Latina women tend to exert a great level of power in the private world of the family. Furthermore, Santiago-Rivera et al. (2002) states that

> if a woman is self-effacing and giving at all times, she may appear to outsiders to be more like a submissive doormat. However, those who know Latinas, especially mothers, often note that women are the silent power in the family.
>
> (p. 50)

No empirical studies were found confirming the idea that Latina women may have more power within the home than it is apparent. However, evidence from dissertation studies has begun to emerge indicating that the endorsement of *marianista* attitudes is associated with higher levels of depression among Latinas. For instance, Sanchez (2004) found a significant positive correlation between depressive symptoms and the endorsement of *marianista* attitudes in a sample of Latina women. In another dissertation study, Cano (2004) reported that *marianismo* significantly predicted depression among Mexican-descent women. These findings are consistent with Gil and Vazquez's (1996) argument that subscribing to a *marianista* attitude may lead to feelings of inadequacy and depression.

In the U.S., Latina women continue to grapple with the impact of sexism coupled with discrimination based on their race, ethnicity, and immigration status. Overall, Latina women confront multiple barriers that often limit their access to resources that are necessary for economic mobility. These challenges stem from Latino/a cultural expectations exemplified by *marianismo* coupled with the sexist, patriarchal, racist, and nativist characteristic of U.S. society.

According to L. G. Castillo, Perez, Castillo, and Ghosheh (2010), one possible reason for the limited research on *marianismo* is the lack of empirically established instruments to assess the construct. In an effort to address the gap in the scientific literature on *marianismo*, L. G. Castillo et al. (2010) developed and validated the Marianismo Beliefs Scale (MBS). Three hundred and seventy participants were used in the study, and the sample consisted of women who self-identified as Mexican American, Cuban American, Puerto Rican, and from countries in Central and South America. MBS confirmatory factor analysis provides evidence that *marianismo* is a multi-dimensional construct influenced by Latino cultural values (e.g., *familismo*, *respeto*, *simpatia*) to inform *marianismo* behaviors. According to the MBS, the multidimensional aspects of *marianismo* include family pillar, virtuous and chaste, subordinate to others, silencing self to maintain harmony, and spiritual pillar.

Immigration and Latinas

Immigration impacts gender-role ideologies and how Latinas adapt to U.S. culture (Gil & Vazquez, 1996). Researchers have reported that traditional Latino/a values, which emphasize family cohesion and interdependence (Baca-Zinn, 1982; de la Rocha, 1994; Gutmann, 1996), may conflict with the U.S. gender ideologies of division of labor, individuality, and independence (Brooks & Bolzendahl, 2004; Domino & Acosta, 1987). As a result, immigrant women may need to adapt or change their attitudes when they move to a country with different views on gender. However, the manner in which immigrant women modify their gender ideologies may vary among individuals as they acculturate to the dominant North American culture. Although empirical research in this area is scant, studies looking at the effects of immigration on Latinas' gender identity and gender-role studies are beginning to emerge.

For instance, using both quantitative and qualitative methodologies, Parrado and Flippen (2005) studied the impact of immigration on gender ideologies among 219 Latina women in the U.S. and 400 Mexican women in four states in Mexico. Their results did not yield significant differences with regard to age or education among the participants. However, their results indicate that the immigrant women in their sample were twice as likely to work outside the home and be involved in family finances compared to Mexican women. With regard to division of labor within the home, both groups had similar results with 37% of women reporting that their husbands contributed to household chores. Although the majority of Mexican women reported believing that women have the right to work, the opportunities available for women to participate in the workforce in Mexico are impacted by the lack of jobs in the country (Gonzalez de la Rocha, 1994; Parrado, 2003). However, access to employment is reported to increase for women who immigrate to the U.S. Another finding included how immigrant women in the U.S. were twice as likely to be employed compared to women in Mexico. Interestingly, women who held jobs in Mexico reported more egalitarian relationships. Although this finding held true for immigrant women in the U.S., it was to a lesser degree. Lastly, immigrant women reported more family pressure to maintain traditional gender roles than did women in Mexico. Moreover, immigrant women were more likely to agree with less egalitarian gender representations than Mexican women (Parrado & Flippen, 2005). Thus we need to consider the central role of women within the Latino family and how their acculturation level can impact the entire family system.

Another study by Franco, Sabattini, and Crosby (2004) looked at the relationship between perceived gender-role ideology and behaviors regarding work and family among Latina and European American females. Specifically, participants were asked about the perceptions of their parents' gender ideologies. No differences were found between the two groups (Latinos and European Americans) with regard to the value their parents placed on work, marriage, and parenting. Furthermore, no significant differences were reported with regard to the amount of time both groups perceived their parents as spending on work, marriage, and parenting. However, Latinas in their sample rated both their fathers and mothers as having more traditional gender-role attitudes compared to European Americans. For example, Latinas reported perceiving their parents as having a more traditional division of household labor than the European American group. Fathers in both groups were perceived as assigning more value to and demonstrating more commitment to their careers than mothers did. Mothers on the other hand, were perceived as assigning more value and showing more commitment to marriage and parenting. The results of this study suggest that within the U.S.-Latino population, parents may hold more traditional gender-role ideologies compared to European American parents. However, it is difficult to know if the differences between Latino and European American parents were due to different levels of acculturation, socioeconomic status, or any other variables, which were not accounted for in the study.

Gender Nonconforming and Queer Latin@s

Historians have concluded that among the Indigenous people of Latin America, gender nonconforming people, who they called two-spirit, were common. These were men with more feminine gender expressions who engaged in traditionally feminine duties. Among Indigenous societies, they belonged in a third sex and were held in high respect. Rather than being stigmatized, Indigenous cultures focused on the spiritual gifts of two-spirited individuals. Some historians have documented that strict enforcement of gender binaries were imported by the Spaniards. Thus their ideology viewed two-spirit people as passive gay men. Since the arrival of the Spaniards and the imposition of their binary gender norms, two-spirit, transgendered, and gender nonconforming people have been subjected to incredible amounts of violence (Kellogg, 2005).

The colonial period was a time of tremendous turmoil and violence for Indigenous and African men and women, as well as for individuals who broke the strict gender binary rules imposed by the Spaniards. Thus it is pivotal for mental health professionals to understand the sociohistorical context in which expectations about gender were created. Moreover, it is necessary to gain specific knowledge on how different aspects of a person's identity (e.g., sexual orientation, gender expression, gender identity, race) impact the challenges they face in contemporary Latin American society. The concept of intersectionality, first introduced and discussed by Black and Brown feminist and queer theorists (Anzaldùa, 1987; Hill-Collins, 1990; Moraga & Anzaldùa, 1981; Smith, 1990) provides us with a framework to discuss the lives of Latino and Latina (Latin@s) queer individuals (Lesbians, Gays, Bisexuals, Transgender, Gender Nonconforming). The term *queer* is deliberately used as a way to demonstrate respect for language that affirms the experience of individuals of color who identify as LGBTQ-GN and to generate a queer critical psychology (Adames, 2009). Viewing human narratives through an intersectional lens rejects the traditional notions of a single human identity (Fuentes & Adames, 2014) and instead embraces "an alternative view of the self, located historically in language, produced in everyday gendered, cultural, [and racial] experiences, and expressed everyday in writing, speaking, and [behavior]" (Bloom, 2002, p. 291). Thing (2010), notes that "Intersectionality theories . . . conceptualize identities as community achievements that are inflected by, and, to a large extent, shaped by the intersection of one's position within various social hierarchies including social class, race-ethnicity, gender, and sexuality" (p. 813).

When considering Queer Latin@s, it is important to consider how context and history impact their multiple identities. Although the literature in this area continues to be underdeveloped, a few scholars have begun to explore the experience of Latin@ queer individuals. For instance, Cerezo, Morales, Quintero, and Rothman (2014) conducted a qualitative study where they interviewed 10 transgender Latina immigrants and asked them about their personal histories, including access to employment, social support networks, and experiences of discrimination in the U.S. Four main themes emerged from the analysis, each with a set of subthemes: 1) motivation for migration (*subthemes*: freedom to express gender identity; transgender acceptance in the U.S.; economic opportunity), 2) psychological distress (*subthemes*: lack of socioemotional supports; target of violence; impact of discrimination on mental health), 3) employment challenges in the U.S. (*subthemes*: challenges with legal documentations; forced entry into survival work, such as sex work), and 4) resiliency (*subthemes*: the healing power of faith; reliance on social support from family of origin and family of choice; civic engagement/drive to help others) (Cerezo et al., 2014, p. 174). The themes discussed by transgender Latinas in this study highlight the continued challenges they experience in the U.S. as members of multiple minoritized groups.

In another study, Morales, Corbin-Gutierrez, and Wang (2013) identified individual and contextual factors impacting the immigration and acculturation of 11 Latino immigrant gay men. They found that Latino gay men immigrate for a number of reasons including, financial motives, lack of safety in their home country due to homophobia, and desire to reunite with a partner. In this study, Latino gay men described frequent experiences of discrimination due to their intersecting identities (e.g., sexual orientation, race, and ethnicity) and gender expression. Participants also noted how the context mediated which identity became more salient and made them targets of discrimination. Lastly, contrary to commonly held stereotypes about Latino gay men engaging in high-risk sexual behaviors, this study did not support such claims. In fact, the results indicated that men were informed about basic knowledge of sexual health and knew where to obtain additional health information related to sexually transmitted illnesses. Overall, the results of these two studies underscore the similar and unique challenges that Queer Latin@s experience in the U.S. Additionally, the studies further demonstrate the need for mental health professionals to consider how "sexual minorities cross [both] physical and psychological borders" (Morales, Corbin-Gutierrez, & Wang, p. 127) when they migrate into the U.S.

Gender and Its Complexities Considered in Treatment of Latin@s

Many mental health providers have neglected the complexities involved when considering gender in the treatment of Latin@s. Ignoring the intricacies of gender in the lives of Latin@s reinforces the interlocking systems of "white supremacist capitalist patriarchy" domination. This phrase, coined by hooks (1994), communicates how different social factors and people's multiple identities (e.g., gender, race, and sexuality) function simultaneously at all times. It is also critical to consider the ways in which history and colonization have shaped Latin@s views regarding gender norms, gender identity, and gender expression. In an effort to assist mental health practitioners appreciate and value the complexities inherent in the socially constructed concept of gender, we recommend they consider the factors involved in their Latin@ clients' gender, gender identity, gender expression, and sex.

Overall, culturally centered and gender-informed treatment requires clinicians to consider the different aspects that make up an individual's internal sense of a gendered self. Figure 4.1 provides an illustration of the interconnected factors that contribute to people's internal sense of gender that clinicians can use to assess and understand the role of gender in the lives of their clients. Moreover, it is important for clinicians to consider how irrational fear and hatred toward people who look, sound, behave, or express themselves in ways that blur the gender scripts of their culture impacts their lives. Lastly, different systems (e.g., family, community, work, school) can impact how affirming and accepting a space is for gender conforming and nonconforming individuals.

In Table 4.1, we list and describe core factors that uniquely impact Latin@ individuals who identify as female, male, or gender nonconforming, as a prelude to recommendations for mental health providers to consider when working with Latin@s across genders.

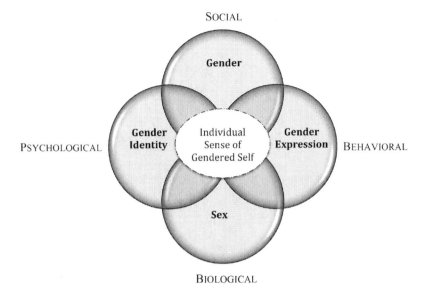

SOCIAL

Gender

PSYCHOLOGICAL

Gender
Identity

Individual
Sense of
Gendered Self

Gender
Expression

BEHAVIORAL

Sex

BIOLOGICAL

Figure 4.1 Four Interconnected Factors Contributing to People's Internal Sense of Gender

Provides an illustration of four interconnected factors that contribute to people's internal sense of gender, which clinicians can use to assess and understand the role of gender in the lives of their clients. Sociohistorical context will impact how affirming society will be of an individual's sense and expression of gender.

Table 4.1 Core Factors Impacting Latin@ Women, Men, and Queer People in the 21st Century

Areas to Assess and Explore	Core Factors
WOMEN:	
1 Living in the Borderlands	• Many Latinas in the U.S. are constantly navigating between the gender expectations of two different cultures, which may lead to feelings of not fully belonging to either culture (Anzaldua, 1987).
2 Economic Inequity	• Latinas have the lowest wages of all groups in the U.S. (Fisher, 2015), which contributes to a lack of economic security. Hence increasing the probability of living in poverty, which has a host of mental health implications.
3 Focusing on Family, Career, or Both	• Given Latina women's membership in multiple marginalized groups, along with the gender norm expectations placed on them, they experience pressure to choose whether to focus on a career, family, or the common challenge of balancing both (Arredondo, 2002).

(*Continued*)

Table 4.1 Continued

Areas to Assess and Explore	Core Factors
4 Sexual Devaluation, Objectification, and Exotization	• U.S. American culture objectifies and exoticizes Latina women by portraying and treating them as hypersexual, emotional, and objects to satisfy the sexual desires of men.
MEN:	
1 Expression of Emotion	• Although Latino men are culturally allowed to be affectionate and show tender feelings toward children and close friends, the display of emotions associated with vulnerability such as pain and fear are perceived as unacceptable and feminine (Gutmann, 1996).
2 Help-Seeking Behaviors	• Although access to mental health services continues to be a problem among Latinos, they do not utilize such services even when they are available. Negative associations between help-seeking behaviors and masculinity contribute to the pattern of underutilization (Hispanics in Philanthropy, 2014).
3 Academic Achievement	• Latino males continue to drop out from high school at higher rates than their White peers (5.4% White boys vs. 14.5% for Latino boys) despite recent significant overall declines in dropout rates. These statistics are higher among young Latino immigrant males (35.8%; Hispanics in Philanthropy, 2014).
4 Involvement with Justice System	• Due to structural inequality, Latino boys and adolescents experience high levels of adjudication and higher probability of being detained in custody. School discipline often results in Latino youth being involved with the justice system. Latino men are disproportionately overrepresented in federal and state prisons and receive harsher sentences (Hispanics in Philanthropy, 2014).
QUEER PEOPLE:	
1 Traversing Different Boundaries	• Latino@s LGBTQ individuals have to learn how to navigate the crossing of multiple socially constructed borders related not only to their gender expression and sexual orientation but also their skin color, physiognomy, and culture.
2 Religious/Spiritual Acceptance	• The second-most religious group in the U.S. are Latin@s. Thus rejection and stigma from religious and some spiritual communities is a significant challenge experienced by LGBTQ Latin@s (Human Rights Campaign Foundation & League of United Latin American Citizens, 2012).
3 Concerns About Family Acceptance	• Given the centrality of family for LGBTQ Latin@s, their acceptance and support is a key factor in their lives (Human Rights Campaign Foundation & League of United Latin American Citizens, 2012).
4 Homophobia and Heterosexism	• Holding membership in a number of stigmatized groups, LGBTQ Latin@s are jeopardized in multiple ways (Adames, 2009).

Recommendations

General Recommendations for Latin@s

1. Therapists are encouraged to be mindful that the establishment of *confianza* (trust) will take time and will likely be impacted by experiences of sexual and gender devaluation, ethnocultural stereotypes, and heterosexism. The establishment of a relationship based on *confianza* will depend on the practitioner's ability to understand the complexities inherent in their client's individual sense of a gendered self.

2. It is pivotal for therapists to acknowledge the strengths and resilience of Latin@s, which have allowed individuals from this community to survive and at times thrive in spite of the myriad of threats and challenges they face as a result of ethnosexual stereotypes and heterosexism.

3. Therapists are encouraged to help Latin@ clients place their sense of a gendered self in a sociohistorical context. Such practice may help clients better understand and identify when their struggles are due to internal conflicts, external oppressive forces, or both.

4. A culturally and gender-centered treatment approach for Latin@s requires therapists to be knowledgeable about Latino history and culture. Such knowledge will allow therapists to integrate Latin@ cultural values (e.g., *personalismo, familismo, respeto*) and worldviews in treatment. For instance, integrating art, music, literature, and *dichos* (proverbs) into treatment may be helpful in achieving this goal.

Recommendations for Latin@ Women

1. Latina-centered treatment requires therapists to understand the complexities inherent in navigating the gender expectations of two different cultures. Clinicians can demonstrate understanding by providing support and affirmation of their Latina clients' cultural values, while also helping them to find a balance between the expectations placed on them by society and their own dreams and goals.

2. Given the multiple and at times unrealistic gender expectations placed on Latinas, clients often feel inadequate and not "Latina enough." Thus it is important for clinicians to assist Latina women in developing their own definition of Latina womanhood. This approach can help clients expand their notions of what a Latina woman looks like and realize that there are many ways to be a Latina woman.

3. Latinas grow up navigating between the expectations and values of different cultures. The strengths and skills that Latinas have acquired as a result of constantly code-switching and engaging in cultural brokering can help women survive and navigate hostile and difficult environments. Clinicians can help Latinas explore and acknowledge the many skills that they already possess and help them learn ways to use their skills in the workplace, school, or at home. Using their internal skills

as a result of code-switching can help Latina women cope when feeling overwhelmed and unable to deal with difficult situations.

4. Latina women can benefit from connecting with other women who can serve as positive role models of Latina womanhood. For instance, therapists can offer group interventions to promote a collective solidarity. Groups can allow Latinas to be exposed to first-person accounts of how other women navigate the many demands placed on their lives. This experience of connecting with other women may allow Latinas to construct new narratives while having their histories, struggles, and triumphs affirmed and validated.

5. Therapists are encouraged to support faith-oriented Latinas to use spirituality as a way of coping with their problems of living. For instance, use of spiritual activities such as *altar* making, blessing ceremonies, pilgrimages, *promesas* (promises to Virgins), and the like can be incorporated into the treatment of spiritually oriented Latinas.

6. Given the history of religion and spirituality in the Americas, we encourage therapists to learn how to differentiate between healthy and unhealthy beliefs. For instance, Latina clients may associate their presenting problems with feelings of guilt and think they are being punished and deserve such pain. These beliefs can be counterproductive to the well-being of Latinas. Therapists can ask Latinas to explore any *dichos* or stories they used in their culture that provide an alternative narrative, such as the *dichos* *"Dios dice, ayudate que yo te ayudare"* (God says help yourself, and I will help you); *"A Dios rogando y con el mazo dando"* (Pray to God but continue rowing to the shore); *"Al que madruga dios lo ayuda"* (God helps those who wake up early).

7. Lastly, therapists are encouraged to help Latinas gain a better understanding of the sociopolitical basis of gender discrimination in the U.S. This awareness can help Latinas recover from ethnosexual victimization.

Recommendations for Latin@ Men

1. Latino men may benefit from exploring their own definition of masculinity and the origin of their description. Helping Latinos develop an awareness regarding the sociohistorical and political nature of masculinity may help them expand the notion of what it means to be a Latino man. Once this understanding has taken place, clinicians can assist Latinos to explore the kind of men they are aspiring to be and reconnect with the definition of *machismo* rooted in the Indigenous culture.

2. Given the socially reinforced stigma associated with the expression of vulnerable emotions among Latino men, they often have a restricted range of emotional expression. Hence we recommend that clinicians use emotional literacy as part of their treatment with Latino men. For instance, using lyrics from Latin music and films to show how Latino characters and songwriters express many emotions, including crying,

which Latino boys and men often do not do in public. Emotional literacy can assist clients in learning how to identify, express, and cope with emotions that are often suppressed (e.g., fear, sadness, disappointment, despair). Regarding the expression of emotions in therapy, clinicians are encouraged to:

  a. Listen, validate, and affirm the verbal expression of emotions used by Latino men in therapy.
  b. Explore how the expression of particular emotions (e.g., anger, frustration) may be perceived as a threat by dominant U.S. society.
  c. Assist Latino men in finding ways to express frustration and anger in prosocial ways (e.g., joining advocacy groups and engaging in artistic expression, such as painting, spoken word).

3. For Latino boys and youth, finding role models who represent different ways in which masculinity can be expressed is of utmost importance. Exposing children to different ways of being a Latino man can free children from the constrictions imposed by society, while allowing them to choose an expression of manhood that is consistent with their cultural values.

Recommendations for Queer Latin@s

1. It is important for therapists to assist Queer Latin@s in connecting with community-based organizations (e.g., advocacy, empowerment groups, and agencies to volunteer). Being connected to these networks can help clients find support and receive affirmation when facing adversity due to rejection of their humanity.
2. Clinicians may also consider helping Queer Latin@s understand and process that most communities may not fully embrace all of their multiple identities. Hence it is important for clients to understand this reality and not blame themselves when people fail to affirm aspects of who they are in different settings. Establishing networks that affirm different aspects of their identities is necessary.
3. Given the many ways in which Queer Latin@s are oppressed in U.S. society, it is critical for clinicians to help them develop and/or strengthen healthy coping skills so they can be more effective in dealing with heterosexism, homophobia, and transphobia.
4. Clinicians are encouraged to consider Queer Latin@s' multiple minoritized identities. In treatment, it is important that therapists not focus on one identity and instead assess the impact of each of their identities on the presenting problem(s).

Conclusion

"One of the first things a colonizing power does is to attack the sense of history of those they wish to dominate" (Levins Morales, 1998, p. 22). This chapter sought to highlight how the socially constructed concept of gender has evolved over time in Latin America. Furthermore, the chapter aimed to describe the impact that a history of colonization has on the current gender expectations of Latin@s in the U.S. To achieve these goals, the chapter begins with a brief discussion on how language impacts the ways people communicate about gender and all of its nuanced complexities. A review of the experiences of men and women during the pre-Columbian and colonization historical eras is then provided. Connections between Indigenous perspectives about masculinity and womanhood were drawn to emphasize the historical underpinnings of gender. The chapter concludes with recommendations for mental health practitioners to consider when working with Latin@ men, women, and queer people. Overall, the chapter helps construct views of gender that are grounded in a historical, cultural, and political context. This perspective offers an ideology that is affirming, nuanced, and contextualized rather than one that is fixed, pathological, and acontextual.

References

Adames, H. Y. (2009, August). Invisible among invisibles: Heterosexism in communities of color. In R. Navarro (Chair) (Ed.), *Addressing and overcoming heterosexism and homophobia in communities of color*. Paper presented at the 117th Annual Convention of the American Psychological Association, Toronto, Canada. doi:10.1037/e618662009- 001

American Psychological Association. (2008). *Report of the APA Task Force on gender identity and gender variance*. Retrieved from http://www.apa.org/pi/lgbt/resources/policy/gender-identity-report.pdf

American Psychological Association. (2012). Guidelines for psychological practice with lesbian, gay, and bisexual clients. *American Psychologist, 67*(1), 10–42. doi:10.1037/a0024659

Anaya, R. (1996). "I'm the King": The macho image. In R. Gonzalez (Ed.), *Muy Macho* (pp. 57–73). New York, NY: Anchor Books.

Anders, G. (1993). Machismo: Dead or alive? *Hispanic, 3*, 14–20.

Andrews, A. R. (2004). *Afro-Latin America: 1800–2000*. New York, NY: Oxford University Press.

Anzaldua, G. (1987). *Borderlands/La Frontera: The New Mesitcza*. San Francisco: Aunt Lute Books.

Arciniega, G. M., Anderson, T. C., Tovar-Blank, Z. G., & Tracey, T. J. G. (2008). Toward a fuller conception of machismo: Development of a traditional machismo and caballerismo scale. *Journal of Counseling Psychology, 55*, 19–33. doi:10.1097/00003727–198306020–00004

Arredondo, P. (2002). Mujeres Latinas-santas y marquesas. *Cultural Diversity and Ethnic Minority Psychology, 8*, 1–12.

Baca-Zinn, M. (1982). Chicano men and masculinity. *Journal of Ethnic Studies, 10*, 20–44.

Baldwin, J., & DeSouza, E. (2001). Modelo de María and machismo: The social construction of gender in Brazil. *Revista Interamericana de Psicología, 35*(1), 9–29.

Bloom, L. R. (2002). Stories of one's own: Nonunitary subjectivity in narrative representation. In S. B. Merriam & Associates (Ed.), *Qualitative research in practice* (pp. 289–309). San Francisco, CA: Jossey-Bass.

Brooks, C., & Bolzendahl, C. (2004). The transformation of US gender role attitudes: Cohort replacement, social-structural change, and ideological learning. *Social Science Research, 33*, 106–133.

Cano, S. (2004). Acculturation, marianismo, and satisfaction with marianismo: An analysis of depression in Mexican American college women. *Dissertation Abstracts International, 64*(9-B), 4645.

Castañeda, S. O. (1996). Guatemalan macho oratory. In R. Gonzalez (Ed.), *Muy Macho* (pp. 35–50). New York, NY: Anchor Books.

Castillo, L. G., Perez, F. V., Castillo, R., & Ghosheh, M. R. (2010). Construction and initial validation of the marianismo beliefs scale. *Counseling Psychology Quarterly, 23*(2), 163-175. doi:10.1080/09515071003776036

Cerezo, A., Morales, A., Quintero, D., & Rothman, S. (2014). Trans migrations: Exploring life at the intersection of transgender identity and immigration. *Psychology of Sexual Orientation and Gender Diversity, 1*(2), 170–180. doi:10.1037/sgd0000031

Chaney, E. M. (1979). *Supermadre: Women in Politics in Latin America.* Austin, TX: University of Texas Press.

De La Cancela, V. L. (1981). Toward a critical analysis of machismo: Puerto Ricans and mental health. *Dissertation Abstracts International, 42*, 368.

De La Cancela, V. L. (1986). A critical analysis of Puerto Rican machismo: Implications for clinical practice. *Psychotherapy: Theory, Research, Practice, Training, 23*(2), 291–296. doi:10.1037/h0085611

de la Rocha, G. M. (1994). *The Resources of Poverty: Women and Survival in a Mexican City.* Oxford, UK and Cambridge, MA: Backwell Press.

Del Priore, M. (1993). *Ao sul do corpo: Condicao feminina, maternidades e mentalidades no Brasil Colonia [To the south of the body: The feminine condition, motherhoods and mentalities in Colonial Brazil.]* Rio de Janeiro, Brazil: Jose Olympio.

Domino, G., & Acosta, A. (1987). The relation of acculturation and values in Mexican Americans. *Hispanic Journal of Behavioral Sciences, 9*, 131–150.

Espada, M. (1996). The Puerto Rican dummy and the merciful son. In R. Gonzalez (Ed.), *Muy Macho: Latino men confront their manhood* (pp. 75–89). New York, NY: Anchor Books.

Estrada, F., Rigali-Oiler, M., Arciniega, G. M., & Tracey, T. J. G. (2011). Machismo and Mexican American men: An empirical understanding using a gay sample. *Journal of Counseling Psychology, 58*, 358–367. doi:10.1037/a0023122

Ferrari, A. M. (2002). The impact of culture upon child rearing practices and definitions of maltreatment. *Child Abuse & Neglect, 26*(8), 793–813.

Fisher, M. (2015). *Women of color and the gender wage gap.* Retrieved from https://cdn.americanprogress.org/wp-content/uploads/2015/04/WomenOfColor WageGapbrief.pdf

Fragoso, J. M., & Kashubeck, S. (2000). Machismo, gender role conflict, and mental health in Mexican American men. *Psychology of Men & Masculinity, 1*, 87–97. doi:10.1037/1524- 9220.1.2.87

Franco, J. L., Sabattini, L., & Crosby, F. J. (2004). Anticipating work and family: Exploring the associations among gender-related ideologies, values, and behaviors in Latino and White families in the United States. *Journal of Social Issues, 60,* 755–766.

Fuentes, M. A., & Adames, H. Y. (2014). Theories, models, and practices for understanding gender, race, and ethnicity in clinical assessment. In M. L. Miville & A. D. Ferguson (Eds.), *Handbook of race-ethnicity and gender in psychology* (pp. 313–328). New York, NY: Springer Science + Business Media. doi:10.1007/978-1-4614-8860-6_14

Gainor, K. A. (2000). Including transgender issues in lesbian, gay, and bisexual psychology: Implications for clinical practice and training. In B. Greene & G. L. Croom (Eds.), *Psychological perspectives on lesbian and gay issues: Vol. 5. Education, research, and practice in lesbian, gay, bisexual, and transgendered psychology: A resource manual* (pp. 131–160). Thousand Oaks, CA: Sage.

Gil, R. M., & Vazquez, C. I. (1996). *The Maria Paradox.* New York, NY: Perigee.

Glass, J., & Owen, J. (2010). Latino fathers: The relationship among machismo, acculturation, ethnic identity, and parental involvement. *Psychology of Men & Masculinity, 11,* 251-267. doi:10.1037/a0021477

Gonzalez, R. (1996). *Muy Macho.* New York, NY: Anchor Books.

Gutmann, M. C. (1996). *The Meanings of Macho: Being a Man in Mexico City.* Berkeley, CA: University of California Press.

Hill-Collins, P. (1990). *Black Feminist Thought: Knowledge, Consciousness, and the Politics of Empowerment.* Boston, MA: Unwin Hyman.

Hispanics in Philanthropy (HIP). (2014). *The right to dream: Promising practices improve odds for Latino men and boys.* Retrieved from http://www.hiponline.org/storage/documents/HIP-MENANDBOYS-THE-RIGHT-TODREAM.pdf

hooks, b. (1994). *Teaching to Transgress: Education as the Practice of Freedom.* New York, NY: Routledge.

Human Rights Campaign & League of United Latin American Citizens. (2012). *Supporting and caring for our Latino LGBT youth.* Retrieved from http://lulac.org/assets/pdfs/LGBTLatinoYouthReport.pdf

Ingoldsby, B. (1991). The Latin American family: Familism vs. machismo. *Journal of Comparative Family Studies, 1,* 57–64.

Keegan, W. F. (1997). "No man [or woman] is an island": Elements of Taino social organization. In S. M. Wilson (Ed.), *The Indigenous people of the Caribbean* (pp. 111–117). Miami, FL: University Press of Florida.

Kellogg, S. (2005). *Weaving the Past: A History of Latin America's Indigenous Women from the Prehispanic Period to the Present.* New York, NY: Oxford University Press.

Lorde, A. (n.d.). *Audre Lorde quotes.* Retrieved from http://www.goodreads.com/author/quotes/18486.Audre_Lorde

Maccoby, E. E. (1988). Gender as a social category. *Developmental Psychology, 24*(6), 755-765. doi:10.1037/0012-1649.24.6.755

Mirandé, A. (1988). Que gacho es ser macho: It's a drag to be a macho man. *Aztlan Journal, 17*(2), 63–89.

Moraga, C., & Anzaldua, G. (1981). *This bridge called my back: Writing by radical women of color.* Watertown, MA: Persephone Press.

Morales, A., Corbin-Gutierrez, E. E., & Wang, S. C. (2013). Latino, immigrant, and gay: A qualitative study about their adaptation and transitions. *Journal of LGBT Issues in Counseling, 7*(2), 125–142. doi:10.1080/15538605.2013.785380

Morales, E. (1996). Gender roles among Latino gay men. In R. J. Green & J. Laird (Eds.), *Lesbians and gays in couples and families: A handbook for therapists* (pp. 272–297). San Francisco, CA: Jossey-Bass.

Morales, L. A. (1998). *The Historian as Curandera*. JSRI Working paper No. 40. The Julian Samora Research Institute. Retrieved from http://learning.hccs.edu/faculty/james.rossnazzal/huma-2319-minorities-in-the-us-mexican-americans/journal-articles/the-historian-as-curandera/view

Ojeda, L., & Piña-Watson, B. (2014). Caballerismo may protect against the role of machismo on Mexican Day Laborers' self-esteem. *Psychology of Men and Masculinity, 15*(3), 288-295.

Parrado, E.A. (2003). International migration and men's marriage in Western Mexico. *Journal of Comparative Family Studies, 35*, 51-72.

Parrado, E. A., & Flippen, C. A. (2005). Migration and gender among Mexican women. *American Sociological Review, 7*, 606-632.

Penalosa, F. (1968). The Mexican family roles. *Journal of Marriage and Family, 30*, 680-689.

Ramírez, R. L. (1993). *Dime capitán: Reflexiones sobre la masculinidad* [Tell me, Captain: Reflections on masculinity]. Rio Piedras, Puerto Rico: Ediciones Huracán.

Riding, A. (1985). *Distant Neighbors: A Portrait of the Mexicans*. New York, NY: Vintage.

Rodriguez, G. G. (1999). *Raising Nuestors Niños*. New York, NY: Fireside Books.

Rodriguez, L. (1996). On macho. In R. Gonzalez (Ed), *Muy Macho: Latino men confronting their manhood* (pp. 187-202). New York, NY: Doubleday Dell.

Ruiz, R. (1981). Cultural and historical perspective in counseling Hispanics. In D. W. Sue (Ed.), *Counseling the culturally different: Theory and practice* (pp. 186-214). New York, NY: Wiley.

Sale, K. (1990). *The conquest of paradise: Christopher Columbus and the Columbian legacy*. New York, NY: Knopf.

Sanchez, M. M. (2004). Latinas' experience of depression. *Dissertation Abstracts International: Section B: The Sciences & Engineering, 64*(10-B), 5232.

Santiago-Rivera, A. L., Arredondo, P., & Gallardo-Cooper, M. (2002). *Counseling Latinos and la familia: A Practical Guide*. Thousand Oaks, CA: Sage Publications.

Smith, D. (1990). *Texts, facts, & feminity: Exploring the relations of ruling*. London: Routledge

Sobralske, M. C. (2006). Health care seeking among Mexican American men. *Journal of Transcultural Nursing, 17*(2), 129-138. doi:10.1177/1043659606286767

Stavans, I. (1996). The Latin phallus. In R. Gonzalez (Ed.), *Muy Macho* (pp. 143-164). New York, NY: Anchor Books.

Tate, C. C., Youssef, C. P., & Bettergarcia, J. N. (2014). Integrating the study of transgender spectrum and cisgender experiences of self-categorization from a personality perspective. *Review of General Psychology, 18*(4), 302-312. doi:10.1037/gpr0000019

Thing, J. (2010). Gay Mexican and immigrant: Intersecting identities among gay men in Los Angeles. *Social Identities, 16*, 809-831.

Torres, J. B. (1998). Masculinity and gender roles among Puerto Rican men: Machismo on the U.S. mainland. *American Journal of Orthopsychiatry, 68*(1), 16-26. doi:10.1037/h0080266

Torres, J. B., Solberg, V. S., & Carlstrom, A. H. (2002). The myth of sameness among Latino men and their machismo. *American Journal of Orthopsychiatry, 72*(2), 163-181. doi:10.1037/0002-9432.72.2.163

Unger, R. K. (1979). Toward a redefinition of sex and gender. *American Psychologist, 34*(11), 1085-1094. doi:10.1037/0003-066X.34.11.1085

Valdés, L. F., Barón, A. Jr., & Ponce, F. Q. (1987). Counseling Hispanic men. In M. Scher, M. Steven, G. Good, & G. A. Eichenfield (Eds.), *Handbook of counseling and psychotherapy with men* (pp. 203–217). Newbury Park, CA: Sage.

Wilson, S. M. (1990). *Hispaniola: Caribbean Chiefdoms in the Age of Columbus.* Tuscaloosa, AL: University of Alabama Press.

5 Adapting to a New Country

Models and Theories of Acculturation Applied to the Diverse Latino/a Population

It's never the change we want that changes everything.

–Junot Díaz, 2007, p. 51

The study of acculturation has focused on capturing, identifying, and assessing the process individuals undergo as a result of coming in contact with a new cultural group. For the past several decades, acculturation has been studied in an interdisciplinary manner and has been the focus of much inquiry in the social sciences. Scholars have studied acculturation from different perspectives ranging from a focus on the cultural/group level to a focus on the psychological/individual level. At the group level, acculturation refers to the changes that result from contact between two distinct and independent cultural groups (Berry, 2003). At the individual level, acculturation describes the extent to which individuals learn the values, behaviors, lifestyles, and language of a host culture, originally referred to as psychological acculturation (Graves, 1967; Szapocznik, Scopetta, Kurtines, & Aaranalde, 1978). The concept of acculturation was further expanded on by Padilla (1980) who explored two additional components: a) cultural awareness, referring to what an individual knows about his or her native and host culture and b) ethnic loyalty, referring to someone's preference for one culture over the other. Cuellar, Arnold, and Maldonado (1995) added to the acculturation literature by suggesting that acculturation involved changes at the affective and cognitive levels. This chapter provides an overview of the dynamic and complex process of acculturation experienced by many Latinos/as in the United States (U.S.). To achieve this goal, the chapter begins with a brief history of the theories of acculturation followed by an overview and critique of the three main acculturation models: *unidirectional*, *bidirectional*, and *multidirectional*. The chapter concludes with an ecological systems perspective on the acculturation of Latinos/as as a prelude to implications on health and social mobility.

Brief History on the Theories and Models of Acculturation

As previously discussed, the concept of acculturation has historically received considerable attention in the social sciences; however, a lack of agreement on how best to define, conceptualize, and assess acculturation persists (Arends-Toth & Van De Vijver, 2006; Berry, 2003; Cabassa, 2003; Kim & Abreu, 2001; Matsudaira, 2006; Ryder, Alden, & Paulhus, 2000). Nonetheless, Redfield, Linston, and Herskovita's (1936) classic and widely used definition describes acculturation as "the phenomena which results when groups of individuals having different cultures come into continuous firsthand contact, with subsequent changes in the original cultural patterns of either or both groups" (cited in Organista, 2007, p. 5). Beyond specific definitions of acculturation, a number of theories providing insight into how the process of acculturation takes place have emerged over decades. The following section provides an overview of theories of acculturation organized chronologically from earlier models to more complex and contemporary paradigms. Specifically, three models will be discussed: unidirectional, bidirectional, and multidirectional frameworks.

Acculturation: A Unidirectional Paradigm

The study of the acculturative process began in the field of sociology with Park and Miller (1921), who were the first scholars to propose a theory of acculturation. Their theory described the "blending process" that results from individuals' encounters with U.S. culture or host culture. The notion of "blending" suggests that for recent immigrants, the process of acculturation is gradual and irreversible. Park and Miller further postulated that although some people may try to resist acculturation, most individuals would be unable to stop the acculturative process. To describe the linear process of acculturation, Park and Miller's model included three consecutive stages: *contact, accommodation,* and *assimilation.* The process begins when individuals come in contact with a new culture (i.e., contact), followed by a focus on how individuals' actively replace their culture of origin with the host culture (i.e., accommodation), and ends with individuals fully blending with members of the host culture (i.e., assimilation). Overall, Park and Miller state that avoidance of conflict is what prompts new immigrants to behave in ways consistent with the customs and norms of the host culture (Park, 1955; Park & Miller, 1921). Given the focus on a linear process and assimilation being the end goal, Park and Miller's theory is classified as unidirectional.

Limitations of Unidirectional Perspectives

Unidirectional models have been critiqued for having a number of problematic assumptions. One, unidirectional frameworks promote the ideology and perception that an immigrant's culture is inferior and needs to be replaced. Unidirectional models of acculturation also assume that it is not possible for immigrants to be fully integrated members of two cultures (i.e., bicultural) given incompatible worldviews of the cultures (Ramirez, 1984). However, the literature suggests that many immigrants show a bicultural identification (Devos, 2006; Padilla, 1994; M. M. Suarez-Orozco & Paez, 2009). Two, unidirectional paradigms assume that only new immigrants go through the acculturation process with no discussion on how both groups (i.e., new immigrants and individuals from the host culture) are impacted by contact and interaction with individuals from different cultures (Rudmin, 2003). Three, unidirectional models fail to acknowledge the power differentials inherent in the relationship between the immigrant and dominant group (Berry, 1997; Cabassa, 2003). Lastly, unidirectional models of acculturation tend to assume that a higher orientation to the host culture is associated with positive outcomes, which is not always the case. In fact, the empirical literature on the *healthy migrant paradox* does not support such assertions. Earlier studies on the *healthy migrant paradox* show that increasing levels of acculturation among Latinos/as are associated with higher rates of depression, substance use, mortality, and adolescent pregnancy (Clark & Hofsess, 1998). Recent studies of Mexican immigrants and their U.S.-born counterparts demonstrate that some mental health disorders show a distinct increase over time and across generations (Alderete, Vega, Kolody, & Aguilar-Gaxiola, 2000; Alegria et al., 2007).

Bidirectional Models of Acculturation

Bidirectional models of acculturation posit that identification with two or more cultures is not mutually exclusive (Nguyen, Messe, & Stollak, 1999). Thus bidirectional models emphasize the possibility of individuals having a bicultural identification and being fully integrated members of two distinct cultures. Individuals who are bicultural have extensive socialization and life experiences in two or more cultures in which they actively participate (Ramirez, 1984). As we can see, bidirectional models reflect the evolution and complexity in thinking about the acculturation process by addressing many of the limitations and critiques of the unidirectional models discussed previously. In this section, a brief overview of bidirectional models of acculturation is provided, along with some of the limitations outlined in the literature. Szapocznik, Kurtines, and Fernandez (1980) argued that traditional unidirectional views of acculturation do not take into account the fact that acculturation is a process that requires adaptation to the host culture without dictating rejection of the culture of origin. They further posited that effective adjustment requires the ability to navigate between two different worlds. In other words, "To learn about the host culture is clearly adaptive, but to simultaneously discard those skills which effectively allow them to interact with the culture of origin, such as language and relationship style is not adaptive" (Szapocznik et al., 1980). They are also credited with proposing the first bidirectional model and measurement of acculturation. Their model suggests that individuals may fall within two separate but interrelated dimensions of acculturation. One dimension includes the level of involvement to either the culture of origin or the host culture (i.e., Marginality) or to both cultures (i.e., Cultural Involvement). The other dimension assesses an individual's bicultural identity, which ranges between monoculturalism to biculturalism. Figure 5.1 provides a visual description of Szapocznik et al.'s (1980) *Bicultural Involvement Model of Acculturation.*

Mendoza and Martinez (1981) proposed another bidirectional model of acculturation. They created an instrument to assess the degree to which individuals acquire the values and practices of the host culture, as well as the degree to which individuals maintain the values and practices of their culture of origin. They identified four acculturation patterns: *cultural resistance* (maintenance of culture of origin and rejection of dominant culture), *cultural shift* (abandonment of culture of origin while substituting it with the dominant culture), *cultural incorporation* (integration of both the culture of origin and the dominant culture), and *cultural transmutation* (alteration of cultures to create a unique subcultural identity; Mendoza & Martinez, 1981).

Another bidirectional model created by Berry (1997, 2003) is one of the most well-known models of acculturation. In his theory, Berry focused on the historical experience of ethnic minority groups in North America, which was pivotal in shaping his understanding of the acculturation process. Specifically, Berry's model underscores the role of power differentials between dominant and nondominant groups. For instance, the dominant group has more power to control, influence, oppress, and turn their ideologies into laws and policies, which can make the process of acculturation

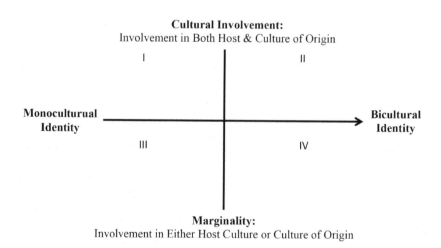

Figure 5.1 Bicultural Involvement Model of Acculturation

From "Bicultural Involvement and Adjustment in Hispanic-American Youths," by J. Szapocznik, W.M. Kurtines, and T. Fernandez, 1980, *International Journal of Intercultural Relations, 4*(3), p. 353–365. Copyright 1981 by Pergamon Press. Adapted with permission.

overly stressful for members of nondominant groups (Berry, 1997; Organista, 2007). Overall, the emphasis on power differentials, which was lacking in previous acculturation models, is central to Berry's model.

Berry's theory of acculturation is composed of three phases: *contact, conflict,* and *adaptation. Contact* refers to the historical conditions under which the two groups first met; that is, the context surrounding the first encounter between a powerful or dominant group and the less powerful or nondominant group. *Contact* may occur through voluntary or involuntary immigration, military, or political intervention (i.e., political asylum), invasion, and forced translocation from the homeland (i.e., slavery). *Conflict* refers the expected tension and hostility that results when the powerful group attempts to dominate and oppress the less powerful. *Conflict* can be categorized as high, medium, or low, with high levels of conflict often resulting in armed conflict. The last phase of the acculturation process according to Berry is *adaptation*. This phase is intended to reduce conflict between the dominant and nondominant groups. Berry (1997) postulated that individuals in both the dominant and nondominant groups "must deal with the issue of how to acculturate," (p. 9) by working out two major issues: 1) *cultural maintenance*, referring to whether or not individuals wish to maintain their cultural identity, and 2) *contact and participation*, referring to whether individuals wish to seek daily interactions with members of the dominant group. According to Berry, answers to these two questions lead individuals, in the nondominant group, to choose one of four different acculturation strategies: *assimilation, separation/segregation, marginalization,* and *integration* (see Table 5.1 for their descriptions). However, Berry (2003) then postulated that due to power differentials between dominant and nondominant groups, the acculturation strategies used by members of nondominant groups are heavily influenced by the sociohistorical context upon which the contact between the two groups occurs (e.g., acculturation expectations, tolerance for diversity). For instance, Berry (1997) argues, "integration can only be 'freely' chosen and successfully pursued by nondominant groups when the dominant society is open and inclusive in its orientation towards cultural diversity" (Berry, 1997, p. 10). Thus, although the acculturation strategies outlined in Table 5.1 were based on the premise that individuals from nondominant groups can decide which strategy of acculturation to utilize, such an assumption is not always accurate. Berry states, "When the dominant group enforces certain forms of acculturation or constrains the choices of nondominant groups or individuals, then other terms need to be used" (2003, p. 24). Table 5.2 lists and describes the acculturation expectations imposed by the dominant group onto nondominant or ethnocultural groups. As previously noted, these expectations impact the acculturation strategies available for ethnocultural groups. Lastly, Figure 5.2 illustrates the relationship between acculturation strategies and acculturation expectations.

Table 5.1 Possible Acculturation Strategies for Nondominant Groups

Strategies	Description
Assimilation	• Individuals embrace and adapt the cultural values and practices of the dominant culture, and there is no attempt to maintain the culture of origin.
Separation/Segregation	• Individuals wish to maintain their culture of origin and are not interested in adopting the cultural values and practices of the dominant culture.
Marginalization	• Little desire to maintain culture of origin exists, and there is no interest in adopting the cultural values and practices of the dominant culture.
Integration	• Individuals wish to simultaneously maintain culture of origin while also adopting elements from the dominant culture.

Note: Table informed by Berry (1997, 2003).

Table 5.2 Acculturation Expectations of Dominant Groups

Expectations	Description
Melting Pot	• When the nondominant group expects assimilation. Of note, when assimilation is demanded by the dominant group. It is referred to as the "pressure cooker."
Segregation	• When the dominant group forces the nondominant group to separate (e.g., de facto and de jure segregation).
Exclusion	• When the dominant groups impose marginalization.
Multiculturalism	• When diversity is an accepted feature of the larger society, allowing individuals to integrate various aspects of varying groups.

Note: Table informed by Berry (1997, 2003).

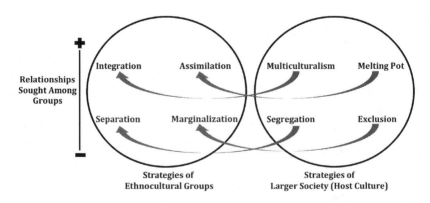

Figure 5.2 Acculturation Strategies for Minoritized and Dominant Ethnic Groups

From "Conceptual Approaches to Acculturation" by J. W. Berry, In *Acculturation: Advances in Theory, Measurement, and Applied Research* (p. 17–37) by K.M. Chun, P. Balls Organista, and G. Marín (Eds.), 2003, Washington, DC: American Psychological Association. Copyright 2003 by American Psychological Association. Adapted with permission.

Limitations of Bidirectional Models

Although bidirectional models exemplify an evolution of the complexity in thinking about the acculturation process, they also pose several limitations. For instance, bidirectional models of acculturation connote a linear progression toward a "fixed state" of acculturation by not taking into account variations in strategies across domains of social functioning (e.g., home, work, and school) and historical time periods (e.g., Great Depression, post 9/11). Furthermore, bidirectional models do not consider the possibility of individuals acculturating to three or more cultures. Finally, bidirectional models fail to unpack within-group acculturation differences. For instance, bidirectional models do not specifically take into account how skin color, physiognomy, level of education, or socioeconomic status impact the process of adaptation.

Multidirectional/Multidimensional Models of Acculturation

In recent years, there has been a move toward a multidirectional conceptualization of acculturation. This includes the notion that acculturation is an ongoing process that can vary along a number of domains, including social context (e.g., home, work, and school) and time (Felix-Ortiz, Newcomb, & Myers, 1994). More specifically, proponents of multidirectional models of acculturation postulate that bidirectional frameworks, which focus on adherence to culture of origin and host culture, have failed to include how the process of acculturation may vary across social settings, time, and cultures (Kim & Abreu, 2001).

Recent research has recognized the importance of conceptualizing acculturation as a multidirectional construct, which takes into account the complexities associated with context, time, and cultures. However, most of the measures developed to assess acculturation adhere to a unidirectional conceptualization of the construct. In their seminal article, Felix-Ortiz et al. (1994) called for new nomenclature of the process of acculturation to emphasize the complexities inherent in the construct since they believed that "the descriptor [acculturation] is problematic because it implies a unidirectional process" (p. 101). In an effort to distinguish multidirectional processes of acculturation from unidirectional and bidirectional paradigms, Felix-Ortiz et al. suggest the use of the term "cultural identity" as the descriptor to capture the multidimensional and complexities of acculturation. The use of "cultural identity" as a construct for acculturation signals a shift in focus from a process that occurs between cultural groups to one that emphasizes the changes at the individual level across social functioning, context, and time. In concert with conceptualizing the multidimensionality of acculturation, while focusing on the changes that occur at the individual level, the *Multidimensional Measure of Cultural Identity* was developed to assess bicultural and monocultural orientation across several domains (Felix-Ortiz et al., 1994). Specifically, proficiency and preference in native and host language, familiarity with dominant and nondominant culture, and adherence to cultural values of both host and native culture make up the scales of the measure.

Although Felix-Ortiz et al.'s model offers a more complex way for us to think about the acculturation process, their model places a strong emphasis on the individual and, in particular, on describing acculturation as part of personality formation. This conceptualization of the acculturation process is likely to be problematic, as it has the potential to place blame on the individual for not attaining high levels of acculturation when attempting to adapt to a new culture. Hence it is paramount for clinicians and researchers to center the role that history, oppression, and context have on the acculturation process for People of Color in the U.S.

Limitations of Multidirectional/Multidimensional Models

Multidirectional models offer the most contemporary and complex conceptualization of the acculturation process; nonetheless, their limitations are worth noting. For instance, the relationship between ethnic/racial identity development and level of acculturation continue to remain unaddressed by multidirectional models, despite the fact that research indicates that these two variables intersect (e.g., Kohatsu, Concepcion, & Perez, 2010). Changes at the psychological, attitudinal, and behavioral levels have also not been teased out by multidirectional models. Finally, the terms "multidirectional" and "multidimensional" are often used interchangeably, even though they could be different constructs. The concept of multidirectionality primarily focuses on the direction of a construct (e.g., high or low levels of functioning in school, work), while multidimensionality deals with multiple domains (e.g., language, attitudes, and behaviors) of a construct.

The Acculturation of Latinos/as Through an Ecological Systems Perspective

As discussed throughout this chapter, acculturation is a complex and multidimensional process involving various systems that may impact the adaptation of Latino/a immigrants to U.S. culture. In an effort to underscore the role of multiple systems on the acculturation of Latinos/as, Bronfenbrenner's (1979) ecological systems theory is used as a framework. Specifically, the impact of the chrono, macro, and micro systems on the acculturative process of Latinos/as is provided in this section. Table 5.3 provides a brief description of each system along with exemplars as a prelude to the application of them to Latinos/as.

Chronosystem

The chronosystem considers the effect of time and historical events on individuals. This system helps identify historical events that have impacted the

Table 5.3 Ecological Systems' Impact on Acculturation

Ecological Systems	Exemplars
Chrono Describes the impact of historical events on Latinos/as' acculturative process.	• Mexican–American War • Spanish–American War • The Great Depression • World War I and II • 9/11 • Proliferation of social media

Macro
Highlights the cultural environment impacting the acculturation of Latinos/as, including the U.S.'s social expectations, beliefs, values, laws, and policies.
	• Values of U.S. culture:
	  – Individuality
	  – Competitiveness
	  – Independence
	• Social expectations:
	  – Low tolerance for differences
	  – Expectations of assimilation
	• Laws and policies:
	  – Proposition 187
	  – Secure Communities Program
	  – SB 1070

Micro Describes the immediate surroundings of the communities where Latinos/as settle upon their arrival to the U.S. that affect their acculturation process. The micro level can include schools, neighborhoods, spiritual/religious organizations/services, etc.	• Availability of ethnic enclave • Diversity of local community • Community violence • Availability of bilingual programs • Local sentiment about immigrants
Individual Differences Unique characteristics of the individual that may facilitate or hinder acculturation.	• Physiognomy (i.e., skin color, phenotype) • Age upon arrival to the U.S. • Nationality, sexual orientation, socioeconomic status, religion, and spirituality • Intersecting identities

acculturative process of Latinos/as in the U.S. Although Chapter 3 provides a more extensive history, this section reviews particular events that are pivotal in understanding the acculturation patterns of Latinos/as. Specifically, Berry's (2003) theory of acculturation (i.e., contact, conflict, acculturation strategies) is used to frame the chronosystem.

Contact

The history of how Latinos/as first came into contact with the U.S. is an important element in understanding the acculturation process of this group.

It is also critical to note that the history of contact between Latinos/as and the U.S. is complex and varies by individual Latino groups. (Chavez-Dueñas, Adames, & Organista, 2014). For instance, some Latinos/as have deep roots in what today is known as U.S. territory (Meier & Ribera, 1993). This is the case for Latinos/as of Mexican descent whose ancestors lived in the southwest part of today's U.S. prior to the Mexican–American War. Other Latino/a groups (i.e., Central Americans, Dominicans, Mexicans, and South Americans) have immigrated to the U.S. for a number of reasons, including better economic opportunities or asylum due to political turmoil in their countries of origin (Organista, 2007). For Cubans, contact with the U.S. resulted from the Spanish–American War and the Cuban Revolution. This led to four major waves of Cubans seeking political asylum to the U.S. Finally, Latinos/as of Puerto Rican descent have a long history in the U.S. resulting from political intervention and colonization (Organista, 2007).

Conflict

High levels of conflict have marked the relationship between the U.S. and the various Latino/a groups. Some of these tensions resulted in armed conflict, such as the Mexican–American and the Spanish–American Wars. Moreover, Latinos/as have been subjected to forced segregation and discrimination that led to massive protests and social movements. Examples of these movements include Puerto Rican revolts of 1950, Zoot Suit Riots, Chicano Civil Rights Movement, Elian Gonzalez's protests, and *The* Immigration Movement.

Adaptation Strategies of Latinos/as

The adaptation strategies of the different Latino/a subgroups (e.g., Mexicans, Cubans) in the U.S. have been impacted by the original conditions of contact, in addition to individual differences and factors stemming from the macro and microsystem. For instance, given the original conditions of contact between Cubans and the U.S. (i.e., legal refugees), members from this group experienced a low degree of conflict with the host culture. As a result, the predominant strategy of acculturation for Cubans ranges from segregation to assimilation (Organista, 2007). Their individual differences, prior resources, and access to opportunities upon arriving in the U.S have impacted the particular form of adaptation available for Cubans. For instance, the first wave of Cubans consisted predominantly of lighter-skinned individuals whose phenotypes resembled those of White European Americans. This wave of Cubans also included individuals from wealthy families with higher levels of education. These experiences and resources facilitated an assimilative adaptation strategy for this particular wave of Cubans (Organista, 2007). Later waves of Cubans included a larger proportion of Afro-Cubans and individuals from lower socioeconomic status and with lower levels of education. Given the differences in phenotypes, skin color, SES, and level of education among individuals from subsequent waves, the acculturation strategies available to them are more limited compared to the first wave of Cubans. The relationship between individual differences, access to resources, and adaptation strategies is illustrated in a recent study on the upper echelons of corporate America. The study by Zweigenhaft and Domhoff (2006) found that among the 1% of Latinos/as that are chief executive officers (CEOs) of Fortune 500 companies, most were of Cuban American descent and described as culturally and racially similar to European Americans. The authors report that the only feature differentiating the Cubans from non-Latino/a CEOs was their international orientation.

The history of Puerto Ricans in the U.S. provides an excellent illustration of the impact of the chronosystem on acculturation. Colonization and the exploitation of land and labor marked the conditions of first contact between Puerto Ricans and the U.S., leading to medium degrees of conflict. As a result, the predominant adaptation for Puerto Ricans has been segregation. Similar to Cubans and other Caribbean Latino/a groups, variations in physiognomy and skin color impact the adaptation strategies available.

Macrosystem

The macrosystem focuses on the effect of the cultural environment on acculturation. Here the values of U.S. culture are likely to impact the degree of acculturative stress. For instance, most Latinos/as are socialized to value collectivism, interdependence, and harmonious collaborative relationships. These types of relationships are not entirely congruent with the dominant U.S. values that tend to foster individualism, competitiveness, and independence. Throughout history, the U.S. has shown a consistent pattern of low tolerance for cultural differences, with high expectations for immigrants to assimilate (e.g., melting pot; pressure cooker). These ideologies and expectations have shaped laws and policies regarding immigration.

A number of anti-immigrant laws and policies have created a hostile environment for Latinos/as in the U.S., contributing further to high levels of acculturative stress (Cornelius, 2009; Organista, 2007). For instance, Proposition 187 was a policy introduced in the state of California in 1994 that made undocumented immigrants ineligible for social services. The policy also mandated educators and human service providers to verify the citizenship of their clients. Although this policy never went into effect, it created fear and anguish among Latino/a immigrants living in California during that time. More recently, the Secure Communities Program and the SB 1070 law, both of which were described in Chapter 3, have had similar effects on recent immigrants.

Microsystem

The microsystem emphasizes the role of the communities where Latinos/as settle upon their arrival in the U.S. in the acculturation process. For instance, the long histories of immigration and settlement of some Latino/a subgroups led to the establishment of ethnic enclaves or geographical areas with a high concentration of ethnic minority groups. For individuals arriving into communities with existing ethnic enclaves, acculturative stress and the process of adaptation may be lower due to language and accessibility of Latin food, places of worship, and the like. Although ethnic enclaves may protect immigrants from external stressors, these communities are often plagued by high levels of poverty and low access to resources, both of which are factors that contribute to high levels of community violence. On the other hand, when immigrants arrive into communities characterized by low levels of diversity, their acculturative stress may be higher due to the stark differences in culture and language. Immigrating into a less diverse community may speed up the acculturative process since individuals are likely to feel the pressure to quickly acquire the skills they need to survive (e.g., English proficiency, learning rules, norms, and expectations).

Implications of Acculturation on Latino/a Health and Social Mobility

Health

In this chapter, the concept of acculturation is underscored as one of the most studied constructs in cultural psychology. Similarly, the process of acculturation for Latinos/as has been the focus of much literature in the social sciences. Although there is an ample amount of literature on acculturation, disagreement regarding the level and impact of acculturation on Latinos/as exists. For instance, some scholars have argued that even after years of U.S. residency, Latinos/as tend to maintain relatively low levels of acculturation; in other words, Latinos/as hold on to their values and traditions (Huntington, 2000; Kluckhohn & Strodtbeck, 1961). Low levels of acculturation among this ethnic group have traditionally been misinterpreted as symbolic of Latinos/as' rejection of the U.S. culture. Historically, low levels of acculturation have been perceived as a threat to the dominant group. For instance, Huntington (2000) argued that low levels of acculturation among individuals of Mexican descent would change the fabric and way of life in the U.S. Many groups with conservative ideologies and anti-immigrant organizations have used these misguided ways of understanding low levels of acculturation among Latinos/as to conclude that members of this ethnic group choose to reject U.S. culture and refuse to follow the "American" way of life and learn English.

Some members of the dominant culture prefer, and at times expect, Latinos/as to adapt to the U.S. culture by assimilating, requiring them to replace their rich ancestral culture, traditions, and language with that of the dominant group. However, social science does not support these erroneous assumptions. In fact, empirical studies report that either low levels of acculturation or a bicultural identity are associated with better adjustment among people of Mexican descent (Buriel, 1984; Ramirez, 1969). Buriel (1984) stated, "Mexican American culture is an advantage rather than a drawback" for individuals of Mexican descent and that "integration with the traditional Mexican-American culture fosters healthy sociocultural adjustment to mainstream American society" (p. 100). Most recently, the CDC reported that despite the many barriers to quality health, such as high rates of uninsured and poor profiles for some social determinants of health, the life expectancies among some Latino/a groups is approximately two years longer compared to European Americans, with overall lower death rates for the nine leading causes of death (CDC, 2015).

Several studies also report an inverse relationship between risk factors and health outcomes among U.S.-born Latinos/as (CDC, 2015; Morales, Lara, Kington, Valdez, & Escarce, 2002). A similar relationship has been observed among Latinos/as with increased time of residence in the U.S. (CDC, 2015; Jones, Pezzi, Rodriguez-Lainz, & Whittle, 2014). However, it is important to note that the pattern of poor health outcomes with longer periods of residency in the U.S. has only been supported for Latinos/as of Mexican descent. This pattern has been referred to as the *Mexican Health Paradox* (MHP) and has been observed in both physical and mental health research. Specific to mental health, MHP has been evident in conditions that are more sensitive to stress, such as anxiety disorders, mood disorders, and substance use and abuse disorders. (Alderete et al., 2000; Vega et al., 1998). Moreover, the *Mexican American Prevalence and Services Survey* (MAPSS), a classic study conducted by Vega et al. (1998), revealed that a positive relationship exists between increasing time in the U.S. and the lifetime prevalence for any mental health disorder among Latinos/as of Mexican descent. Interestingly, the same pattern has not been documented among other Latino/a groups. For instance, Puerto Ricans generally fare worse while Cubans fare the best on most health and adjustment indicators compared to other Latinos/as and non-Latino/a Whites (CDC, 2015; Horevitz & Organista, 2012). Organista (2007) postulates that differences in health indicators among Latino/a groups result from an "inverse relation between acculturative stress and adjustment." He states that Puerto Ricans have experienced a "double legacy of conquest and colonization followed by racialized discrimination and hyper-segregation among African Americans in the United States" (Organista, 2007, p. 21). Moreover, Horevitz and Organista (2012) posit that the apparent declining mental health of Mexican Americans in the U.S. can be accounted for by stressful events associated with the acculturative process at the group level. They also argue that with longer time in the U.S., there is a higher probability of experiencing social exclusion and discrimination particularly for Latinos/as who are minorities within a minority such as Afro-Latinos/as, Latinos/as of Indigenous descent, and dark-skinned Latinos/as. Within-group differences and their impact in the acculturative process are addressed in the next section.

Social Mobility

The complex and nonlinear relationship between acculturation and social mobility can be readily observed when looking at the differences between generations of Latinos/as (e.g., first generation: Latinos/as who were born in Latin America and immigrated to the U.S.; second generation: Latinos/as who were born in the U.S., but whose parents immigrated to the U.S. from Latin America; and third generation: Latinos/as and their parents who were born in the U.S., but whose grandparents immigrated to the U.S. from Latin America) across different economic indicators (e.g., poverty levels, high school graduation rates) and adjustment factors (e.g., language proficiency). For instance, a recent study suggests that second generation Latinos/as reported higher levels of English proficiency and were less likely to drop out of high school, live in poverty, and become teenage parents (Pew Research Center, 2013). In another study, Rumbaut (2008) merged two samples from California's *Children of Immigrants Longitudinal Study* and the *Immigration and Intergenerational Mobility Metropolitan Los Angeles* to identify factors that may facilitate mobility, including acculturation, education, incarceration, and teenage and nonmarital childbearing. Samples were compared between first-, second-, and third-generation Mexicans. Results suggest that Mexican immigrants are twice as likely to drop out of high school than they are to graduate from college; however, the second generation reverses the pattern, with college graduates exceeding high school dropouts. Although first-generation Latinos/as can certainly adopt a bicultural identity, factors such as age at the time of immigration, reason for immigration, SES, etc., can facilitate or hinder their process of adaptation to the U.S. culture. On the other hand, having been born to immigrant parents living in the U.S. facilitates the process of acculturation for second-generation Latinos/as.

Results from the Pew Research Center (2013) and Rumbaut (2008) studies are consistent with previous reports (Buriel, 1984; Grebler, Moore, & Guzman, 1970) that support the assertion that bicultural Latinos/as tend to fare better in U.S. society. A bicultural identity provides Latinos/as with the tools and flexibility to navigate between two distinct cultures, which many monocultural Latinos/as may lack. For example, first-generation or immigrant Latinos/as face challenges that compromise their ability to move up the social ladder, such as low levels of English proficiency when compared to their native-born counterparts (48% vs. 98%, respectively). Given their immigration to the U.S., first-generation Latinos/as are also likely to experience higher levels of acculturative stress as they seek to adapt to the new society. With regard to jobs, Latino/a immigrants are more likely to be employed or looking for employment compared to second-generation Latinos/as (64% vs. 56%, respectively); however, immigrants are more likely (52% vs. 27%) to work in lower-skilled and higher-risk occupations, such as food preparation, construction, building grounds, cleaning, maintenance, and the like.

Second-generation Latinos/as are often influenced by two cultures. On one hand, they may have been influenced by traditional values from their culture of origin, which can help them to maintain their emotional connections to family, a strong sense of ethnic identity, and pride in their community. On the other hand, having been raised in the U.S., they are able to learn the social rules, norms, and expectations of the dominant culture, as well as the language and skills necessary to succeed in U.S. society. Thus second-generation Latinos/as are often experts at cultural and language code-switching. For second-generation Latinos/as, acculturation provides them with the resources they need to deal with some of the obstacles that may impair their ability to succeed in the dominant culture (Alvarez-Rivera, Nobles, & Lersch, 2013), which can reduce their acculturative stress. Lastly, third-generation Latinos/as and beyond have often lost their connection to their Latino/a culture, which, according to studies, helps serve as a protective factor for first- and second-generation Latinos/as. Thus third-generation Latinos/as may lack the protection that the Latino/a culture (e.g., values, customs, beliefs) provides. The lack of cultural protection is often exacerbated for third-generation Latinos/as who often adapt to the cultural values and customs of the dominant group, which has a history of devaluing and oppressing individuals of Latino/a descent.

Conclusion

This chapter offers a lens to understand the complexity involved in the process of adaptation to a different culture. Among Latinos/as, the level of acculturation moderates the extent to which individuals adhere to cultural values, practices, and beliefs. The chapter provided a brief history of acculturation followed by an overview and critique of the three main acculturation models: *unidirectional*, *bidirectional*, and *multidirectional*. The chapter concluded with an ecological systems perspective on the acculturation of Latinos/as as a prelude to implications on the health and social mobility of individuals of Latino/a descent.

References

Alderete, E., Vega, W. A., Kolody, B., & Aguilar-Gaxiola, S. (2000). Lifetime prevalence of the risk factors for psychiatric disorders among Mexican migrant farmworkers in California. *American Journal of Public Health*, 90(4), 608–614. doi:10.2105/AJPH.90.4.608

Alegría, M., Mulvaney-Day, N., Torres, M., Polo, A., Cao, Z., & Canino, G. (2007). Prevalence of psychiatric disorders across Latino subgroups in the United States. *American Journal of Public Health*, 97(1), 68–75. doi:10.2105/AJPH.2006.087205

Alvarez-Rivera, L. L., Nobles, M. R., & Lersch, K. M. (2013). Latino immigrant acculturation and crime. *American Journal of Criminal Justice*, 39, 315–330.

Arends-Toth, J., & Van De Vijver, F. J. R. (2006). Assessment of psychological assessment. In D. L. Sam & J. W. Berry (Eds), *The Cambridge handbook of acculturation* (pp. 58–77). Cambridge, UK: Cambridge University Press.

Berry, J. W. (1997). Immigration, acculturation, and adaptation. *Applied Psychology: An International Review*, 46(1), 5–34. doi:10.1080/026999497378467

Berry, J. W. (2003). Conceptual approaches to acculturation. In K. M. Chun, P. Balls Organista & G. Marín (Eds.), *Acculturation: Advances in theory, measurement, and applied research* (pp. 17–37). Washington, DC: American Psychological Association. doi:10.1037/10472-004

Bronfenbrenner, U. (1979). *The ecology of human development*. Cambridge, MA: Harvard University Press.

Buriel, R. (1984). Integration with traditional Mexican-culture and sociocultural adjustment. In J. L. Martinez & R. H. Mendoza (Eds.), *Chicano psychology* (2nd ed., pp. 95–128). New York: Academic Press.

Cabassa, L. J. (2003). Measuring acculturation: Where we are and where we need to go. *Hispanic Journal of Behavioral Sciences*, 25(2), 127–146. doi:10.1177/0739986303025002001

Centers for Disease Control and Prevention. (2015). Vital signs: Leading causes of death, prevalence of diseases and risk factors, and use of health services among Hispanics in the United States from 2009 to 2013. *Morbidity and Mortality Weekly Report*, 64(17), 469-478.

Chavez-Dueñas, N. Y., Adames, H. Y., & Organista, K. C. (2014). Skin-color prejudice and within-group racial discrimination: Historical and current impact on Latino/a populations. *Hispanic Journal of Behavioral Sciences*, 36(1), 3–26. doi:10.1177/0739986313511306

Chun, K. M., Balls Organista, P., & Marin, G. (2003). *Acculturation: Advances in theory, measurement, and applied research*. Washington, DC: American Psychological Association.

Clark, L., & Hofsess, L. (1998). Acculturation. In S. Loue & S. Loue (Eds.), *Handbook of immigrant health* (pp. 37–59). New York, NY: Plenum Press.

Cornelius. (2009). Ambivalent reception: Mass public responses to the "New" Latino Immigration to the United States. In M. M. Suaréz-Orozco & M. M. Paez (Eds.), *Latinos remaking America* (pp. 165–189). Los Angeles, CA: University of California Press.

Cuellar, I., Arnold, B., & Maldonado, R. (1995). Acculturation rating scale for Mexican Americans-II: A revision of the original ARSMA scale. *Hispanic Journal of Behavioral Sciences*, 17(3), 275–304.

Devos, T. (2006). Implicit bicultural identity among Mexican American and Asian American college students. *Cultural Diversity and Ethnic Minority Psychology*, 12(3), 381–402. doi:1037/1099–9809.12.3.381

Diaz, J. (2007). *The brief and wondrous life of Oscar Wao*. New York: Riverhead Trade.

Felix-Ortiz, M., Newcomb, M. D., & Myers, H. (1994). A multidimensional measure of cultural identity for Latino and Latina adolescents. *Hispanic Journal of Behavioral Sciences*, 16(2), 99–115.

Graves, T. D. (1967). Psychological acculturation in a tri-ethnic community. *Southwestern Journal of Anthropology*, 23, 337–350.

Grebler, L., Moore, J. W., & Guzman, R. C. (1970). *The Mexican American people*. New York: The Free Press.

Horevitz, E., & Organista, K. C. (2012). The Mexican health paradox: Expanding the explanatory power of the acculturation construct. *Hispanic Journal of Behavioral Sciences, 35*(1), 3–34. doi:10.1177/0739986312460370

Huntington, S. (2000). The special case of Mexican immigration: Why Mexico is a problem. *The American Enterprise, 11*(8), 20–22.

Jones, S. E., Pezzi, C., Rodriguez-Lainz, A., & Whittle, L. (2014). Health risk behaviors by length of time in the United States among high school students in five states. *Journal of Immigrant and Minority Health, 18*(1), 150–160. doi:10.1007/S10903–014–0151–3

Kim, B. S. K., & Abreu, J. M. (2001). Acculturation measurement: Theory current instruments, and future directions. In J. G. Ponterotto, J. M. Casas, L. A. Suzuki & C. M. Alexander (Eds.), *Handbook of multicultural counseling* (2nd ed., pp. 394–424). Thousand Oaks, CA: Sage.

Kluckhohn, F. R., & Strodtbeck, F. L. (1961). *Variations in value orientations.* Evanston, IL: Row, Peterson.

Kohatsu, E. L., Concepcion, W. R., & Perez, P. (2010). Incorporating levels of acculturation in counseling practice. In J. G. Ponterotto, J. M. Casas, L. A. Suzuki & C. M. Alexander (Eds.), *Handbook of multicultural counseling* (2nd ed., pp. 343–456). Thousand Oaks, CA: Sage.

Matsudaira, T. (2006). Measures of psychological acculturation: A review. *Transcultural Psychiatry, 43*, 461–487.

Meier, M. S., & Ribera, F. (1993). *Mexican Americans/American Mexicans: From Conquistadors to Chicanos.* New York: Hill and Wang.

Mendoza, J. L., & Martinez, R. (1981). The measurement of acculturation. In A. Barón, Jr. (Ed.), *Explorations of Chicago psychology* (pp. 71–82). New York: Praeger.

Morales, L. S., Lara, M., Kington, R. S., Valdez, R. O., & Escarce, J. J. (2002). Socioeconomic, cultural, and behavioral factors affecting Hispanic health outcomes. *Journal of Health Care for the Poor and Underserved, 13*(4), 477–503.

Nguyen, H., Messe, L., & Stollak, G. (1999). Toward a more complex understanding of acculturation and adjustment. *Journal of Cross-Cultural Psychology, 30*, 5–26.

Organista, K. C. (2007). *Solving Latino psychological and health problems: Theory, practice, and populations.* Hoboken, NJ: John Wiley & Sons.

Padilla, A. M. (1980). The role of cultural awareness and ethnic loyalty in acculturation. In A. M. Padilla (Eds.), *Acculturation: Theory, models, and some new findings* (pp. 47–84). Boulder, CO: Westview Press.

Padilla, A. M. (1994). Bicultural development: A theoretical and empirical examination. In R. G. Malgady & O. Rodriguez (Eds.), *Theoretical and conceptual issues in Hispanic mental health* (pp. 20–51). Melbourne, FL: Robert E. Krieger Publishing Co.

Park, R. E. (1955). *Race and culture.* Glencoe, IL: Free Press.

Park, R. E., & Miller, H. A. (1921). *Old world traits transplanted.* New York, NY: Harper & Brothers.

Pew Research Center. (2013). *Between two worlds: How young Latinos come of age in America.* Pew Research Center. Retrieved from http://www.pewhispanic.org/2009/12/11/between-two-worlds-how-young-latinos-come-of-age-in-america/

Ramirez, M. (1969). Identification of with Mexican-American values and psychological adjustment in Mexican-American adolescents. *International Journal of Social Psychiatry, 11*, 151–156.

Ramirez, M. (1984). Assessing and understanding biculturalism-multiculturalism in Mexican-American adults. In J. L. Martinez & R. H. Mendoza (Eds), *Chicano psychology* (2nd ed., pp. 75–93). New York, NY: Academic Press.

Redfield, R., Linston, R., & Herskovita, M. J. (1936). Memorandum of the study of Acculturation. *American Anthropologist, 38*, 149–152.

Rudmin, F. W. (2003). Critical history of the acculturation psychology of assimilation, separation, integration, and marginalization. *Review of General Psychology, 7*(1), 3–37.

Rumbaut, R. G. (2008). The coming of the second generation: Immigration and ethnic mobility in Southern California. *Annals of the American Academy of Political and Social Science, 620*(1), 196–236. doi:10.1177/0002716208322957

Ryder, A. G., Alden, L. E., & Paulhus, D. L. (2000). Is acculturation unidimensional or bidimensional? A head-to-head comparison in the prediction of personality, self-identity, and adjustment. *Journal of Personality and Social Psychology, 79*, 49–65.

Suarez-Orozco, M. M., & Paez, M. M. (2009). The research agenda. In M. M. Suarez-Orozco & C. Suarez-Orozco (Eds.), *Latinos remaking America* (pp. 1–38). Los Angeles, CA: University of California Press.

Szapocznik, J., Kurtines, W. M., & Fernandez, T. (1980). Bicultural involvement and adjustment in Hispanic-American youths. *International Journal of Intercultural Relations, 4*, 353–365.

Szapocznik, J., Scopetta, M., Kurtines, W., & Aranalde, M. A. (1978). Theory and measurement of acculturation. *Interamerican Journal of Psychology, 12*, 113–130.

Vega, W. A., Kolody, B., Aguilar-Gaxiola, S., Alderete, E., Catalano, R., & Caraveo-Anduaga, J. (1998). Lifetime prevalence of DSM-III-R psychiatric disorders among urban and rural Mexican Americans in California. *Archives of General Psychiatry, 55*, 771–778. doi:10.1001/archpsyc.55.9.771

Zweigenhaft, R., & Domhoff, G. W. (2006). *Diversity in the power elite: How it happened, why it matters.* Lanham, MD: Rowham and Littlefield Publishers.

6 Skin Color Matters

Toward a New Framework That Considers Racial and Ethnic Identity Development Among Latinos/as

If you allow a people to control the way you think, you do not have to assign them to an inferior status, if necessary they will seek it out for themselves.

–Carter G. Woodson, 2008, p. 55

One of the most central and complex tasks of human development is to gain an understanding of one's personal and collective identities (Erikson, 1968; Parham, Ajamu, & White, 2010). The ways individuals grapple with, explore, and make decisions about the process of becoming who they are undoubtedly impacts their life trajectories. Understanding the complex process in which people develop their beliefs, attitudes, and feelings about themselves and others, as well as how sociohistorical factors impact these processes is vital for mental health practitioners to consider. Hence it is not surprising that the study of personal and collective identity has become one of the most researched and discussed areas in the field of psychology.

In psychology, personal identity refers to the adoption of specific personal attitudes, feelings, characteristics, and behaviors about the self. It involves the process of answering two questions: "Who am I at the core of my being?" and "What are my personal standards, morals and values?" (White & Cones, 1999). Alternatively, group identity or group orientation is often defined as the process of learning the collective group history (see Chapter 1) and identifying with a larger social group of people with similar values, characteristics, worldviews, beliefs, and practices. Affiliation with social groups guides an individual's feelings, thoughts, and behaviors. Ethnic and racial identities are specific types of social group identities, which are aspects of the self that are important for People of Color in the United States (U.S.).

This chapter focuses on the development of racial and ethnic identity, two paradigms situated within the larger umbrella of the study on social identities. First, definitions of terms pertinent to the study of race and culture are provided as a foundation for understanding the complexities inherent in the existing ethnic- and racial-identity development models. Second, Latino/a specific ethnic-identity paradigms are reviewed, and the ramifications of using race and ethnicity interchangeably in the study of Latino/a social identity are discussed. Lastly, a new conceptual framework that integrates both race and ethnicity to understand these two social constructs among Latinos/ as is provided, as a prelude to implications for research and practice.

Latinos/as are Racial, Ethnic, and Cultural Beings

Race, ethnicity, and culture are socially constructed concepts which have evolved throughout time, contributing to the complexity of their current definitions. Historically, these three ambiguous concepts have been used interchangeably, and in some instances, ethnicity and culture have been used as proxies for race (Helms & Cook, 1999). This conundrum is particularly evident when we consider how the U.S. Census Bureau has categorized Latinos/as. For instance, in the 1960s, Latinos/as were classified as Spanish, in the 1980s as Hispanics, and in 2000 as Hispanics/Latinos. Interestingly, with regard to racial categorization, Latinos/as were classified as being one race until the 2000 census, when individuals from this group were allowed for the first time in U.S. history to classify themselves as belonging to any race. This is a clear example of how the concepts of race and ethnicity were initially used synonymously by the U.S. government to classify the heterogeneous Latino/a population, thus contributing to the notion that ethnicity equates to race. Some scholars also posit that ethnicity and culture are conflated with race because "[race] is so emotionally laden that people try to find 'nicer' terms to substitute it" (Helms & Cook, 1999, p. 19). Overall, the consensus among many scholars in the social sciences is that race, ethnicity, and culture are socially constructed concepts that are distinct yet often interrelated. Thus the perennial effects of race, ethnicity, and culture need to be considered when studying, assessing, and treating Latino/a populations. In an effort not to substitute emotionally laden concepts for terminology that is more comfortable, the following section provides definitions of race, ethnicity, and culture grounded in the existing psychological literature.

Race

Much controversy has circulated around what constitutes the construct of "race," with a number of divergent definitions (i.e., biological, cultural, sociopolitical) proposed by scholars across the social sciences (Bonilla-Silva, 2014; Haller, 1996; Helms, 1990; Smedley & Smedley, 2005). Janet E. Helms (1994), one of the most cited, influential, and respected theorists and scientists on the study of race, underscores that the different definitions of race (i.e., biological, cultural, sociopolitical) may each "have relevance for how race becomes one of an individual's collective identities" (Helms, 1994, p. 297). In the field of psychology, race often refers to how groups of people are categorized according to their shared physical characteristics, including skin color, physiognomy, and other hereditary traits (Chavez-Dueñas, Adames, & Organista, 2014; Cokley, 2007; Helms & Cook, 1999), as well as the social, political, and economic implications of such socially constructed classification for individuals and groups. According to A. Smedley and Smedley (2005), race is a socially fabricated conception about human differences (i.e., predominantly based on skin color, nose width, hair texture, lip thickness) historically and currently used as a justification and rationalization for limiting and restricting access to power, privilege, and wealth of non-White individuals. Overall, we posit that it is not the physical features associated with "race" that cause discrimination, "it is the culturally invented ideas and beliefs about these differences" (Smedley & Smedley, 2005, p. 20) that lead to the horrendous oppression, harm, injustices, and inequities in society experienced daily by People of Color. As discussed in Chapter 2, the Latino/a community is composed of individuals across the entire skin-color spectrum, from the darkest Indigenous and African skin colors to the lightest white skin colors. Moreover, Latinos/as can have phenotypes ranging from African and Indigenous to European. As a result, Latinos/as can be classified as members of any racial category (e.g., Black, White, Native American).

Ethnicity and Culture

The constructs of ethnicity and culture are often used synonymously, although some differences exist between the two words. Ethnicity refers to an individual's lineage, including the national, regional, or tribal origins of a person's oldest remembered ancestors (Helms & Cook, 1999). Alternatively, culture refers to the "complex constellation of [learned] mores, values, customs, traditions, and practices that guide and influence a people's cognitive, affective, and behavioral response to life circumstances" (Parham et al., 1999, p. 14). Accordingly, culture is dynamic, passed from generation to generation, and constantly adapting to social-historical events. In the U.S., culture is often defined by surface-level elements, such as a group's food, language, clothing, and music (Gallardo, Yeh, Trimble, & Parham, 2012; Parham et al., 2010). However, when discussing this complex concept, it is critical to examine domains of culture at the deep structural level (e.g., ontology, axiology, epistemology; see Chapter 8 for a more detailed discussion). In addition to differentiating ethnicity from culture, it is important to also distinguish it from race. Although the terms race and ethnicity have often erroneously been used interchangeably, it is critical to understand that ethnicity can vary within members of the same racial group (e.g., Africans, Afro-Latinos/as, African Americans) and that members of the same ethnic group can be of different races (e.g., White Latinos/as, Afro-Latinos/as, Indigenous Latinos/as).

Ramifications of Using Race and Ethnicity Interchangeably With the Latino/a Population

The interchangeable use of race, ethnicity, and culture has a number of implications for Latinos/as. In fact, Cokley (2007) explains that such erroneous practices prevent scholars from differentiating and identifying the underlying psychological mechanisms of each construct. In addition, the interchangeable use of the terms impacts the way researchers study racial and ethnic identity among Latino/a populations. Consequently, most theories and empirical research have looked at Latinos/as' identities through an ethnic lens; however, such theories and studies are often void of racial considerations (Chavez-Dueñas et al., 2014). Interestingly, a disproportionate number of studies with Latinos/as have solely looked at ethnic identity development to the exclusion of racial identity (Cokley, 2007). This practice offers an incomplete picture of Latinos/as, given that individuals from this group are both ethnic and racial beings (Chavez-Dueñas et al., 2014; Cokley, 2007). In an effort to provide and gain a more holistic view of the racialized and ethnicized experiences of Latinos/as, it is important to discuss models designed to describe the process of racial and ethnic identity development.

Ethnic Identity Development Models

As discussed previously in this chapter, ethnicity refers to an individual's national, regional, or tribal lineage. Consequently, ethnic identity refers to "a social identity based on the culture of one's ancestors' national or tribal group(s) as modified by the demands of the culture in which one's group currently resides" (Helms, 1994, p. 293). The authors of this volume (Adames & Chavez-Dueñas) suggest that ethnic identity is an aspect of the self that includes a sense of acceptance and congruence regarding an individual's membership in a socially constructed ethnic group. Furthermore, it involves an individual's perceptions and feelings about members of his or her own ethnic group, as well as members of the dominant/majority group. In this definition, dominance refers to the group with structural/systemic power and not a numerical majority.

One of the most well-known theorists in the study of ethnic identity is Jean S. Phinney. She defines ethnic identity as a multidimensional and fluid construct that develops from an individual's sense of belonging to a cultural group. Her theory of ethnic identity development is informed by Tajfel's (1981) social identity theory, coupled with the statuses included in Marcia's (1993) theory of identity development, which operationalizes Erikson's (1968) theory of general/global identity. Hence, Phinney's theory of ethnic identity development includes four stages: I) *Diffused*, II) *Foreclosed*, III) *Moratorium*, and IV) *Achieved*. The *Multigroup Ethnic Identity Measure* (MEIM) grounded in Phinney's theory (1992) assesses ethnic identity development across diverse ethnic groups and is a measure used widely in ethnic identity studies.

Specifically, the MEIM measures three domains of ethnic identity: a) *Achievement* (i.e., degree that an individual explores and commits to an ethnic group), b) *Ethnic Behaviors* (i.e., degree to which an individual participates in activities specific to his or her ethnic group), and c) *Affirmation and Belonging* (i.e., degree to which an individual feels positive about his or her ethnic group). Although the MEIM has three subscales (i.e., achievement, ethnic behaviors, affirmation and belonging), only the total score (sum of all three subscales) is used to assess the degree to which an individual has achieved an ethnic identity. A revised version of the MEIM was published in 2007 (Phinney & Ong), which provides a multidimensional and dynamic conceptualization of ethnic identity and further assesses exploration and commitment, two processes believed to be critical in the development of ethnic identity.

Although the MEIM is a widely used instrument, predominantly because of its use with all ethnic groups (Yip, Douglass, & Sellers, 2014), a number of scholars have pointed to some of the measure's limitations. For instance, Umaña-Taylor, Yazedjian, and Bamaca-Gomez (2004) posit that the method of having a sum score to measure the complexities embedded in the concept of ethnic identity is problematic. For instance, the MEIM's total score suggests that only individuals who have a positive commitment to their ethnic identity have an achieved identity. Such assumption makes it difficult for researchers and clinicians to extrapolate which aspect of an individual's ethnic identity formation is associated with a less optimal or negative outcome. To this end, Umaña-Taylor et al. (2004) outlines how the MEIM is not consistent with Erikson's (1968) original identity formation, which requires exploration and commitment. Given these critiques, Umaña-Taylor et al. (2004) developed the *Ethnic Identity Scale* (EIS), which was designed to better align the assessment of ethnic identity development with Erikson's theory (1968) while still mirroring Marcia's theory (1993) of identity.

The EIS is a measure of ethnic identity that captures the three theoretical domains of the construct (i.e., *exploration, affirmation, resolution*). For each of the three domains, a score is provided. Moreover, the measure adds complexity to the construct of affirmation by capturing how individuals can have a positive or negative effect (affirmation) on their ethnic group. Overall, the EIS captures the variability in ethnic identity development leading to a typology that

> captures the experiences of individuals who feel that their ethnicity is an important component of their social selves, engage in a process of exploration, resolve their feelings, and choose to affirm [or not] the role that their ethnic identity plays in their lives.
>
> (Umaña-Taylor et al., 2004, p. 14)

Another major critique of Phinney's scholarly work is her conceptualization of ethnic identity development and her description of race in her theory, a concern raised by a number of scholars (e.g., David, Okazaki, & Giroux,

2014; Fischer & Moradi, 2001; Helms, 2007). For instance, one critique centers on Phinney's definition of race as an ambiguous concept, which is subsumed within the concept of ethnic identity (David et al., 2014; Helms, 2007). Helms (2007) and other scholars (Fischer & Moradi, 2001) have argued in favor of a clear distinction between the concepts of race and ethnicity. Proponents of having two distinct constructs note that racial identity develops as a result of living in a racist society, which is not the case for ethnic identity. Moreover, racial identity highlights dynamics of power and privilege not addressed by Phinney's ethnic identity theory (Fischer & Moradi, 2001; Helms, 2007; Moya & Markus, 2010). While Phinney proposes to combine both concepts (race and ethnicity) into a unitarian construct (Phinney, 1996), other researchers have argued for the separation in the measurement of racial and ethnic identity (Helms, 2007). Additionally, Cokley (2007) asserts that "race and ethnicity should be treated as separate yet related constructs, so too should racial identity and ethnic identity" (p. 518).

Racial Identity Development Models

Given that people may phenotypically classify Latinos/as into all possible racial groups, the experience of Black Latinos/as or Afro-Latinos/as may, in some ways, be similar to that of U.S. African Americans. For instance, systemic discrimination, historical and contemporary forms of racism, and continued oppression, marginalization, and dehumanization are racialized experiences shared by Afro-Latinos/as and Black Americans. Similarly, Latinos/as with white or lighter skin and European features have some commonalities with European Americans. For instance, there is empirical and theoretical literature to support how White Latinos/as, and those with lighter skin, benefit from racial privilege (e.g., Chavez-Dueñas et al., 2014; Montalvo, 2004; Ramos, Jaccard, & Guilamo-Ramos, 2003; Zweigenhaft & Domhoff, 2006). Furthermore, racial inequities among Latinos/as based on skin color and physiognomy have been well documented in the literature. For instance, one of the earliest studies conducted to assess the impact of skin color reported that darker and more Indigenous phenotypical Latinos/as had lower levels of educational attainment (9.5 and 7.8 years, respectively), income ($12,721 and $10,450, respectively), and higher levels of perceived discrimination compared to their White and lighter-skinned, European-looking Latino/a counterparts (Arce, Murguia, & Frisbie, 1987). A more recent study of diversity within the upper echelons of corporate America found that among CEOs of Fortune 500 companies, only 1% were of Latino/a descent (Zweigenhaft & Domhoff, 2006) and most of them were of elite Cuban American background. These individuals were described as culturally and racially similar to European Americans, with their international orientation being the only feature differentiating them from non-Latino/a CEOs (Zweigenhaft & Domhoff, 2006). Overall, race has a profound impact on how individuals are viewed by others, as well as how they perceive themselves, which is at the core of racial identity development. Racial identity development is defined as "the significance and qualitative meaning that individuals attribute to their membership within [the] racial group within their self-concepts" (Sellers, Smith, Shelton, Rowley, & Chavous, 1998, p. 23). The next sub-sections provide a brief review of the main racial identity development models used to understand how Blacks, Whites, and People of Color gain an understanding of themselves as racial beings.

Black Racial Identity Development

The study of racial identity development dates back to the 1970s with Charles Thomas's (1971) concept of *Negromachy*, which he described as a Black person's inappropriate dependence on White society for self-definition. Thomas posited that *Negromachy* resulted in confusion about self-worth. One of the first models of Black racial identity, developed by Jackson (1976), proposes a stage identity paradigm titled the *Social Identity Development Model* (SIDM). The SIDM describes how the oppressed (e.g., Black Americans) move through a process of attaining a liberated identity within the bounds of an oppressive environment. The model has five stages: 1) *Naive*, 2) *Acceptance*, 3) *Resistance*, 4) *Redefinition*, and 5) *Internalization*, with two of the stages encompassing two possible states of consciousness, including a) active/conscious/explicit and b) passive/unconscious/implicit. The SIDM stages are summarized in Table 6.1.

Table 6.1 Jackson's Social Identity Development Model (SIDM) for the Oppressed

Stage	Descriptions
NAIVE:	**No Racial Consciousness:** Describes the innocence of the oppressed when they are born into a racist society. Individuals are taught about social-group memberships and the social status of People of Color.
STAGE I	**Active Acceptance:** *Conscious Identification* Explicitly identifying with the logic of the oppressor and the structural system of inequality. *Rationalization* Agreeing and actively supporting the oppressor, as well as the logic and system that supports the oppression, while ignoring the contradictions that are inherent in the logic of actively participating in one's own oppression.

(*Continued*)

Table 6.1 Continued

Stage	Descriptions
	Beginning to Acknowledge The oppressed individual begins to acknowledge some of the contradictions in the logic of his or her thinking.

Passive Acceptance:

Unconscious Identification
The oppressed individual implicitly identifies with the oppressor's logic, denies the existence of oppression, or denies any personal involvement with the oppressor. The denial of differences is used as a means for not seeing oppression.

Acknowledgment
The oppressed acknowledges the existence of specific types of overt discrimination and begins to see such instances as more than random exceptions.

STAGE II   **Active Resistance:**

Openly Questions
The individual openly questions personal and institutional support for oppressive practices and policies and is interested in gaining a deeper understanding of how oppression works and the many ways in which it is expressed.

Experiences Pain and Anger
The oppressed individual recognizes feelings of anger, pain, and rage resulting from the oppression. He or she confronts people who actively participate in and support oppression; the oppressed person attempts to abandon beliefs, attitudes, and behavioral patterns learned in Stage I (acceptance stage).

Realizes Sense of Power
The oppressed individual recognizes the ability that he or she has to make changes within his or her immediate environment, to develop a clearer sense of who he or she is not, and to define who he or she actually is.

Passive Resistance:

Questions and Challenges
The person begins to question and challenge oppression in settings and situations where there is no personal risk.

Experiences Frustration, Pain, and Anger
The individual experiences feelings of frustration, anger, and pain; he or she continues to take greater risks by challenging oppression more openly.

Increasing Sense of Power
Each time the person challenges oppression directly, he or she feels an increased sense of personal power and a desire to redefine him or herself.

Stage	Descriptions
STAGE III	**Redefinition:**
	Redefinition of Racial-Group Membership
	The person begins to redefine what it means for them to be who they are. The individual searches for new ways to redefine his or her racial group and membership in that racial group.
	New Racial-Group Identity
	The process of searching, investigating, and dialoguing with members of the same racial group results in the person redefining him or herself in terms that are independent of his or her perceived strengths and weaknesses of White people and White culture.
	Rename Personal Role in Oppression
	The individual renames his or her role in the manifestation of oppression.
STAGE IV	**Internalization:**
	Application of Racial Identity
	New racial identity is expressed in various roles in the person's life.
	Internalization of New Identity
	As the person feels more comfortable expressing his or her new racial identity across settings, this identity is internalized.
	Internalized Identity is Nurtured
	The internalized identity needs to be nurtured so that it can be sustained even in hostile environments that work to resocialize individuals into an oppressed identity.

Note: Table informed by Jackson, B. W., III, 1976.

Two other prolific scholars credited with advancing the study of Black racial identity development are Janet E. Helms and William E. Cross Jr., whose theories are briefly reviewed in the following section. Additionally, Helms's (1990) and Hardiman's (1982) models of White racial identity developments are discussed to assist in understanding the process of racial identity development among White populations. Lastly, this section concludes with a brief review of the *Racial/Cultural Identity Development Model (R/CID)* proposed by Atkinson, Morten, and Sue (1989).

Cross's Theory of Nigrescence

Although Cross is well known for developing the concept of *Nigrescence* into a theory of racial identity development, it is important to note that Frantz Fanon (1967) coined the term "Nigrescence." The process of developing a Black identity under conditions of oppression and marginalization captures the essence of Nigrescence. Cross (1971) utilized the concept of Nigrescence to describe the process Black Americans go through as they develop a Black consciousness and identity. A major tenant of the Nigrescence theory is that Black individuals move from a stage of self-degradation to one where they feel self-pride. The original model included five stages, which was later revised to a four-stage model that included seven identities. The four stages outlined by the revised theory include 1) *Pre-Encounter*, 2) *Encounter*, 3) *Immersion/Emersion*, and 4) *Internalization-Commitment*. Each of the stages and the seven identities are described in Table 6.2.

Table 6.2 Cross's Racial Identity Model

Stages	Descriptions
Pre-Encounter	• This stage has two identities: I) *Assimilation*, II) *Anti-Black* • The Assimilation Identity characterizes individuals who look at the world through a "pro-American" view and attach low salience to racial issues. Individuals in the Anti-Black identity have internalized negative stereotypes of the Black community, and experience self-hate or rejection of the self and/or hate toward their racial group.
Encounter	• Stage where individuals experience a personal racial event(s), which dismantles previously held beliefs regarding their racial group and themselves as racial beings.
Immersion/Emersion	• Individuals in this stage experience cognitive dissonance, which requires taking on a new frame of reference, while at the same time attempting to dismantle their old identities. • This stage contains two identities: I) *Intense Black Involvement Identity* II) *Anti-White Identity* • Intense Black Involvement is characterized by the idealization and glorification of everything that is Black (e.g., people, music, food). The Anti-White identity describes an individual who has a strong rejection of White people and White culture.
Internalization	• This stage includes three identities: I) *Black Nationalist, II) Biculturalist, III) Multiculturalist* • A focus on Black community empowerment is the hallmark of Black Nationalist. An individual with a Biculturalist Identity has achieved a state of self-acceptance with a pluralistic perspective that includes other cultural orientations. The Multiculturalists perspective includes a focus on two or more identities that are salient for the person.

Note: Table informed by Cross, W. E., Jr., & Vandiver, B. J., 2001.

Helms's Racial Identity Theory

Although Helms is well known for her model of White racial identity development (discussed later in this chapter), she also contributed to Black racial identity theory. Specifically, Helms expanded Cross's theory of Nigrescence by suggesting that "each stage [i.e., *Pre-encounter, Encounter, Immersion/Emersion, Internalization*] be considered a distinct worldview" (Helms, 1990, p. 19), by which she meant cognitive templates that people use to organize (especially racial) information about themselves, other people, and institutions. Helms also posited that an individual's racial identity consists of three components that influence each other: ascribed identities, personal identities, and reference-group identities. According to her theory, each component is influenced by environmental factors proximal to the individual. Helms further postulates that it might be best to think of each stage as bimodal, with each stage of identity having an active (conscious) or passive (unconscious) expression. Lastly, Helms is credited with conducting extensive empirical studies on racial identity development (Cokley & Chapman, 2009).

White Racial Identity Development

Helms's White Racial Identity Development Model

Janet E. Helms developed the most influential and sophisticated White racial identity theories. Her model has been at the center of much empirical research (e.g., Carter, 1990; Helms & Carter, 1990; Sue & Sue, 2013) and is the most widely cited model of all the White racial identity development models (Spanierman & Soble, 2010). In her model, Helms explains that developing a healthy racial identity for White individuals involves "the capacity to recognize and abandon the normative strategies of white people for coping with race" (1999, p. 89). For instance, White individuals are privileged due to their race compared to non-Whites. Consequently, they are socialized to implicitly and, at times, explicitly believe that they are superior to non-Whites. The process of developing a healthy White identity requires individuals to acknowledge the unearned entitlements and privileges bestowed onto them by society and actively work to end racism and the oppression of People of Color. In addition, developing a healthy White identity requires movement through two phases: a) abandonment of racism and b) defining a nonracist White identity (Helms, 1990, 2008). Unlike earlier models of racial identity, Helms's replaced the construct of "stages" with "ego statuses." She asserts, "statuses are cognitive-affective-conative intrapsychic principles for responding to racial stimuli in one's internal and external environments" (Helms, 1990, p. 84). This small yet significant change in terminology allows researchers and practitioners to understand and treat the process of racial identity development as malleable and not part of an individual's fixed personality structure. Table 6.3 provides a summary of Helms's White Racial Identity Statuses.

Table 6.3 Helms's White Racial Identity Development Model

Statuses	Descriptions
CONTACT *I am innocent.*	• Individuals do not see themselves as a racial being (i.e., White person); instead, they claim to be color-blind, have limited knowledge of People of Color, and interactions with racially diverse others are characterized by naïveté.
DISINTEGRATION *How can I be White?!*	• Characterized by feelings of shame, guilt, and anxiety caused by unresolvable ethical dilemmas related to race, which forces the individual to choose between own-group loyalty and humanism.
REINTEGRATION *We Whites have the best because we are the best.*	• Idealization of Whites and White culture; denigration and intolerance of People of Color and their cultures. Feelings of White superiority are implicitly and explicitly expressed in this status.
PSEUDO-INDEPENDENCE *Let's help People of Color become more like us Whites.*	• Individuals strive to be perceived as good White people. They may be able to articulate feelings of racial equity, but they continue to believe that Whites and White culture are superior to People of Color and their cultures. Individuals profess a desire to help People of Color by making them more like the dominant group.
IMMERSION/ EMERSION *I am White.*	• People search for an understanding and personal meaning of racism, whiteness, and White privilege. Feelings of anger and frustration toward other Whites who they perceive as being less knowledgeable about race are experienced. This status requires White people to take responsibility for racism and to understand their role in perpetuating it. They are also likely to experience feelings of guilt, anger, and anxiety.
AUTONOMY *I see color and I like it.*	• Characterized by an informed commitment to seeking opportunities to increase racial diversity in their personal lives in order to learn from such experiences. Individuals find ways to use their racial privilege to eliminate racism and to avoid engaging in behaviors that promote racial oppression. Internalization of an anti-racist White perspective.

Note: Table informed by Helms, J. E., 2008; Helms, J. E. & Cook, D. A., 1999.

Hardiman's Model of White Racial Identity Development

Rita Hardiman (1982) is another scholar considered a pioneer in the study of whiteness and White racial identity development. Her theory emerged from qualitative analyses of the autobiographies of six White anti-racist authors (Spanierman & Soble, 2010). Hardiman was particularly interested in examining the psychological impact of racism on members of the dominant group and the process by which they develop a nonracist racial identity. Specifically, Hardiman (1982) focused on the development of a racial consciousness, the events creating cognitive dissonance, and the factors leading to the motivation for change. Although her theory has received little empirical attention, it offers important information about the process experienced by White individuals as they become aware of their racial privilege and work to develop a healthy White racial identity. Table 6.4 provides a detailed description of her theory.

Table 6.4 Hardiman's Model of White Racial Identity Development

Stage	Descriptions
NAIVE: STAGE I	**No Racial Consciousness:** Describes the innocence of oppressors when they are born into a racist society. Individuals are taught about the status of their racial (White) group. **Active Acceptance:** *Conscious Identification* There is a conscious identification with the social hierarchical system(s) that give members of the oppressor group unearned power and privilege. *Reinforcement of Oppressive Ideologies* The oppressor operates and disseminates prejudicial thoughts about the oppressed, while actively blaming and rewarding members of the oppressed group(s) who support racist and oppressive logic systems used by oppressors. Individuals from the oppressor group punish oppressed individuals who question and challenge the system. *Recognition and Questioning* Oppressors begin to explicitly recognize that some of the issues about the system, raised by members of the oppressed group, may have some validity; they begin to overtly question the beliefs about the system they have embraced. **Passive Acceptance:** *Unconscious Identification* Individuals demonstrate an implicit identification with the social system that gives their racial group unearned power and privilege. *Denial and Blaming of the Oppressed* Members of the oppressing group deny the existence of racial oppression and blame members of racial minority groups for it. *Begins to Acknowledge* Individuals begin to implicitly recognize the existence of some forms of injustice in society and begin to admit that the oppressed may not be causing their own oppression.

(Continued)

Table 6.4 Continued

Stage	Descriptions
STAGE II	**Active Resistance**

Openly Questions
The oppressor observes and questions their social support for signs of oppression. They challenge oppression when noticed among people and institutions.

Acknowledges Participation in Oppressive System
Individuals admit their own oppressive behavior(s) and implicit support of oppressive institutions. Experiences shame, guilt, and anger due to their roles in supporting the system of oppression.

Actively Rejects Own Oppressive Behavior
Oppressors reject their own oppressive behavior and the system that teaches racist ideologies. They actively reject the status and privileges gained from an oppressive system and begin to feel the need for a redefinition of their racial identity.

Passive Resistance:
Questions and Challenges
Looks for examples of oppression within their social network and the institutions they are embedded in. Questions and challenges oppressive behaviors in ways that are socially and professionally safe.

Recognition
Acknowledges oppression's existence and its pervasiveness in society; such recognition contributes to a desire to leave or distance the self from such racist systems.

Experiences Alienation
Frustration and alienation are experienced, which results in individuals engaging in antioppressive work. Individuals begin this process by owning their participation in the oppressive system and rejecting the tenets of oppression. Individuals feel the need to redefine their racial identity.

STAGE III   **Redefinition:**

Redefinition of Racial Identity
Searches for new ways of defining one's racial group and one's membership in it.

New Group Name and Definition
The individual begins a process of searching, investigating, and dialoguing with members of the same racial group, which results in the person redefining what it means to be a member of the group that oppresses.

Renaming Personal Role in Oppression
Individuals gain a better understanding of the different manifestations of oppression. The new awareness requires individuals to examine their roles in the various manifestations of oppression.

Stage	Descriptions
STAGE IV	Internalization: *Application of New Name* New racial identity is expressed in various roles within the person's life. *Internalization of New Identity* As individuals feel more comfortable expressing their new racial identity across settings, this identity is internalized. *Nurtured New Identity* Needs to nurture new racial identity in order to sustain it while in a hostile environment that seeks to resocialize individuals into an oppressor identity.

Note: Table informed by Hardiman, R., 1982.

People of Color Racial Identity Development

The majority of the racial identity development models have focused on a single racial group (i.e., Cross, 1971; Helms, 1990). However, the Racial/Cultural Identity Development (R/CID) model proposed by Atkinson et al. (1989) describes the experiences of oppression shared across individuals from racial and ethnic minority groups. The R/CID model is a conceptual framework that seeks to describe the process experienced by minority individuals as they develop an understanding of their own cultural heritage, the dominant culture, and the relationship between both groups. The model is made up of five stages: 1) *Conformity*, 2) *Dissonance*, 3) *Resistance and Immersion*, 4) *Introspection*, and 5) *Integrative Awareness*. Each stage is described next in more detail.

The first stage of the R/CID model is *Conformity*, which characterizes an individual exhibiting a preference for the values of the dominant culture. Individuals in this stage identify with White Americans, see the dominant group as the norm, and have "bought into societal definitions about their minority status in society" (Sue & Sue, 2013, p. 296). In addition, negative feelings toward members of their own minoritized cultural group accompany the *Conformity* stage. The second stage is *Dissonance*, characterized by an event that calls into question the beliefs, attitudes, and values held by the individual in the *Conformity* stage. This experience leads into cognitive dissonance, where minoritized individuals begin to question their attitudes toward their cultural group and the dominant group. Moreover, people in the *Dissonance* stage experience a challenge in their self-concept as they attempt to make sense of conflicting pieces of information. During the *Resistance and Immersion* stage (third), ethnic minority individuals are likely to experience intense emotions, such as shame, guilt, and anger, resulting from their previously held admiration for the dominant group and rejection of their own cultural group. This stage is further marked by minoritized individuals' unequivocal and all-encompassing endorsement of their cultural group's attitudes, beliefs, and values along with an overall rejection of the values and beliefs held by the dominant culture. In this stage, "the person seems dedicated to reacting against white society and rejects white social, cultural, and institutional standards as having no personal validity" (Sue & Sue, 2013, p. 301). In the fourth stage (*Introspection*), people spend more time and energy developing an understanding of themselves as members of a cultural minority group. They no longer see their group through an idealistic lens and are able to discern their individual perspectives and beliefs from those of their cultural group (e.g., members of a minority group would be able to reject homophobic ideologies even if this is common among members of their cultural group). The last stage of the R/CID model is *Integrative Awareness*, which is marked by a sense of security in the individual's ability to see both positive and negative aspects of different cultures. Lastly, individuals in this stage demonstrate a commitment to ending all forms of oppression.

Ethnic Identity Development Models for Latinos/as

Ethnoracial Model of Latino/a Identity Orientations

One of the few identity models developed specifically for Latino/a populations is the *Ethnoracial Model of Latino/a Identity Orientations* created by Ferdman and Gallegos in 2001. The model was originally intended to assist leaders in business organizations in understanding the complexities of identity among individuals in the Latino/a community. Scholars (e.g., Evans, Forney, Guido, Patton, & Renn, 2010) have also applied the model to the development of college students. For instance, considerations have been offered on how the model can be used to understand the experiences of race and racism among Latino/a college students (Evans et al., 2010). Considerations include 1) the idea that race is not a central component of the Latino/a experience, but skin color is relevant; 2) because Latinos/as do not fit easily into the U.S. racial framework, placing Latinos/as into a restricted racial category can be challenging; and 3) Latinos/as tend to use many variables when self-identifying (e.g., family, education, appearance). Ferdman and Gallegos (2001) used these three considerations to develop the Ethnoracial Model of Latino/a Identity Orientations, which consists of six identities that serve as lenses Latinos/as may employ when viewing themselves as ethnoracial beings. Two of the underlying assumptions central to the Ethnoracial Model of Latino/a Identity Orientations include the idea that (a) no orientation is better or worse than the other and (b) identity is fluid and constantly changing as a result of contextual and social forces affecting the individual. The six identities are based on five factors, which include

1) the individual's identity lens, 2) identity preference, 3) overall view of Latinos/as as a group, 4) view of Whites as a whole, and 5) consideration of race (Evans et al., 2010; Ferdman & Gallegos, 2001). The following are the six identities identified by Ferdman and Gallegos.

1. **White Identified:** Latinos/as who are White-identified are characterized by being highly acculturated to the U.S.-dominant American culture. They are also likely to view society from a White American perspective. These individuals tend to have internalized the negative stereotypes about the Latino/a community reinforced by U.S.-dominant society. They tend to see themselves as different and superior to other People of Color. Lastly, they often do not self-identify as Latinos/as.

2. **Undifferentiated Denial:** Latino/a individuals who espouse "culturally blind" ideologies characterize this identity. In other words, they deny or pretend that they do not see cultural and ethnic differences. Moreover, undifferentiated Latinos/as do not connect with members of their own ethnic group, as they lack awareness about cultural characteristics that make this group unique. Individuals not exposed to Latino/a culture are more likely to develop an undifferentiated denial style, which may lead into cultural confusion or disorientation when encountering discrimination.

3. **Latinos/as as Other:** This identity represents individuals who have a general association with and consciousness of being Latino/a, but do not have an in-depth sense of the history, traditions, or cultural markers associated with each of the subgroups represented in this collective category. Thus individuals in this identity view themselves as non-White and feel connected to the group as a whole. However, they tend not to see much differentiation within this heterogeneous group. As a result, individuals in this group do not identify closely with any Latino/a subgroup; instead, their primary identification is as minorities or People of Color.

4. **Subgroup Identified:** Subgroup identified Latinos/as see themselves as members of their own distinct Latino/a subgroup (e.g., Mexican, Dominican, Cuban). These individuals tend to see their subgroup, its culture, and its people more positively than other Latino/a subgroups.

5. **Latino/a Identified:** This identity is composed of Latinos/as who see their ethnic group in a unitary and unified way. They advocate for the group as a whole, are aware of the uniqueness of each subgroup, but they do not overemphasize within-group differences.

6. **Latino/a Integrated:** This identity characterizes individuals who see their membership in the Latino/a group as a central aspect of themselves. They are aware of how race is dynamic, contextual, and socially constructed, while also understanding how their own experience is shaped by their multiple identities (e.g., gender, sexual orientation, religion orientation).

Bernal's Mexican American Ethnic Identity Development Model

Another model specific to Latinos/as is the *Mexican American Ethnic Identity Development Model* created by Bernal, Knight, Garza, Ocampo, and Cota (1990). The model was created for Mexican Americans; however, some scholars postulate that Bernal et al.'s model can be applied to most Latinos/as (Miville, 2010). The Mexican American Ethnic Identity Model describes the components that comprise ethnic identity development for Mexican Americans. Such components include 1) *ethnic self-identification categorization* (labeling self as part of an ethnic group), 2) *ethnic constancy* (ethnic characteristics are permanent across time and place), 3) *ethnic role behaviors* (engaging in practices that are congruent with cultural values, customs, etc.), 4) *ethnic knowledge* (knowing that specific behaviors, values, customs, etc., are part of one's ethnic group), and 5) *ethnic preferences and feelings* (having a desire to be part of one's ethnic group; Bernal et al., 1990). Phinney (1992) later used the same components to construct her theory of ethnic identity. However, both models differ in a number of ways. For instance, while Phinney's model proclaims to be applicable to all ethnic groups (see earlier section in this chapter for full description), Bernal et al.'s model was developed solely for U.S. Latinos/as. Conceptually, different frameworks guide both models. Bernal et al.'s model integrates elements of cognitive social learning, cognitive development theory, and self-system theory (Bernal et al., 1990), whereas an Eriksonian and social identity theory are the underlying frameworks that guide Phinney's model (Phinney & Ong, 2007).

Limitations of the Existing Racial and Ethnic Identity Development Models When Applied to Latinos/as: A Call for New Paradigms

The topic of social identity development among minoritized communities highlights the complexities embedded in the study of an individual's sense of membership in his or her ethnic and racial groups. The models reviewed in this chapter provide a diverse array of perspectives in the study of racial and ethnic identity development. While models of racial identity development have exclusively focused on U.S. Blacks and Whites (e.g., Cross, 1971; Helms, 1990), models of ethnic identity development (e.g., Phinney, 1992; Umaña-Taylor et al., 2004) have predominantly been applied to Latinos/as. The exclusive use of ethnic identity models for Latinos/as mask the racial heterogeneity of this community. Viewing Latinos/as primarily through an ethnic identity lens ignores the racial heterogeneity of this community and perpetuates *Mestizaje Racial Ideologies* (MRIs), referred to as the historical socialization of Latinos/as that maintains denial, deflection, and minimization of the skin-color hierarchy (Adames, Chavez-Dueñas, &

Organista, 2016). MRIs place Latino/a individuals from the entire color spectrum into a racial category that de-emphasizes the impact of skin color and phenotype on their lives (Adames et al., 2016; Chavez-Dueñas et al., 2014).

As previously discussed, dominant theories that inform research on social identity among Latinos/as in the U.S. have predominantly focused on ethnicity while minimizing or neglecting the role of race. This practice is evident in Phinney's (1992) model, which blurred the distinction between race and ethnicity and at times used ethnicity as a euphemism for race (Helms, 1990; Helms & Cook, 1999). Interestingly, the only two models developed exclusively to study the process of Latino/a identity development, the Mexican American Ethnic Identity Model (Bernal et al., 1990) and the Ethnoracial Model of Latino/a Identity Orientations (Ferdman & Gallegos, 2001), have either reinforced the ideology of MRIs, or demonstrated an unclear understanding about the construct of race as applied to Latino/a populations. For example, although Ferdman and Gallegos (2001) assert that race is a central component of Latino/a identity, they describe it as being fluid and chosen by the individual rather than it being ascribed by others, which is incongruent with most definitions of race. The authors of this volume (Adames & Chavez-Dueñas) assert that it is difficult, if not impossible to gain a good understanding of the Latino/a experience using models that have traditionally neglected the role of race and skin color. Hence it is necessary to develop models of social identity that capture both the racialized *and* ethnicized experiences of Latinos/as. Neglecting either aspect of identity will only provide a partial, incomplete, and erroneous understanding of the individuals in this group. A framework that integrates both racial *and* ethnic identity is offered in the next section.

C-REIL: A New Framework for Centering Racial *and* Ethnic Identity for Latino/a Populations

Chapters 1 through 5 provide information on the historical context (e.g., historical roots of Latinos/as, skin-color differences and colorism, history of Latinos/as in the U.S.), sociocultural foundations (e.g., acculturation, models of social identity), and evolving social realities pivotal to consider when providing culturally and racially congruent mental health services to Latinos/as. The information provided in the first six chapters serves as a foundation for developing a more nuanced and complex understanding of this heterogeneous population. This section proposes an alternative framework that provides a more complex understanding of the study of Latino/a social identities (i.e., race and ethnicity). The framework depicted in Figure 6.1 is titled C-REIL (*Centering Racial & Ethnic Identity for Latinos/as*) and was constructed by integrating the body of research and literature discussed in the first five chapters of this volume.

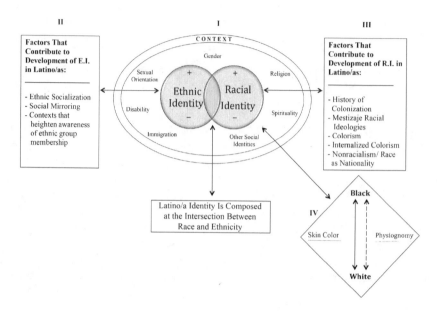

Figure 6.1 Centering Racial and Ethnic Identity for Latino/a Framework (C-REIL)

Assumptions of the C-REIL Framework

Overall, we strongly assert that centering race and ethnicity in the study of Latino/a social identities would enable researchers and practitioners to develop a more accurate, nuanced, and comprehensive understanding of the Latino/a experience. Such understanding would provide a foundation for conducting racially and ethnically congruent assessment and treatment of Latino/a clients. A number of assumptions guide the underpinnings of this alternative framework. One, we affirm that although many social identities (e.g., gender, sexual orientation, immigration) are important in the understanding of the Latino/a experience, race and ethnicity are the main sources of most social inequities, including disparities in education, health, socioeconomic status, and the like. Two, context determines which aspects (e.g., race, gender, disability) of identity become more salient. Three, Latinos/as in the U.S. are the product of a historically and contemporarily oppressive culture that impacts individuals' view of themselves and others. Four, members of the dominant group are socialized to engage in behaviors that reinforce and maintain the ethnic and racial hierarchy endemic to U.S. society, which has a negative impact on the racial and ethnic identities of Latinos/as.

The C-REIL Framework

The C-REIL framework offers a unique perspective on Latino/a social identities given its explicit integration of race and ethnicity. In fact, the C-REIL framework places race and ethnicity at the center of an individual's intersecting identities. For instance, the experience of a person who identifies as an Afro-Latina lesbian woman will be shaped by her sexual orientation and gender, with her race and ethnicity providing a unique racialized experience compared to a White Latina lesbian woman. The framework also underscores the significance of the sociohistorical and sociopolitical factors that shape the experiences of Latinos/as in the U.S. The C-REIL framework seeks to bridge the divide between the study of racial and ethnic identity among Latinos/as.

Part I

The first component of the C-REIL framework explicitly focuses on race and ethnicity, as well as the context in which the individual develops and currently resides. Taking these factors into consideration allows us to appreciate how the experience of Latinos/as is not universal; instead, it is impacted by individuals' sense of acceptance and congruence (i.e., +/–) regarding their membership in the Latino/a community (ethnic identity), as well as the meaning individuals ascribe to being members of a racial group (racial identity). Moreover, how Latinos/as view themselves, and how others categorize them, may be impacted by the racial and ethnic makeup of the community where they grew up (e.g., predominantly Latino/a vs. White European American community), as well as by the sociohistorical time and political climate (i.e., context) of the U.S. For instance, a child of Latino/a immigrants residing in a predominantly White European American community and growing up during a time of high anti-Latino/a immigrant sentiment may develop feelings of shame that can result in rejection of his or her Latino/a heritage. Despite the challenges this individual may face as a result of grappling with her ethnicity, race (e.g., skin color, physiognomy) can facilitate or hinder his or her ability to assimilate into the U.S. White dominant culture. Assimilation can allow individuals who have that option (i.e., phenotypically White Latinos/as) to access resources often denied to those who are phenotypically identified as People of Color. The previous example illustrates how context can impact the ways in which individuals choose to identify and how others categorize them. Although this framework predominately focuses on the role of race and ethnicity, it is also important to note that race and ethnicity intersect with other social identities (e.g., gender, sexual orientation) to produce racialized and ethnicized experiences of those different identities.

Part II

The second component of the C-REIL framework highlights the factors that contribute to the development of ethnic identity among Latinos/as. A number of social factors impact how individuals come to understand their membership in the community, as well as the meaning and feelings associated with being Latino/a. The literature has identified three elements that contribute to the development of ethnic identity, including a) parental ethnic socialization (Else-Quest & Morse, 2015), b) social mirroring (e.g., media, peers, teachers) (Spencer, Fegley, & Harpalani, 2003; C. Suarez-Orozco & Suarez-Orozco, 2001), and c) social contexts that heighten the awareness or salience of ethnic identity (French, Seidman, Allen, & Aber, 2006; Garcia Coll et al., 1996). In the next section, each factor is applied briefly to Latinos/as.

ETHNIC SOCIALIZATION

Ethnic identity development is influenced by a wide variety of social agents, including the family. Within the Latino/a community, families serve as the primary mechanism for the transmission of historical, cultural, and heritage knowledge about an individual's ethnic group, which reinforces his or her sense of ethnic group membership and pride (i.e., ethnic socialization). An important component of ethnic socialization is preparing children for experiences of oppression due to their membership in a minoritized ethnic group (Else-Quest & Morse, 2015). Part of equipping children for navigating an oppressive society requires parents to promote a sense of mistrust (i.e., healthy cultural suspicion; White & Cones, 1999), which "emphasizes the need for caution in interethnic interactions, specifically with members of the dominant group" (Else-Quest & Morse, 2015, p. 55). Empirical research supports that parental ethnic socialization plays a significant role in the development of ethnic identity (Huynh & Fuligni, 2008; Umaña-Taylor, Alfaro, Bamaca, & Guimond, 2009; Umaña-Taylor & Guimond, 2010).

SOCIAL MIRRORING

Members of ethnic minority groups develop a keen eye for discerning where their group is situated within the U.S. social hierarchy. This phenomenon has a number of implications for the development of a healthy ethnic identity. For instance, a person's sense of self is influenced by the reflections mirrored by members of society about their ethnic group (e.g., social media, traditional media, adult caretakers, teachers, peers, employers). Winnicott (2005) explains that when the reflected images are positive, individuals are better equipped to experience a sense of self-worth. Instead, members of minoritized communities are often rendered invisible in many spheres of society, including history books, mainstream media, higher education (e.g., professors, deans, presidents of colleges and universities), positions of authority, and the like. Winnicott further asserts that when reflections are negative, individuals may find it difficult to maintain a positive sense of self. For instance, the Latino/a population is often portrayed as one that is uneducated, unintelligent, aggressive, promiscuous, and hyper-emotional. When multiple outlets mirror these negative images of Latinos/as, the outcome may be an internalization of such messages, which may have a detrimental effect on the individual's ethnic identity. Overall, "nonrecognition or misrecognition can inflict harm, can be a form of oppression, imprisoning someone in a false, distorted, and reduced mode of being" (Taylor, 1994, p. 75).

CONTEXTS THAT HEIGHTEN THE AWARENESS OF ETHNIC-GROUP MEMBERSHIP

The context in which individuals function can modulate the level of awareness they have regarding their ethnic group and their sense of connection to that group. For example, in the years following 9/11, Latinos/as and immigrants in particular, experienced increasing levels of oppression and rejection. The increased attention paid to national security has led to a number of legislations that criminalize and demonize the presence of undocumented immigrants in the U.S. The negative perceptions of immigrants depicted in the media have impacted the entire Latino/a community, regardless of their citizenship status and generation in the U.S. Hence, for some Latinos/as, the sociohistorical and political context contributes to a heightened awareness about their membership in a minoritized and oppressed group. Some Latinos/as cope with the negative rhetoric by focusing on the positive aspects of their culture, while others deal with it by distancing themselves from the community. Yet for others, these events have served as an "encounter," making the individuals more prone to questioning and exploring their membership in the Latino/a community. Examining the social, political, and historical context is critical to the understanding of how Latinos/as develop particular beliefs, attitudes, and feelings about their membership in their community.

Part III

An imperative prerequisite to the development of a Latino/a racial identity is the ability for Latino/as to recognize themselves as racial beings regardless of context. As such, the third component of the C-REIL focuses on the factors that contribute to the development of racial identity among Latinos/as. These factors include history of colonization, MRIs, colorism, internalized colorism, and nonracialism/race as nationality. Within the context of Latinos/as, each factor is briefly discussed.

HISTORY OF COLONIZATION

The meaning Latinos/as ascribe to being members of a racial group has its foundations in the complex history of its people. On one end, Latinos/as have rich histories of ancestral roots and traditions; on the other end, their collective narrative is plagued by conquest, colonization, and slavery. During the colonial period, Latin America was divided into a caste society, also referred to as a system of stratification (Chavez-Dueñas et al., 2014; Soler Castillo & Pardo Abril, 2009). This system was based on skin color and phenotypical characteristics (see Chapter 2 for more detailed information). The social stratification system of the colonial period had the Spaniards (elite Whites) and their descendants strategically occupying the top of the hierarchy. Such a stratification system was designed to allow Spaniards to hold and control political, social, and economic power at the cost of impoverishing Indigenous and African groups (Chavez-Dueñas et al., 2014; Ogbu, 1994; Organista, 2007; Soler Castillo & Pardo Abril, 2009). People's placement within the stratification system determined their privilege and power within that context. The Spaniards possessed the power to discriminate on the basis of skin color and phenotype as one of the main strategies to maintain the stratification of race, ethnicity, and power throughout the colonization and post-colonization period (Casaus Arzu, 2009; Chavez-Dueñas et al., 2014; Soler Castillo & Pardo Abril, 2009). Today, the legacy of racial hierarchy, established during the conquest and colonial times, remains alive, is thriving, and has continued implications for how Latinos/as choose to identify racially and how others categorize them.

MESTIZAJE RACIAL IDEOLOGIES

Latinos/as can trace their racial heritage to three different predominant groups: Indigenous, Black, and White. The mixing of these three racial groups in the period following the colonization of the Americas is often referred to as *mestizaje* (Adames et al., 2016; Chavez-Dueñas et al., 2014; Gates, 2011). This term was initially used to connote that all individuals of Latino/a descent were racially mixed. Additionally, *mestizaje* was constructed as a way to deny that a racial/color hierarchy had been established, where Latinos/as with lighter skinned and more European-looking phenotypes had more power and social status than individuals with darker skin and more Indigenous and/or African phenotypes. All individuals of Latino/a descent were socialized not to identify themselves racially and were indoctrinated into adopting MRIs despite living with the effects of the established racial hierarchy (Adames et al., 2016; Chavez-Dueñas et al., 2014; Montalvo & Codina, 2001). When Latinos/as perceive the world and themselves through MRIs, they are likely to conclude that they are mixed regardless of how they are racially categorized by others. For example, a dark-skinned Colombian male may identify as *mestizo* even though he is likely to be categorized and treated as a Black man in the U.S. Thus MRIs may influence the way in which Latinos/as identify racially and the meaning they ascribe to being labeled as members of a racial group. Part IV of the C-REIL depicts the complexity of variations in skin color and phenotype within Latino/a communities.

COLORISM AND INTERNALIZED COLORISM

Within Latino/a populations, racial identity is influenced by colorism, a form of within-group racial discrimination that reinforces a system of stratification based on skin color. Historically, a system based on colorism placed white-skinned individuals at the top and darker-skinned people at the bottom of the racial stratification. Colorism is the result of three centuries of colonization, where White individuals often abused their power and privilege to oppress people with darker skin complexions and those who had African or Indigenous phenotypes. Sadly, the legacy of colorism is alive and visible in today's Latino/a communities. For instance, most people of Afro and Indigenous descent are rendered invisible in society (e.g., education, media, government). Furthermore, traditions and beliefs rooted in the rich ancestral African and Indigenous cultures are often devalued throughout the Americas. Unfortunately, many Latinos/as have either explicitly or implicitly accepted the dominant society's racist views, stereotypes, and biases toward darker-skinned people. Internalized colorism is likely to complicate the development of a healthy racial identity. Latinos/as with darker skin and African and/or Indigenous features may minimize, invalidate, and dislike themselves, which may contribute to a negative self-concept. For White Latinos/as or those with lighter skin and European features, internalized colorism may promote the denial of White privilege.

NONRACIALISM: RACE AS A NATIONALITY

A necessary precursor to the development of a racial identity is the ability to recognize oneself as a racial being. However, for many Latino/a individuals, this poses a significant challenge due to a) the history of their countries of origin and b) the various ways in which Latinos/as have been racially categorized by the U.S. Census Bureau at various points in time. First, as previously discussed, Latino/a populations in the U.S. share a history of colonization that reinforced strict systems of stratification based on phenotype and skin color. Ironically, Latinos/as also share a systemic denial of race as a social category. Such denial stems from two main factors: a) a desire to increase cohesion within national populations by creating a high level of patriotism where all individuals would solely identify by their national origin rather than by their phenotypic characteristics and b) the assumption that erasing race as a demographic category from national censuses would lead to a decrease in social inequities. This history and its impact can be observed in contemporary Latin American countries where information regarding the racial composition of its nations is not recorded and thus not available. As a result, when Latinos/as are asked to classify themselves racially, many are confused and tend to report their nationality as their race. This can be observed in the latest reports of the U.S. Census Bureau detailed earlier in this chapter. Second, throughout the history of the U.S., Latinos/as have been racially categorized in multiple ways, with nationality being used at a point in time to categorize them racially (see the section on "Latinos/as as Racial, Ethnic, and Cultural Individuals" provided earlier in this chapter). As noted from this brief discussion, Latinos/as continue to grapple with making sense of their race, which serves to further complicate and possibly impede the development of a healthy racial identity.

Implications for Research and Clinical Practice

Research

1. The preponderance of research on Latino/a social identities has focused on ethnic identity while ignoring the influence of racial identity. However, there is a dire need for researchers to examine the racial realities, as well as the process of racial identity development for individuals of Latino/a descent.
2. Most of the literature on racial and ethnic identity development among Latinos/as has predominantly used quantitative methodologies. Given the underresearched state of Latino/a racial identity development, exploratory and qualitative methods of inquiry are warranted to understand the phenomena of race and colorism in the identity development of individuals from this population. Thus researchers currently conducting studies with Latino/a populations are encouraged to pay closer attention to how racial and ethnic identity may serve as mediating and moderating variables.
3. Despite the similarities that Afro-Latinos/as share with U.S. Black Americans and Indigenous Latinos/as share with Native Americans, the existing models of racial identity development do not address the particular sociohistorical and political factors that have shaped their racial identity experiences (i.e., the process of understanding their race). Thus scholars are encouraged to explore specific factors that may impact the racial identity development of minoritized Latinos/as populations (i.e., Indigenous and Afro-Latinos/as) and investigate how such factors are similar or different when compared to their U.S. counterparts (i.e., U.S. Black Americans, Native Americans).
4. Scholars have noted that some measures of ethnic identity (e.g., MEIM, EIS) lack specific attention to the roles of power and oppression, which have a remarkable effect on ethnic identity development (Fischer & Moradi, 2001). However, power and oppression are not a monolithic phenomenon among Latinos/as, given the multiple nationalities and diverse ethnic groups that make up the pan-ethnic Latino/a population. Hence scholars developing measures of Latino/a ethnic identity development need to consider the role of power embedded within the Latino/a community.

Clinical Practice

1. Mental health clinicians working with Latinos/as are encouraged to assess their clients' racial and ethnic identities. Integrating this important components into the assessment process may assist clinicians in

determining how Latino/a clients perceive the world and interact with others who are racially and ethnically similar or different. Additionally, the information provided by such assessment can lead clinicians into developing a more nuanced understanding of what their clients believe is the etiology of their presenting problem(s) and what they believe will help alleviate their symptoms. A thorough assessment of clients' racial and ethnic identity development can assist in developing treatment plans tailored to Latinos/as across the color gradient and across the statuses/stages of their racial and ethnic identities.

2. For first-generation/immigrant Latinos/as in the U.S., treatment may need to center on the challenges they experience as they go through a racialization process, whereby they are assigned to specific racial categories. The racialization process may lead to feelings of confusion, pain, and shame that may further complicate the adaptation process of Latino/a immigrants. Clinicians can help clients process through these feelings while affirming the difficulties inherent in the potential need to redefine their ethnic and racial identities.

3. Research has found a connection between individuals with strong racial and ethnic identities and protective factors that help People of Color from oppressed communities navigate hostile and racist terrains (e.g., Caldwell, Kohn-Wood, Schmeelk-Cone, Chavous, & Zimmerman, 2004; Ponterotto & Park-Taylor, 2007; Seaton, Scottham, & Sellers, 2006). Most of the available literature discusses how the process of racial and ethnic socialization takes place in the home for ethnic and racially minoritized children. We posit that clinicians can also help foster a process of racial and ethnic socialization in therapy. For instance, clinicians can encourage clients to develop an appreciation of their race and culture. This can be achieved by customizing treatment plans to include ways clients can become more familiar with their racial and ethnic roots.

References

Adames, H. Y., Chavez-Dueñas, N. Y., & Organista, K. C. (2016). Skin color matters in Latino/a communities: Identifying, understanding, and addressing Mestizaje Racial Ideologies in clinical practice. *Professional Psychology: Research and Practice, 47*(1), 46–55. doi:http://dx.doi.org/10.1037/pro0000062

Arce, C. H., Murguia, E., & Frisbie, P. W. (1987). Phenotype and life chances among Chicanos. *Hispanic Journal of Behavioral Sciences, 9*(1), 19–32.

Atkinson, D. R., Morten, G., & Sue, D. W. (1989). A minority identity development model. In D. R. Atkinson, G. Morten, & D. W. Sue (Eds.), *Counseling American minorities* (5th ed., pp. 35–52). Boston: McGraw-Hill.

Bernal, M. E., Knight, G. P., Garza, C. A., Ocampo, K. A., & Cota, M. K. (1990). The development of ethnic identity in Mexican-American children. *Hispanic Journal of Behavioral Sciences, 12*(1), 3–24. doi:10.1177/07399863900121001

Bonilla-Silva, E. (2014). *Racism without racists: Color-blind racism and the persistence of racial inequality in America* (4th ed.). Lanham, MD: Rowman & Littlefield Publishers.

Caldwell, C. H., Kohn-Wood, L. P., Schmeelk-Cone, K. H., Chavous, T. M., & Zimmerman, M. A. (2004). Racial discrimination and racial identity as risk or protective factors for violent behaviors in African American young adults. *American Journal of Community Psychology, 33*(1), 91–105.

Carter, R. T. (1990). The relationship between racism and racial identity among White Americans: An exploratory investigation. *Journal of Counseling and Development, 69,* 46–50.

Casaus Arzu, M. (2009). Social practices and racist discourse of the Guatemalan power elites. In T. A. Van Dijk (Ed.), *Racism and discourse in Latin America* (pp. 171–216). Lanham, MD: Lexington Books.

Chavez-Dueñas, N. Y., Adames, H. Y., & Organista, K. C. (2014). Skin-color prejudice and within-group racial discrimination: Historical and current impact on Latino/a populations. *Hispanic Journal of Behavioral Sciences, 36*(1), 3–26. doi:10.1177/0739986313511306

Cokley, K. (2007). Critical issues in the measurement of ethnic and racial identity: A referendum on the state of the field. *Journal of Counseling Psychology, 52,* 224–239.

Cokley, K., & Chapman, C. (2009). Racial identity theory: Adults. In H. A. Neville, B. M. Tynes, & S. O. Utsey (Eds.), *Handbook of African American Psychology* (pp. 283–297). Thousand Oaks, CA: Sage Publications.

Cross, W. E., Jr. (1971). The Negro-to-Black conversion experience. *Black World, 20*(9), 13–27.

Cross, W. E., Jr., & Vandiver, B. J. (2001). Nigrescence theory and measurement: Introducing the Cross Racial Identity Scale (CRIS). In J. G. Ponterotto, J. M. Casas, L. A. Suzuki, & C. M. Alexander (Eds.), *Handbook of multicultural counseling* (2nd ed., pp. 371–393). Thousand Oaks, CA: SAGE.

David, E. R., Okazaki, S., & Giroux, D. (2014). A set of guiding principles to advance multicultural psychology and its major concepts. In F. Leong, L. Comas-Díaz, G. C. Nagayama Hall, V. C. McLloyd, & J. E. Trimble (Eds.), *APA handbook of multicultural psychology, Vol. 1: Theory and research* (pp. 85–104). Washington, DC: American Psychological Association. doi:10.1037/14189–005.

Else-Quest, N. M., & Morse, E. (2015). Ethnic variations in parental ethnic socialization and adolescent ethnic identity: A longitudinal study. *Cultural Diversity and Ethnic Minority Psychology, 21*(1), 54–64. doi:10.1037/a0037820

Erikson, E. H. (1968). *Identity: Youth and crisis.* New York, NY: Norton.

Evans, N. J., Forney, D. S., Guido, F. M., Patton, L. D., & Renn, K. A. (2010). *Student development in college: Theory, research, and practice.* San Francisco, CA: Jossey-Bass.

Fanon, F. (1967). *Black skin, white masks.* New York: Grove.

Ferdman, B. M., & Gallegos, P. I. (2001). Racial identity development and Latinos in the United States. In C. L. Wijeyesinghe & B. W. Jackson III (Eds.), *New perspectives on racial identity development: A theoretical and practical anthology* (pp. 32–66). New York: New York University Press.

Fischer, A. R., & Moradi, B. (2001). Racial and ethnic identity. In J. Ponterotto, J. M. Casas, L. A., Suzuki, & C. M. Alexander (Eds.), *Handbook of multicultural counseling* (2nd ed., pp. 341–370). Thousand Oaks, CA: Sage.

French, S. E., Seidman, E., Allen, L., & Aber, J. L. (2006). The development of ethnic identity during adolescence. *Developmental Psychology, 42*(1), 1–10. doi:10.1037/0012-1649.42.1.1

Gallardo, M. E., Yeh, C. J., Trimble, J. E., & Parham, T. A. (2012). *Culturally adaptive counseling skills: Demonstrations of evidence-based practice.* Thousand Oaks, CA: Sage Publications.

Garcia Coll, C., Lamberty, G., Jenkins, R., McAdoo, H. P., Crnic, K., Wasik, B. H., & Garcia, H. V. (1996). An integrative model for the study of developmental competencies in minority children. *Child Development, 67*(5), 1891–1914. doi:10.2307/1131600

Gates, H. L. (2011). *Black in Latin America.* New York: New York University Press.

Haller, J. S., Jr. (1996). *Outcasts from evolution: Scientific attitudes of racial inferiority, 1859-1900.* Urbana, IL: University of Illinois Press.

Hardiman, R. (1982, July). White identity development: A process oriented model for describing the racial consciousness of White Americans. *Dissertation Abstracts International, 43*, 104.

Helms, J. E. (1990). *Black and white racial identity: Theory research, and practice.* Westport, CT: Greenwood Press.

Helms, J. E. (1994). The conceptualization of racial identity. In E. Trickett, R. Watts, & D. Birman (Eds.), *Human diversity: Perspectives on people in context* (pp. 285–311). San Francisco, CA: Jossey-Bass.

Helms, J. E. (2007). Some better practices for measuring racial and ethnic identity constructs. *Journal of Counseling Psychology, 52*, 235–246.

Helms, J. E. (2008). *A race is a nice thing to have: A guide to being a white person or understanding the white persons in your life* (2nd ed.). Alexandria, VA: Microtraining Associates.

Helms, J. E., & Carter, R. T. (1990). Development of the White racial identity attitude inventory. In J. E. Helms (Ed.), *Black and White racial identity: Theory, research, and practice* (pp. 66–80). Westport, CT: Greenwood Press.

Helms, J. E., & Cook, D. A. (1999). *Using race and culture in counseling and psychotherapy: Theory and process.* Needham Heights, MA: Allyn & Bacon.

Huynh, V. W., & Fuligni, A. J. (2008). Ethnic socialization and the academic adjustment of adolescents from Mexican, Chinese, and European backgrounds. *Developmental Psychology, 44*(4), 1202–1208. doi:10.1037/0012–1649.44.4.1202

Jackson, B. W., III. (1976). Black identity development: Further analysis and elaboration. In L. H. P. Golubchick (Ed.), *Urban, social, and educational issues* (pp. 158–164). Dobuque, IA: Kendall and Hunt.

Marcia, J. E. (1993). The relational roots of identity. In J. Kroger (Ed.), *Discussions on ego identity* (pp. 101–120). Hillsdale, NJ: Erlbaum.

Miville, M. L. (2010). Latina/o identity development: Updates on theory, measurement, and counseling implications. In J. G. Ponterotto, J. M. Casas, L. A. Suzuki, & C. M. Alexander (Eds.), *Handbook of multicultural counseling* (3rd ed., pp. 241–251). Thousand Oaks, CA: Sage Publications.

Montalvo, F. F. (2004). Surviving race: Skin color and the socialization and acculturation of Latinas. *Journal of Ethnic & Cultural Diversity in Social Work, 13*(3), 25–43.

Montalvo, F. F., & Codina, G. E. (2001). Skin color and Latinos in the United States. *Ethnicities, 1*, 321–341. doi:10.1177/146879680100100303

Moya, P. M. L., & Markus, H. R. (2010). Doing race: An introduction. In H. R. Markus & P. M. L. Moya (Eds.), *Doing race: 21 essays for the 21st century* (pp. 1–102). New York, NY: Norton.

Ogbu, J. U. (1994). Racial stratification and education in the United States: Why inequality exists. *Teachers College Record, 98*, 264–298.

Organista, K. C. (2007). *Solving Latino psychosocial and health problems: Theory, practice, and populations.* Hoboken, NJ: John Wiley & Sons.

Parham, T. A., Ajamu, A., & White, J. L. (2010). *The psychology of blacks: Centering our perspectives in the African consciousness* (4th ed.). Boston, MA: Prentice Hall.

Parham, T. A., White, J. L., & Ajamu, A. (1999). *The psychology of Blacks: An African centered perspective* (3rd ed.). Upper Saddle River, NJ: Prentice Hall.

Phinney, J. S. (1992). The multigroup ethnic identity measure: A new scale for use with adolescents and young adults from diverse groups. *Journal of Adolescent Research, 7,* 156–176.

Phinney, J.S. (1996). When we talk about American ethnic groups, what do we mean? *American Psychologist, 51,* 1–10.

Phinney, J. S., & Ong, A. D. (2007). Conceptualization and measurement of ethnic identity: Current status and future directions. *Journal of Counseling Psychology, 54*(3), 271–281. doi:10.1037/0022–0167.54.3.271

Ponterotto, J. G., & Park-Taylor, J. (2007). Racial and ethnic identity theory, measurement, and research in counseling psychology: Present status and future directions. *Journal of Counseling Psychology, 54*(3), 282–295.

Ramos, B., Jaccard, J., & Guilamo-Ramos, V. (2003). Dual ethnicity and depressive symptoms: Implications of being Black and Latino/a in the United States. *Hispanic Journal of Behavioral Sciences, 25,* 147–173. doi:10.1177/0739986303025002002

Seaton, E. K., Scottham, K. M., & Sellers, R. M. (2006). The Status Model of racial identity development in African American adolescents: Evidence of structure, trajectories, and well-being. *Child Development, 77*(5), 1416–1426.

Sellers, R. M., Smith, M. A., Shelton, J. N., Rowley, S. J., & Chavous, T. M. (1998). Multidimensional model of racial identity: A reconceptualization of African American racial identity. *Personality and Social Psychology Review, 2*(1), 18–39. doi:10.1207/s15327957pspr0201_2

Smedley, A., & Smedley, B. D. (2005). Race as biology is fiction, racism as a social problem is real: Anthropological and historical perspectives on the social construction of race. *American Psychologist, 60*(1), 16–26.

Soler Castillo, S., & Pardo Abril, N. G. (2009). Discourse and racism in Colombia: Five centuries of invisibility and exclusion. In T. A. Van Dijk (Ed.), *Racism and discourse in Latin America* (pp. 131–170). Lanham, MD: Lexington Books.

Spanierman, L. B., & Soble, J. R. (2010). Understanding whiteness: Previous approaches and possible directions in the study of White racial attitudes and identity. In J. G. Ponterotto, J. M. Casas, L. A. Suzuki, & C. M. Alexander (Eds.), *Handbook of multicultural counseling* (3rd ed. pp. 283–299). Thousand Oaks, CA: SAGE.

Spencer, M. B., Fegley, S. G., & Harpalani, V. (2003). A theoretical and empirical examination of identity as coping: Linking coping resources to the self processes of African American youth. *Applied Developmental Science, 7*(3), 181–188. doi:10.1207/S1532480XADS0703_9

Suarez-Orozco, C., & Suarez-Orozco, M. M. (2001). *Children of immigration.* Cambridge, MA: Harvard University Press.

Sue, D. W., & Sue, D. (2013). *Counseling the culturally diverse: Theory and practice* (6th ed.). Hoboken, NJ: Wiley.

Tajfel, H. (1981). *Human groups and social categories.* Cambridge, England: Cambridge University Press.

Taylor, C. (1994). The politics of recognition. In A. Gutmen (Ed.), *Multicultural-ism: Examining the politics of recognition* (pp. 25–73). Princeton, NJ: Princeton University Press.

Thomas, C. (1971). *Boys no more.* Beverly Hills: Glencoe Press.

Umaña-Taylor, A. J., Alfaro, E. C., Bamaca, M. Y., & Guimond, A. B. (2009). The central role of familial ethnic socialization in Latino adolescents' cultural orientation. *Journal of Marriage and Family, 71*(1), 46–60. doi:10.1111/j.1741–3737.2008.00579.x

Umaña-Taylor, A. J., & Guimond, A. B. (2010). A longitudinal examination of parenting behaviors and perceived discrimination predicting Latino adolescents' ethnic identity. *Developmental Psychology, 46,* 636–650.

Umaña-Taylor, A. J., Yazedjian, A., & Bamaca-Gomez, M. (2004). Developing the Ethnic Identity Scale using Eriksonian and social identity perspectives. *Identity: An International Journal of Theory and Research, 4,* 9–38.

White, J. L., & Cones, J. H., III. (1999). *Black man emerging: Facing the past and seizing the future in America.* New York, NY: Routledge.

Winnicott, D. W. (2005). *Playing and reality.* New York, NY: Routledge.

Woodson, C. G. (2008). *The mis-education of the Negro.* Washington, DC: BN Publishing.

Yip, T., Douglass, S., & Sellers, R. M. (2014). Ethnic and racial identity. In F. L. Leong, L. Comas-Díaz, G. C. Nagayama Hall, V. C. McLoyd, & J. E. Trimble (Eds.), *APA handbook of multicultural psychology, Vol. 1: Theory and research* (pp. 179–205). Washington, DC: American Psychological Association. doi:10.1037/14189–010

Zweigenhaft, R. L., & Domhoff, G. W. (2006). *Diversity in the power elite: How it happens, why it matters.* Lanham, MD: Rowman & Littlefield Publishers.

Part III

Culturally Responsive and Racially Conscious Clinical Practice With Latinos/as

7 Toward a Complex Understanding of Mental Health Service Utilization Among Latinos/as

Considering Context, Power, and Within-Group Differences

When mental health professionals begin to understand the worldview within which other people live, the door opens to begin to comprehend another person's emotional experience.

–Dr. Joseph L. White and Henderson, 2008, p. 37

As the population of Latinos/as continues to grow, the need for mental health services is likely to also increase. It is important for mental health providers and organizations to identify, comprehend, and develop strategies to address factors that may be contributing to the underutilization of mental health care by Latinos/as who reside in the United States (U.S.) (Chavez-Dueñas, Torres, & Adames, 2011). In this chapter, a framework is provided to help organize the challenges that Latino/a individuals may experience when seeking mental health services. Some of these challenges include systemic and individual barriers that may impact access to mental health services by individuals in the Latino/a community. Current sociohistorical context may also exacerbate barriers to services. Overall, the aim of this chapter is to provide a framework that illustrates the factors that contribute to the maintenance of service underutilization among Latinos/as, while highlighting the impact of within-group differences (e.g., language, socioeconomic factors, documented status, and skin color) and sociohistorical context.

Challenges Experienced by Latinos/as When Seeking Mental Health Services

The underutilization of mental health services by Latinos/as has been well documented in the literature (Gonzalez & Gonzalez-Ramos, 2005; U.S. Department of Health and Human Services, 2001). Among Latinos/as with a mental health diagnosis, less than 1 in every 11 seek mental health services. These figures are even higher among Latino/a immigrants with a mental health illness with less than 1 in every 20 individuals seeking mental health care. When Latinos/as seek mental health services, they are more likely to drop out of treatment in comparison to their non-Latino/a White counterparts

(CECC, 2009; Owen, Imel, Adelson, & Rodolfa, 2012; U.S. Department of Health and Human Services, 2001; Wierbicki & Pekarik, 1993). Economic variables and insurance coverage are factors that have been identified as contributing to the underrepresentation and accessibility of Latinos/as to mental health services (Alegria et al., 2002; Vega & Lopez, 2001). When economic factors are not a challenge to mental health service utilization, differences in access to care continue to persist. For instance, Latinos/as with similar levels of health insurance still receive fewer services than non-Latino/a Whites (Smedley, Stith, & Nelson, 2003; Thomas & Snowden, 2002). Underrepresentation of Latinos/as in mental health services is not fully explained by economic barriers (Chavez-Dueñas et al., 2011; Richman, Kohn-Wood, & Williams, 2007). Language and cultural factors also need to be considered. Cultural and linguistic variables have also been used to explain the disparities in mental health service utilization among Latinos/as (CECC, 2009; Gilmer et al., 2007).

Scholars have organized the barriers to mental health service utilization by Latinos/as into two categories: individual and systemic challenges (Barrio et al., 2008; Martinez & Carter-Pokras, 2006; U.S. Department of Health

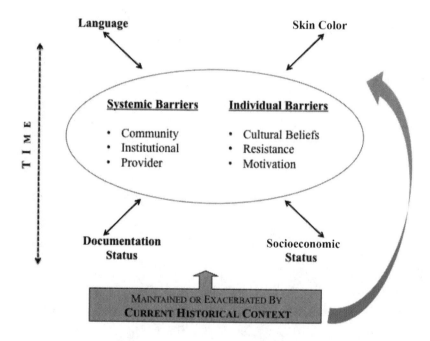

Figure 7.1 Systemic and Individual Barriers (SIB) Model

This model builds on the work of Chavez-Dueñas et al. (2011). The role of skin color, SES, language, and documentation status were added to the figure to illustrate how these variables impact mental health service utilization while also considering current sociohistorical context.

and Human Services, 2001). Chavez-Dueñas et al. (2011) have placed the two categories within a model that helps explain how the current historical climate maintains or exacerbates individual and systemic barriers. In an effort to build on this body of work, Figure 7.1 illustrates how within-group differences may also impact the challenges experienced by Latinos/as when seeking mental health services. Specifically, the model focuses on skin color, language, socioeconomic status, and documentation status variables that represent the heterogeneity within the Latino/a community. These within-group differences are also likely to impact mental health service utilization. A more comprehensive description of the model is provided within the following sections, including major challenges at the systemic and individual level, as well as the role of sociohistorical context in mental health service utilization. The chapter concludes with recommendations for agencies and mental health providers to address these complex challenges.

Three Major Challenges at the Systemic Level

Challenges at the systemic level consist of three subdomains: community, institution, and provider. These subdomains are described in the next section.

Community-Level Challenges

At the community level, individuals are often faced with not knowing where mental health services are offered. However, even when services are located, they often are not available in clients' native language, a language they feel comfortable communicating in, or the agency may lack therapists on staff who are bilingual and bicultural. In agencies where language is not a concern, monolingual Spanish-speaking clients may be placed on long waiting lists.

Institution-Level Challenges

Latinos/as residing in predominantly non-Latino/a communities are often fearful of accessing health and human services (Gresenz, Rogowski, & Escarce, 2009; Moya & Shedlin, 2008). The long history of discrimination that many Communities of Color have experienced from institutions, coupled with distrust of social and governmental agencies, may help explain the apprehension associated with seeking services. These worries are exacerbated among undocumented Latino/a immigrants who often fear being reported to ICE officials. For Latinos/as who are not impacted by fear or mistrust of public and human services, insurance coverage may affect their ability to access mental health services (Chavez-Dueñas et al., 2011). For instance, according to the U.S. Census Bureau (2004), approximately 33% of Latinos/as were uninsured compared to 11% of non-Latino/a Whites. These figures are higher for non-English speaking and immigrant Latinos/as (Rios-Ellis et al., 2005). Not surprisingly, lack of health insurance is connected to poor health outcomes across racial/ethnic groups (Institute of Medicine, 2009).

Provider-Level Challenges

A system of education that does not focus on teaching practices that meet the unique needs of ethnic minority communities contributes to the challenges clients face at the provider level (White & Henderson, 2008). For mental health professionals working with Latinos/as, such lack of training can be classified into three areas: Spanish-language proficiency, multicultural competency, and Latino/a-specific cultural competencies (Chavez-Dueñas et al., 2011). A number of reports highlight the lack of available Spanish-speaking providers trained to meet the needs of U.S. Latinos/as (Aguilar-Gaxiola et al., 2002). There are few, if any, Spanish/English and bilingual/bicultural staff in mental health agencies and fewer master's- and doctoral-level professionals (Adames, 2008; Guarnaccia, Martinez, & Acosta, 2005), which underscores the need for Spanish-speaking mental health professionals. The provision of services in the language of the client is not only ethically responsible but also directly linked to treatment outcomes. Health outcome research suggests that clients who receive services from providers who do not speak their language are more likely to be noncompliant with treatment regimens and often miss their appointments (American College of Physicians, 2004; Thompson, 2005).

In addition to language proficiency, mental health providers may lack adequate training in Latino/a-specific cultural competencies (Cho & Solis, 2001). In order to provide culturally responsive treatment for Latinos/as, training programs need to increase practitioners' awareness, knowledge, and skills in working with individuals from this specific community (Arredondo, Gallardo-Cooper, Delgado-Romero, & Zapata, 2014; Santiago-Rivera, Arredondo, & Gallardo-Cooper, 2002).

Challenges at the Individual Level

Factors at the individual level that contribute to mental health service underutilization are important to consider. A number of factors at the individual level that decrease the participation of Latinos/as in mental health services include cultural beliefs, resistance to seeking treatment, and readiness for change (Comas-Diaz, 2006; Guarnaccia, Martinez, & Acosta, 2005). Within the Latino/a community, mental illness is often stigmatized, decreasing the likelihood that individuals will seek mental health care (Guarnaccia et al., 2005). As a result, Latinos/as are more likely to seek help for their mental health ailments from alternative sources before they contact a mental health provider. These sources often include their primary care physicians, spiritual guides, and/or traditional healers (APA, 2014; Applewhite, 1995; Comas-Diaz, 2006).

The Role of the Sociohistorical Context in Mental Health Service Utilization

In order to fully understand the challenges faced by Latinos/as when seeking mental health services, it is imperative to place both systemic and individual barriers within the historical context in which they are embedded. Contextualizing systemic and individual barriers provides further information that will enable providers to comprehend the challenges faced by Latinos/as seeking mental health services. What follows is a description of two important sociohistorical factors to consider when contextualizing systemic and individual barriers to mental health service utilization for Latinos/as. These variables include the growth in the U.S. Latino/a population and the economic downturn of 2007–2008.

The unprecedented changes in the U.S. demographics made Latinos/as more visible in many spheres of U.S. society (U.S. Census Bureau, 2011). The significant increase of Latinos/as in the U.S., consisting of both U.S.-born and immigrant Latinos/as, is associated with an increase in anti-Latino/a sentiment (Chavez-Dueñas et al., 2011; Cornelius, 2009; Rocha et al., 2011). Moreover, the Federal Bureau of Investigation (2004) reports that the number of anti-Latino/a hate crimes has increased by 35% since 2003. Another sociohistorical event that has affected Latinos/as in recent years is the collapse of the housing market and the U.S. banks. The impact of these difficult economic times on the mental health of U.S. Latinos/as has also been documented, with research indicating that Latino/a immigrants are often used as scapegoats during times of financial hardship (Cornelius, 2009; Flores et al., 2008). These alarming behavioral trends have the potential to cause increased levels of psychological distress and anxiety, prompting the need for mental health care. The literature on Latino/a mental health service underutilization, though growing, is still quite limited specifically with regard to recommendations designed to address the complexity of systemic and individual barriers within a current historical context. The following recommendations, modified from Chavez-Dueñas et al. (2011) are designed to minimize the aforementioned challenges faced by Latinos/as when seeking mental health services.

Addressing Challenges to Mental Health Service Utilization

Recommendations to Decrease the Impact of Systemic Barriers

1. Increase the availability of bilingual English/Spanish mental health service providers.

    a. This recommendation highlights the need to support and increase the pipeline of bilingual mental health providers. Unfortunately, many bilingual Latinos/as face both financial and practical challenges that may prevent and discourage them from completing a graduate degree in the mental health field. Academic institutions and departments can address some of these challenges by:

 – Providing tuition waivers, having scholarships available, offering information about loan repayment programs, and paying for internships.
 – Helping students address some of the more practical challenges they may face, such as daycare services, night and weekend educational programs, satellite campuses in Latino/a communities, and academic support specific to issues related to limited English-language proficiency.
 – Developing mentorship programs to help students cope with the challenges of isolation often faced in higher education may increase the likelihood of degree completion.

b. Mental health agencies are encouraged to invest in recruiting and maintaining bilingual and bicultural mental health professionals. In order to do this successfully, it is important for agencies to advertise positions in outlets frequently used by Latinos/as and other Spanish-speaking providers, including Latino/a organizations, professional associations, newsletters, and listservs.

c. Agencies may also want to consider using paraprofessional staff such as peer health promoters also known as *"promotores de salud"* in Spanish. These professionals can facilitate the sharing of information, provide support, and connect clients to important resources.

d. When appropriate, it is important to provide clients with adequate interpretation services. Although the use of interpreters may not be the most effective option, some organizations and professionals resort to this practice given the scarcity of bilingual mental health professionals. When using these services, both the interpreters and mental health providers should be formally trained in the process of translation in mental health care.

2. Increase mental health service providers' level of cultural competence.

a. In order to provide effective mental health services, formalized training and specific education in the areas of diagnosis and treatment of Latinos/as and their families are warranted. In order to apply such knowledge into their clinical practice, providers need to understand the cultural factors that interact with the mental health of Latinos/as. Since cultural competence is an ongoing process, culturally responsive education should take place at both the graduate and the continuing education level.

b. It may also be helpful for mental health providers to establish and maintain consultative relationships with other providers surrounding issues of cultural competence.

c. It is also important for the field of mental health to hold providers and agencies accountable for the lack of cultural competence training, knowledge, and skills. To this end, we recommend the following:

– Licensing boards are encouraged to include specific questions about the Latino/a community in their examination of licensure candidates.

– Accrediting bodies are encouraged to be more strategic in their assessment of institutions' commitment to train students in areas of multicultural competence in general and Latinos/as in particular.

– Agencies providing services to Latinos/as need to be accountable for hiring individuals who are trained to treat Latinos/as or provide ongoing training and supervision to their staff.

3. Both agencies and providers are encouraged to learn about the best practices for working with Latinos/as. This can be accomplished by joining national organizations (e.g., National Latino/a Psychological Association), subscribing to journals, (e.g., *Hispanic Journal of Behavioral Sciences*; *Journal of Latino/a Psychology*), and professional bulletins (e.g., *Latina/o Psychology Today*) that specifically address the needs of this population.

4. Facilitate access to services. Agencies and mental health providers may need to revisit the manner in which services are offered (e.g., requiring clients to attend therapy once a week), the flexibility of their schedules (e.g., 9:00 a.m. to 5:00 p.m.), and their locations (e.g., local office in the community, facilitate transportation, home visits).

5. Develop partnerships with local agencies and providers. Improving communication and developing collaborations among agencies and providers can result in positive outcomes that include the sharing of resources, reduction of waiting lists, and facilitation of referrals.

6. Recognize and reward agencies that have gone beyond the expectations to address the challenges Latinos/as face when seeking mental health services. These agencies should receive public recognition and, when possible, economic rewards such as grants.

7. Agencies offering services to the Latino/a community are encouraged to be strategic about recruiting, hiring, and retaining bilingual and bicultural Latinos/as to serve at all levels of the organization, including positions of leadership and administration.

Recommendations for Individual-Level Barriers

1. Design and implement specific educational campaigns to reduce stigma surrounding mental health services. Many Latinos/as can benefit from social marketing campaigns that focus on normalizing mental health

illness, which can help individuals to better understand the advantages of seeking mental care.

2. Given that Latino/a clients may not be familiar with the process of psychotherapy/counseling, it is imperative to offer information and clarify their expectations about treatment. Providing education about psychotherapy/counseling may increase motivation for engagement and change.

Recommendations to Address Within-Group Differences

Agencies and providers are encouraged to become familiar with the heterogeneity within the Latino/a community and understand how such diversity impacts mental health service utilization. For instance, Latinos/as who are undocumented, lack health insurance, and/or have African or Indigenous phenotypes may have different experiences compared to Latinos/as who are U.S. citizens, are phenotypically White, and who have access to health insurance. To minimize any additional challenges faced by specific members of the Latino/a community, the following recommendations are offered:

1. When developing outreach campaigns designed to raise awareness about mental health services for the Latino/a community, it is important for agencies to ensure that promotional materials, such as pamphlets and websites, make visible the diversity that exists within the Latino/a population. Materials can be printed in both English and Spanish and include individuals with different skin colors and gender.

2. Most agencies focus on the importance of professional experience and language fluency when hiring staff to work with Latinos/as. We recommend that hiring managers also consider the broad range of life experiences that exist within the Latino/a population. Hence agencies are encouraged not to employ a professional solely because he or she identifies as Latino/a or speaks Spanish. To assist managers in selecting ideal candidates, they are encouraged to pay close attention to candidates' ethnic and racial identities (see Chapter 6). Overall, just because someone identifies as a Latino/a, it does not necessarily mean that he or she will have training to effectively work with all individuals from the Latino/a community.

3. Agencies are encouraged to clearly state and make visible a statement that affirms the organization's commitment not to discriminate based on documented status and language. This statement can be a step toward fostering a space in which clients can feel more comfortable discussing their concerns without fear.

4. Advertising mental health services that meet the needs of particular groups within the Latino/a community (e.g., therapy groups for undocumented youth, Latino/a immigrant parents, Afro-Latinos/as) would reach a broader Latino/a clientele.

5. Agencies and mental health service providers are encouraged to become mindful of the inferences they make regarding various Latino/a subgroups (e.g., undocumented, Spanish-speaking, uninsured, Afro-descendants, and Indigenous). Paying attention to and honoring the strengths of these individuals versus viewing them as victims is encouraged. For instance, providers who focus on strengths can help clients understand how they have overcome obstacles in their lives and take ownership for their resiliency.
6. Undocumented people have limited access to health care benefits. Thus it is critical for agencies to offer services at a lower cost or sliding-scale fee. Grants and partnership with funding sources can assist with these endeavors.

References

Adames, H. Y. (2008). An overview of the field of psychology. In A. Kracen & I. Wallace (Eds.), *You can get into a psychology graduate program: Advice from successful graduate students and prominent psychologists* (pp. 9–32). Washington, DC: APA Books.

Aguilar-Gaxiola, S., Zelezny, L., Garcia, B., Edmonson, C., Alejo-Garcia, C., & Vega, W. A. (2002). Translating research into action: Reducing disparities in mental health care for Mexican Americans. *Psychiatric Services, 52*(12), 1563–1568.

Alegría, M., Canino, G., Rios, R., Vera, M., Calderon, J., Rusch, D., & Ortega, A. N. (2002). Mental health care for Latinos: Inequalities in use of specialty mental health services among Latinos, African Americans, and non-Latino Whites. *Psychiatric Services, 53,* 1547–1555.

American College of Physicians. (2004). Racial and ethnic disparities in mental healthcare. *Annals of Internal Medicine, 41,* 3.

American Psychiatric Association. (2014). *Mental health disparities: Hispanics/Latino.* Retrieved from http://www.psychiatry.org/file%20library/practice/diversity/diversity%20resources/fact-sheet—-latinos.pdf

Applewhite, S. (1995). Curanderismo: Demystifying the health beliefs and practices of elderly Mexican Americans. *Health & Social Work, 20*(4), 247–253.

Arredondo, P., Gallardo-Cooper, M., Delgado-Romero, E. A., & Zapata, A. L. (2014). *Culturally responsive counseling with Latinas/os.* Alexandria, VA: American Counseling Association.

Barrio, C., Palinkas, L. A., Yamada, A., Fuentes, D., Criado, V., Garcia, P., & Jeste, D. V. (2008). Unmet needs for mental health services for Latino older adults: Perspectives from consumers, family members, advocates, and service providers. *Community Mental Health Journal, 44,* 57–74.

Center for Excellence in Culturally Competent Mental Health (CECC). (2009). *Cultural profile: Hispanic/Latino Americans.* Retrieved from http://ssrdqst.rfmh.org/sites/ssrdqst.rfmh.org.cecc/userfiles/profiles/Hispanics%20Profile.pdf

Chavez-Dueñas, N. Y., Torres, H. L., & Adames, H. Y. (2011). Barriers to mental health utilization among Latinos: A contextual model and recommendations. *Journal of Counseling in Illinois, 1*(2), 49–58.

Cho, J., & Solis, B. M. (2001). *Health families culture and linguistics resources survey: A physician perspective on their diverse member population.* Los Angeles, CA: LA Care Health Plan.

Comas-Diaz, L. (2006). Latino healing: The integration of ethnic psychology into psychotherapy. *Psychotherapy: Theory, Research, Practice, Training, 43*(4), 436–453.

Cornelius, W. A. (2009). Ambivalent reception: Mass public responses to the "New" Latino immigration to the United States. In M. M. Suarez-Orozco & M. M. Paez (Eds.), *Latinos remaking America* (pp. 165–189). Berkeley, CA: University of California Press.

Federal Bureau of Investigation. (2004). *Hate crime statistics.* Washington, DC: U.S. Department of Justice. Retrieved from http://www.icpsr.umich.edu/icpsrweb/NACJD/studies/23544/version/1

Flores, E., Tschann, J. M., Dimas, J. M., Bachen, E., Pasch, L. A., & de Groat, C. L. (2008). Perceived discrimination, perceived stress, and health among Mexican-origin adults. *Hispanic Journal of Behavioral Sciences, 30*(4), 401–424.

Gilmer, T., Ojeda, V.D., Folsom, D., Fuentes, D., Garcia, P., & Jeste, D.V. (2007). Initiation and use of public mental health services by persons with severe mental illnesses and limited English proficiency. *Psychiatric Services, 58*(12), 1555–1562.

Gonzalez, M. J., & Gonzalez-Ramos, G. (2005). Health disparities in the Hispanic population: An overview. In M. J. Gonzalez & G. Gonzalez-Ramos (Eds.), *Mental health care for new Hispanic immigrants: Innovative approaches in contemporary clinical practice* (pp. 1–19). New York, NY: Haworth.

Gresenz, C. R., Rogowski, J., & Escarce, J. J. (2009). Community demographics and access to health care among U.S. Hispanics. *Health Services Research, 44*(5), 1542–1562.

Guarnaccia, P. J., Martinez, I., & Acosta, H. (2005). Mental health in the Hispanic immigrant community: An overview. In M. Gonzalez & G. Gonzalez-Ramos (Eds.), *Mental health care for new Hispanic immigrants: Innovative approaches in contemporary clinical practice* (pp. 21–46). New York, NY: Haworth Press.

Institute of Medicine. (2009). *America's uninsured crisis: Consequences for health and health care.* Washington, DC: The National Academies Press.

Martinez, I.L., & Carter-Porkas, O. (2006). Assessing health concerns and barriers in a heterogeneous Latino community. *Journal of Health Care for the Poor and Underserved, 17,* 899–909.

Moya, E. M., & Shedlin, M. G. (2008). Policies and laws affecting Mexican-origin immigrant access and utilization of substance abuse treatment: Obstacles to recovery and immigrant health. *Substance Use & Misuse, 43*(12–13), 1747–1769.

Owen, J., Imel, Z., Adelson, J., & Rodolfa, E. (2012). No-show: Therapist racial/ethnic disparities in client unilateral termination. *Journal of Counseling Psychology, 59*(2), 314-320.

Richman, L. S., Kohn-Wood, L. P., & Williams, D. R. (2007). The role of discrimination and racial identity for mental health service utilization. *Journal of Social and Clinical Psychology, 26*(8), 960–981.

Rios-Ellis, B., Agilar-Gaxiola, S., Cabassa, L., Caetano, R., Comas-Diaz, L., Flores, Y., Gonzalez, H., . . . Ugarte, C. (2005). *Critical disparities in Latinos/as mental health: Transforming research into action.* Washington, DC: National Council of La Raza.

Rocha, R. R., Longoria, T., Wrinkle, R. D., Knoll, B. R., Polinard, J. L. and Wenzel, J. (2011), Ethnic Context and Immigration Policy Preferences Among Latinos and Anglos. *Social Science Quarterly, 92,* 1–19. doi:10.1111/j.1540-6237.2011.00754.x

Santiago-Rivera, A. L., Arredondo, P., & Gallardo-Cooper, M. (2002). *Counseling Latinos and la familia: A practical guide.* Thousand Oaks, CA: Sage Publications.

Smedley, B. D., Stith, A. Y., & Nelson, A. R. (2003). *Unequal treatment: Confronting racial and ethnic disparities in health care.* Institute of Medicine. Washington, DC: National Academic Press.

Thomas, K. C., & Snowden, L. R. (2002). Minority response to health insurance coverage for mental health services. *Journal of Mental Health Policy and Economics, 4,* 35–41.

Thompson, W. (2005). *Getting in the door: Language barriers to health services at New York City's hospitals.* New York City Comptroller, NY: Office of Policy Management. Retrieved from http://www.comptroller.nyc.gov/bureaus/opm/reports/jan10–05_geting-in-the-door.pdf

U.S. Bureau of the Census. (2004). *U.S. interim projections by age, sex, race, and Hispanic origin.* Washington, DC: Government Printing Office. Retrieved from http://www.census.gov/ipc/www.usinterimproj/

U.S. Bureau of the Census. (2011). *The Hispanic population: Census 2011 brief.* Washington, DC: Government Printing Office. Retrieved from http://www.census.gov/compendia/statab/brief.html

U.S. Department of Health and Human Services. (2001). *Mental health: Culture, race and ethnicity—A supplement to mental health: A report of the Surgeon General.* Rockville, MD: U.S. Department of Health and Human Services, Public Health Office, Office of the Surgeon General.

Vega, W. A., & Lopez, S. R. (2001). Priority issues in Latino mental health services research. *Mental Health Services Research, 3,* 189–200.

White, J. L., & Henderson, S. J. (2008). The browning of America: Building a new multicultural, multiracial, multiethnic paradigm. In J. L. White & S. J. Henderson (Eds.), *Building multicultural competency: Development, training and practice* (pp.17–49). New York, NY: Rowman & Littlefield Publishers.

Wierbicki, M., & Pekarik, G. (1993). A meta-analysis of psychotherapy dropout. *Professional Psychology: Research and Practice, 24*(2), 190–195. doi:10.1037/0735–7028.24.2.190

8 Roots of Connectedness
Application of Latino/a Cultural Values in Mental Health Care

Roots are not in landscape or a country, or a people; they are inside you.

–Isabel Allende, 2000, para. 6

"Culture is a complex constellation of [learned] mores, values, customs, tradition, and practices that guide and influence a people's cognitive, affective, and behavioral response to life circumstances" (Parham, White, & Ajamu, 1999, p. 14). Culture is passed from generation to generation, is dynamic and constantly adapting to social-historical events. In the United States (U.S.), culture is often thought of as being composed of surface-level elements, such as food, language, clothing, and music (Gallardo, Yeh, Trimble, & Parham, 2012; Parham et al., 2010). Scholars have postulated that when looking at culture, it is also critical to also examine domains at the deep structural level. Ani (1994) provided five fundamental aspects of culture that are thought to play a central role in developing a better knowledge of what culture is at a deep structural level rather than superficially (e.g., focusing on food, clothing, music). The five domains include *ontology* (nature of reality), *axiology* (one's value orientation), *cosmology* (one's relationship to the divine force in the universe), *epistemology* (systems of knowledge and discovering truth), and *praxis* (one's system of human interaction). Gallardo et al. (2012) used the five domains of culture at the deep structural level to build a useful template that compares and contrasts each domain among the five major ethnic minority groups in the U.S. (i.e., African American, Latinos/as, Asian Americans, American Indian/Alaska Natives, Middle Eastern American). Table 8.1 builds upon these two bodies of work by describing how each domain of culture at the deep structural level is manifested among Latinos/as and maps cultural values to the five domains.

Culture serves as the general foundation upon which value orientation or cultural values are formed. Traditional cultural values are beliefs and practices deemed important for individuals within an ethnic group (Kluckhohn & Strodtbeck, 1961). They influence ethnic-group norms and patterns of interpreting reality (Kluckhohn & Strodtbeck, 1961; Parham et al., 2010) and drive preferences for what are considered culturally congruent

Table 8.1 Application and Mapping of Latino/a Cultural Values to the Five Domains of Culture at the Deep Structural Level

Domains	Definitions Applied to Latinos/as	Manifestations	Latino/a Cultural Values
Ontology Nature of Reality	• An integration of personal and familial lived experiences, religious/spiritual insight and history (i.e., an understanding that life is a combination of one's will and efforts and divine intervention), ancestral knowledge and connection, and an understanding that Western forms of health and health care can be limitations to one's growth and well-being.	• The nature of reality for Latinos/as may be influenced by the family and the divine (e.g., God, the creator, or other higher powers).	• Familismo • Spirituality • Obediencia
Axiology Value System	• Latino/a culture is collectivistic. One's worth is based on one's contribution to the group's well-being and advancement. It is present and past oriented and supports group/cultural survival and ownership—language preservation and acquisition—while making connections to cultural traditions. Representation of motherhood is connected to spirituality and seen as protector, love, and source of strength for all.	• Among Latinos/as, maintaining harmonious relationships with others is highly valued.	• Familismo • Respeto • Personalismo/Simpatía • Vergüenza • Amabilidad • Lealtad • Obediencia • Responsabilidad • Ser-trabajador • Honestidad • Humildad
Cosmology Relationship to the Divine	• Spiritual/religious connection represented as integration of family and culture. Divinity falls on a spectrum of ancestral hierarchy that dictates reverence for those who have preceded us and to our creator. A relationship with the Divine fosters connection to, conservation of, and protection of Mother Earth and reverence for women and the strength seen therein (e.g., Virgin de Guadalupe).	• A strong connection to a higher power and/or to the motherland may be a source of spiritual connection for Latinos/as.	• Respeto • Spirituality • Obediencia • Honestidad • Humildad

Epistemology System of Knowing and What Is Truth	Knowledge stems from oral history (i.e., ancestral and cultural history) and direct lived experiences. Western sciences can be limited and may not be seen as universal truth or insights and understanding. The more one is connected to culture and the more solidified one is in one's identity development, the more one understands the limitations to universally accepted truths and discovers and defines one's own reality.	• Latinos/as may seek knowledge from four sources: family, traditional healers, spiritual guides, and Western medicine.	• *Familismo* • *Spirituality* • *Respeto* • *Obediencia* • *Honestidad* • *Humildad*
Praxis Systems of Human Interaction	Religious/spiritual guidance viewed as standard for one's thoughts and behaviors, along with family guidance and shared wisdom. Shared lived experiences influence the integration and acceptance into one's behavioral repertoire and provide a source of validation for the way one lives one's life.	• Core elements of the Latino/a culture include reverence to the individual one is interacting with and to the collective group (e.g., ethnic group, family), while maintaining harmony in one's interpersonal interactions.	• *Familismo* • *Respeto* • *Dignidad* • *Confianza* • *Personalismo/ Simpatía* • *Vergüenza* • *Amabilidad* • *Lealtad* • *Obediencia* • *Responsabilidad* • *Ser-trabajador* • *Honestidad* • *Humildad*

Note: This table builds upon the work of Ani (1994) who provided five domains of elements of culture at the deep structural level. Gallardo et al. (2012) expanded Ani's work by applying the domains to the five major ethnic minority groups in the U.S. (i.e., African American, Latino/a, Asian American, American Indian/Alaska Native, Middle Eastern American). Adapted from *Culturally Adaptive Counseling Skills: Demonstrations of Evidence-Based Practice*. Copyright 2012 by Sage Publication. Adapted with permission. Adames and Chavez-Dueñas (this volume) build upon these two bodies of work in this table by describing how each domain is manifested among Latinos/as and mapping the Latino/a cultural values to each of the five domains.

behaviors and practices. Overall, cultural values serve as a set of guiding principles that impact every area of an individual's life (Carter, 1991; Kluckhohn & Strodtbeck, 1961). Gaining knowledge and understanding of traditional cultural values is important to gain a full grasp of the uniqueness of cultural groups, which can serve to inform the development of culturally congruent treatment interventions (Carter, 1991; Parham et al., 2010).

This chapter provides an overview of the five main traditional Latino/a cultural values followed by a brief overview of the available research in this area. A discussion of the importance of considering Latino within-group differences when applying the traditional cultural values to Latinos/as is offered. The chapter concludes with ways in which providers can integrate the cultural values into mental health treatment.

Major Traditional Latino/a Cultural Values

Familismo

Familismo is one of the key values that are significant for Latinos/as patients and their families. *Familismo* is closely associated with placing a strong emphasis on familial ideals; it involves broad networks of support that extend beyond the nuclear family to include aunts, uncles, grandparents, godparents, and other close family friends. Moreover, family structures, processes, and interactions are highly informed by the collectivistic norms of the Latino/a culture (Falicov, 1998), emphasizing obligation, affiliation, and cooperation. *Familismo* consists of three components: 1) perceived obligation to provide support to the family, 2) reliance on family for support, and 3) use of family as behavioral and attitudinal referents (Lawton, Gerdes, Haack, & Schneider, 2014; Marin & Marin, 1991). In Latino/a families, individual identity is commonly secondary to family identity, requiring individuals to prioritize family needs over individual needs. This family-centered socialization breeds considerable emotional connectedness and interdependence "within and across generations over the lifecycle" (Organista, 2007, p. 142). *Familismo* promotes and maintains "solidarity, family pride, and sense of belongings and obligations to one's blood ties" (Falicov, 1998, p. 163) and to close friends who acquire formal kinship through religious or familial rituals (e.g., godparents).

Personalismo/Simpatía

Another Latino value that greatly influences mental health care is *personalismo*, also referred to as *Simpatía*; it is a value that places considerable emphasis on the personal, smooth, interactions of people while avoiding conflict or confrontation. Latinos/as tend to be relationship-centered and prefer formal but warm and supportive interactions to casual interactions

(Organista, 2007). According to Falicov (1998), when establishing relationships with professionals, Latinos require rapport building that includes warmth, formality, and regard. A significant emphasis is placed on professional relationships where the nature of professional care is as important as the treatment received.

Respeto

Respeto (respect) is another highly referenced Latino value that can impact mental health care ideologies and practices. The value of *respeto* reveals the hierarchical structures that may exist in Latino/a communities, contributing to differential behaviors toward others based on a number of factors, such as age, gender, social or economic status, and authority. This value becomes highly evident in adult-child relationships, where children are expected to listen to adults (e.g., the elderly, parents, teachers) and comply with their requests (Falicov, 1998). This value can also significantly influence professional relationships, as Latinos/as perceive professionals as highly regarded authorities who are not to be questioned, which could lead to misunderstandings or noncompliance (Carteret, 2012).

Confianza

Confianza (trust) is a value that is characteristic of the Latino culture, where individuals are invested in establishing relationships that are based on reciprocal trust. Moreover, *confianza* can be understood when someone expresses his or her deeper feelings only to an inner circle of familiar confidants. Overall, *confianza* connotes that the other person(s) in the relationship has one's best interest in mind (Bracero, 1998; Lewis-Fernandez & Kleinman, 1994).

Dignidad

A less-referenced, but equally important, Latino cultural value that relates to mental health care is *dignidad* (dignity). Fundamentally, *dignidad* is associated with worthiness (Triandis, Marin, Lisansky, & Betancourt, 1984) and feeling valued (Chochinov, 2002). It is understood as a concept that includes an individual's sense of self-worth, as well as that individual's experience of others valuing them. In short, this value recognizes that individuals are inherently worthy and meant to be respected (Santiago-Rivera, Arredondo, & Gallardo-Cooper, 2002).

VALOR-SH2

There are additional Latino/a cultural values that are not as well researched or documented in the mental health and social science literature. These cultural values include *Vergüenza, Amabilidad, Lealtad, Obediencia, Responsabilidad,*

Ser Trabajador, Honestidad, and *Humildad.* We have organized these cultural values into the acronym **VALOR-SH2,** in which the word "valor" means "to have courage" in Spanish. Table 8.2 provides a list of these eight additional cultural values grounded in Latino/a culture along with their respective English translations and meanings.

Table 8.2 VALOR-SH2: Less-Referenced Latino/a Cultural Values

Cultural Value	English Translation	Meaning
Vergüenza	Avoidance of shame for self, family, and group	• *Vergüenza* is an experience resulting from failure to meet the expectations of one's family, community, or cultural group. It also includes being cognizant of not engaging in behaviors that may humiliate or dishonor one's self, one's family, social groups one represents, or others.
Amabilidad	Amiable	• A characteristic of a person who is pleasant, helpful, and cordial. Latinos/as are socialized to treat others with *amabilidad* (affable) regardless of their specific feelings toward the other person. *Amabilidad* is different from *personalismo* as it highlights when the individual goes "the extra mile" to help others while focusing on their needs and well-being.
Lealtad	Loyalty	• *Lealtad* is an essential element in the development of trust in human relationships. This value is characterized by an individual carrying out his or her responsibilities in light of changing circumstances, adversaries, or conflict in the relationship. *Lealtad* is an obligation that one has toward others and groups. Essentially, *lealtad* connotes that the other person has demonstrated a strong emotional connection, commitment, and loyalty to an individual, family, and/or group. It can also mean that the person demonstrates commitment and loyalty to their verbalized values; hence they "walk the talk."
Obediencia	Obedience	• *Obediencia* is an important cultural value for Latino/a parents who seek to teach their children to follow the guidance of elders, teachers, and other adults in order to develop a behavioral pattern that is consistent with cultural and social norms and expectations. In order to preserve the social order and demonstrate respect for the wisdom that comes with life experience,

Cultural Value	English Translation	Meaning
		children are socialized to *ser obedientes* (be obedient) to those who are in positions of authority.
Responsabilidad	Responsibility	• Within the Latino/a culture, *responsabilidad* is a value describing the socialization of individuals in which a high emphasis is placed on developing a strong sense of accountability for one's actions, making a commitment to following through with one's word and/or promises, and being reliable to others. *Responsabilidad* also connotes a duty and desire to care for one's family and community.
Ser Trabajador	Strong Work-Ethic	• *Ser trabajador* is a traditional cultural value that emphasizes the importance of being productive, hardworking, and diligent in the completion of tasks/activities. Regardless of occupation or social status associated with the job, Latinos/as often believe that working hard is one of the most important traits a person can demonstrate. *Ser trabajador* can help individuals earn the respect of their community. This concept can become part of individuals' identities and help them feel useful within their families and society. Given the strong focus on being hard working, one of the worse adjectives a Latino/a can be called is lazy.
Honestidad	Honesty	• *Honestidad* is a value where individuals strive to be sincere with their words, feelings, and actions. This value is fundamental in developing trustful and harmonious relationships with others in which security and credibility are reciprocated. In addition, *honestidad* is about being truthful with one's self.
Humildad	Humility	• Within the Latino/a culture, *humildad* is a characteristic in which an individual does not focus on his or her own triumph and virtues, but does recognize his or her own shortcomings. In addition, *humildad* means that a person's actions are not motivated by a desire for social status or monetary gain. His or her actions are driven by values (intrinsic) and not external rewards (extrinsic).

Note: These eight additional cultural values are organized into the acronym VALOR-SH2. In Spanish, the word "valor" means "to have courage," which is an appropriate descriptor for a group of people who have a history of resilience and perseverance.

A Selective Review of the Empirical Literature on Latino/a Cultural Values

There is a large body of scholarship looking at the impact of cultural values on the lives of Latinos/as living in the U.S. (Arredondo, Gallardo-Cooper, Delgado-Romero, & Zapata, 2014; German, Gonzales, & Dumka, 2009; Kaplan, Napoles-Springer, Stewart, & Perez-Stable, 2001; Ma et al., 2014; Santiago-Rivera et al., 2002; Unger et al., 2006; Villar & Concha, 2012). Within the Latino/a community, cultural values also play a critical role in identity, attitudes, and practices (Villarruel et al., 2009). For instance, a number of studies have looked at the role of cultural values in family dynamics, health education, academic achievement, and mental health services. The following section provides a brief overview of the literature in this area of inquiry.

Cultural Values and La Familia Latina/o

Recent studies have found that traditional Latino/a cultural values are associated with higher family cohesion and lower family conflict among youth. For example, a study by Lorenzo-Blanco and colleagues (2012) examined how acculturation, enculturation, and Latino/a cultural values were associated with depressive symptoms among 1,922 Latino/a youths. These findings highlight two important areas for mental health professionals working with Latino/a youths to understand: 1) the effect of acculturation on traditional cultural values among youth and 2) the relationships between family conflict and cohesion and depression. First, results indicate that among Latino/a youths, high levels of *familismo* and *respeto* were reported regardless of the level of acculturation and enculturation. In other words, Latino/a youths adapting to the U.S. culture did not impact these *familismo* and *respeto* values. In light of previous studies that have reported a negative association between acculturation and *familismo* (Miranda, Estrada, & Firpo-Jimenez, 2000), these findings are interesting since they are not what many would anticipate. Second, *familismo* and *respeto* were associated with lower levels of family conflict and higher levels of family cohesion among youth of both sexes. Family cohesion was associated with lower levels of depressive symptoms (Lorenzo-Blanco, Unger, Baezconde-Garbanati, Ritt-Olson, & Soto, 2012). Overall, the results of this study highlight the protective nature of cultural values (i.e., *familismo* and *respeto*) for Latino/a youths, as they are associated with improving family functioning (i.e., lower levels of family conflict and higher levels of family cohesion), while decreasing symptoms of depression.

A study by German et al. (2009) investigated the relationship between *familismo*, deviant peer affiliations, and externalizing problems among 598 low-income Mexican adolescents in the U.S. as measured by parent and adolescent completion of *familismo* scales, teachers' and parents' ratings of externalizing behaviors, and adolescents' reports of peer affiliation. Results demonstrate that, *familismo* serves as a protective factor for externalizing problems. In this study, higher levels of *familismo* reported by parents and adolescents were associated with lower externalizing behaviors as reported by teachers but not parents. These results suggest that parents and teachers may have different sets of behavioral expectations for adolescents where *familismo*, as measured in this study, may serve specifically as a mediator of acting-out behaviors within the school context or to teachers' perceptions of problematic behaviors (German et al., 2009). Of interest, *familismo* did not reduce deviant peer affiliation.

Overall, there is extensive literature highlighting *familismo* and positive outcomes among Latino/a adolescents (Ma et al., 2014). *Familismo* has been associated with higher levels of academic achievement (Gonzales et al., 2008), lower levels of deviant behavior (Vega, Gil, Warheit, Zimmerman, & Apospori, 1993), and lower levels of interpersonal violence (Sommers, Fagan, & Baskin, 1993) among Latino/a adolescents.

Culture Values and Latino/a Health

An intriguing finding in health research with Latinos/as populations is a phenomenon known as the immigrant paradox. According to this theory, Latino/a immigrants demonstrate good physical and mental health initially upon arrival to the U.S. Their overall good health is evident despite the many barriers to health care faced by this community, coupled with high rates of poverty and stress related to adjusting to a new country, as well as racism, discrimination, exclusion, learning a different language, and the like, hence the paradox (Horevitz & Organista, 2013).

With increasing time in the U.S. and across generations, the wellness of Latinos/as shows a rapid decline in health outcomes (Horevitz & Organista, 2013; Organista, 2007; Ruiz, Steffen, & Smith, 2013). These changes have been attributed to acculturation. More recently, social scientists have posited that prolonged exposure to systemic and individual racism, discrimination, and poverty, coupled with the erosion of protective factors, contributes to the decline in health among U.S. Latinos/as rather than just acculturation (Horevitz & Organista, 2013; Organista, 2007). Traditional Latino/a cultural values may serve as factors that protect Latino/a immigrants from the pernicious effects of racism and oppression (Ma et al., 2014; Villar & Concha, 2012).

A number of studies have investigated the role of cultural values as protective factors in health, including mental health, substance use, birth rates, and infant mortality of U.S. Latinos/as (James, 1993; Ma et al., 2014; Perez & Cruess, 2014; Ruiz, Steffen, & Smith, 2013; Scribner & Dwyer, 1989). For instance, Ma et al. (2014) looked at whether Latino/a cultural values served as a protective factor against sexual risk behavior among Latino youths. They found that U.S. Latino/a youths who reported a stronger endorsement of *respeto* had lower intentions of having sex in high school and reported higher self-efficacy when using condoms. *Simpatía* was associated with sexual abstinence and greater sexual self-efficacy for male and female adolescents. Moreover, *simpatía* was related with being chronologically older at the age of the first sexual encounter. Other studies have found that cultural values, specifically *simpatía, respeto*, and *familismo* serve as protective factors against smoking (Castro, Stein, & Bentler, 2009; Kaplan et al., 2001; Unger et al., 2002). *Familismo* has been found to shield Latinos from life's struggles, as it provides emotional, economic, and social support (Cohen, 1979; Mannino & Shore, 1976; Valle & Martinez, 1980). Furthermore, *familismo* has been associated with lower levels of drug and alcohol use among Latinos/as in the United States, and with positive health outcomes (Coohey, 2001; Pabon, 1998; Unger et al., 2002). For instance, Gil, Wagner, and Vega (2000) conducted a study in which they looked at the relationship between acculturation, *familismo*, and alcohol use among Latino/a adolescents. The results revealed that acculturative stress affected alcohol use by reducing the protective factors of Latino/a cultural values, such as *familismo* and parental respect. Overall, a review of the literature on the impact of traditional values on Latinos/as (e.g., *familismo, respeto, simpatía*) suggests that these values may shield against the effects of migration, discrimination, and acculturation (Arredondo et al., 2014; Miller & Rollnick, 2013; Perez & Cruess, 2014; Santiago-Rivera et al., 2002).

Latino/a Cultural Values in Mental Health Care and Within-Group Differences

Cultural values influence different aspects of clients' lives, including mental health treatment outcomes and retention. For instance, differences in cultural values between the client and the therapist may create challenges in communication (Carter, 1991; Sitaram & Haapanen, 1979). Moreover, traditional cultural values affect how Latinos/as understand mental illness, requiring the therapist to be familiar with his or her client's culture (Lawton, Gerdes, Haack, & Schneider, 2014). Research has also revealed that cultural values related to interpersonal relationships (e.g., *simpatía* and *respeto*), family (e.g., *familismo*) play an important role in the provision of mental health services of U.S. Latinos/as. Specifically, interventions that take into account a client's cultural values result in better treatment outcomes among individuals from this population. The integration of traditional Latino/a cultural values in mental health treatment can also increase retention (Kalibatseva & Leong, 2014). Thus it is paramount that therapists working with this community gain knowledge regarding how and when it is appropriate to integrate traditional values into the treatment of Latino/a individuals. This knowledge can serve to inform the development of treatment interventions that are culturally congruent and responsive to the client's needs (Carter, 1991).

As noted in Chapter 2, Latinos/as are a heterogeneous group, rich in diversity, manifested through differences in generational status, race, socio-economic status, ethnicity, degree of bilingualism, nationality, level of accul-turation, and stage of ethnic identity. Despite these differences, Latinos/as are united by a common language, a history of colonization (Chavez-Dueñas, Adames, & Organista, 2014), and traditional cultural values that focus on interdependence, collectivism, and a group orientation to family unity (Adames, Chavez-Dueñas, Fuentes, Salas, & Perez, 2014; Romero, Cuel-lar, & Roberts, 2000; Saetermoe, Beneli, & Busch, 1999; Santiago- Rivera et al., 2002). Traditional Latino/a cultural values are based on collective experiences believed to influence thoughts, goals, and behaviors that impact preferred styles of communication (Añez, Silva, Paris, & Bedregal, 2008; Chandler, 1979; Inclan, 1985; Szapocznik, Scopetta, & King, 1978).

When considering the extent to which an individual of Latino/a descent will adhere to the traditional cultural values described in this chapter, level of acculturation and stage of ethnic and racial identity need to be considered. In the context of this book, acculturation is defined as the process through which individuals adjust to a new culture, which involves the incorporation of new cultural beliefs, values, norms, language, and behaviors (see Chapter 5). Ethnic identity is an aspect of the self that includes a sense of acceptance and congruence regarding one's membership in a socially constructed ethnic group (see Chapter 6). Lastly, racial identity involves a self-referential commitment to the racial group into which society has ascribed an individual (see Chapter 6; Helms & Cook, 1999). An understanding of where the client falls on these three domains will help clinicians understand how much traditional cultural norms, values, and beliefs influence Latino/a clients. Hence mental health practitioners need to account for all of these factors (i.e., race, ethnicity, acculturation) when treating Latinos/as. Figure 8.1 depicts the *CLEAR-Model* to help illustrate vari-ous factors to consider when deciding whether to integrate traditional Latino/a cultural values when assessing and treating individuals of Latino/a descent.

Integration of Latino/a Cultural Values in Mental Health Care

The next section provides concrete ways to understand, assess, and incorpo-rate the main Latino/a cultural values presented earlier (i.e., *familismo, per-sonalismo/simpatía, respeto, confianza,* and *dignidad*) into mental health care.

Manifestations of Familismo *in Mental Health Care*

The concept of "family" may be different for Latinos/as and can expand beyond what is considered the nuclear family. For instance, a family member can include individuals related to the client by blood as well as close friends, godparents, grandmothers, and neighbors. Family members typically influ-ence many aspects of clients' lives, including dating, choosing a career, and

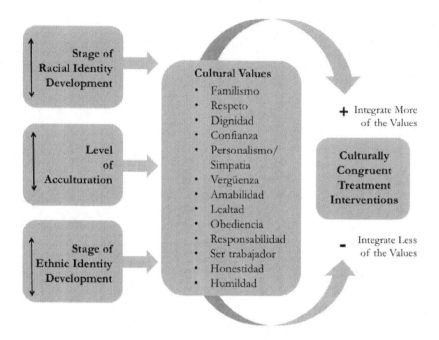

Figure 8.1 CLEAR-Model: Integrating Cultural Values and Latinos/as' Ethnic Identity, Acculturation, and Racial Identity Into Mental Health Treatment

The client's level of acculturation and stage of ethnic and racial identity influences the extent to which cultural values are adhered to and should be integrated into mental health treatment, as depicted by the plus and minus signs.

spiritual beliefs. Hence mental health providers can expect large numbers of individuals who may all be considered "part of the family" to impact decisions made by clients, including whether to seek mental health care. The devotion and emotional connectedness with the family may impact how clients' describe and understand the problems in living, including concerns about mental health. Latinos/as are also likely to have a strong sense of responsibility toward members of their families, particularly their parents. This may be observed in clients' willingness to sacrifice their own goals and at times their well-being for the benefit of the family unit or an individual family member in need. In sessions, this may be observed by family-centered themes throughout the client's narratives and week-to-week recount of events. At times, clients may want to spend the session discussing problems experienced by family members and seek advice for how best to help them. Lastly, given the high value placed on the family's opinion, clients may ask whether family members can be part of therapy sessions. As a result, providers may need to be prepared for the best way to accommodate their clients' requests by integrating treatment goals and ethical and professional standards with cultural responsiveness.

Familismo: Strategies for Mental Health Providers

1. Have explicit conversations with clients regarding the role they would like their families to play in their mental health care and allow clients to decide which people are considered members of their family.

2. Once the necessary forms have been signed and permission is granted, actively engage family members by allowing the client to decide when he or she would like family members to be involved in his or her mental health care.

3. It is important for practitioners to have a good understanding of the ethical guidelines and legal policies regarding clients' protected information. Thus it is necessary for therapists to help clients' understand what confidentiality means and how it is protected.

4. Providers demonstrate their respect and care for the family unity by offering referrals and resources to anyone in the family who may be experiencing a mental health concern and may be in need of services.

5. We encourage mental health providers to avoid using individualistic perspectives to interpret the behavior of clients who have a strong sense of *familismo*. It is important to keep in mind that a Latino/a client's strong family cohesion is a protective factor.

6. In cases where the family unit or an individual family member is causing harm to the client (e.g., physical abuse), it may be helpful for the therapist to empathize with how difficult it can be for Latinos/as to distance themselves from family. At the same time, the therapist needs to help the client brainstorm for ways in which he or she can maintain family harmony while not compromising his or her well-being and safety. If the situation is one where maintaining family harmony is not possible, the therapist can focus on assisting the client in making a decision about potential ways to handle the event(s).

Manifestations of Personalismo/Simpatía in Mental Health Care

Latino/a individuals prefer communication styles that are pleasant, free of conflict (Añez, Silva, Paris, & Bedregal, 2008), and conducive to the maintenance of harmonious relationships. As a result, Latino/a clients place a strong emphasis on how they feel around the therapist and whether they perceive the provider as being warm and caring. These perceptions can be influenced by how the therapist interacts with the client and how caring and warm he or she seems to the client. *Personalismo* can also be observed in the client's avoidance of disagreement with the therapist's opinion during therapy. Latinos/as are likely to engage in indirect forms of communication (e.g., by speaking through metaphors known as *dichos*) (Zuñiga, 1992). This style of relating can be observed among family members and between the family unit and providers. In fact, it is not unusual for clients to agree with treatment goals while in session, but not follow through with them. For instance, a client may agree to consult with a psychiatrist and have a psychological evaluation as part of his or her treatment plan, and the therapist may end the session feeling as if the client is in complete agreement with the goals. However, it is not atypical for clients to go home following such an encounter to discuss their options in greater detail with family members. Following such conversations, clients may change their minds. Consequently, they may not follow through with the referrals and are also not likely to communicate directly with the provider about their decision(s). These divergent messages may be confusing for mental health providers unfamiliar with Latino/a culture and may be interpreted as clients' ambivalence regarding their goals for treatment or as resistance to change.

Personalismo/Simpatía: Strategies for Mental Health Providers

1. It is important for the staff (e.g., administrative, clerical, clinical) who are typically the first point of contact between the client and the mental health field to find ways to help clients feel welcomed and cared for. This can include having the staff use warm and welcoming voices, going the extra mile by offering clients information that may facilitate their participation in treatment (e.g., best directions for getting to the office), and using formal greetings.
2. It is important for providers working with Latinos/as to be mindful of how they communicate verbally (e.g., tone of voice, use of welcoming words) and nonverbally (e.g., eye contact, smiles). They may also need to find concrete ways to demonstrate a warm, caring attitude and a desire to be helpful.
3. Mental health care providers are encouraged to provide Latino/a clients and their families with information regarding all viable options for treatment. After delivering such information, therapists should provide clients with ample time to consider options.
4. Mental health care providers are encouraged to communicate both verbally and nonverbally in ways that foster harmonious interactions through the use of *personalismo*, which includes listening, warmth, attentiveness, and caring, as well interacting in ways that are free of conflict.
5. It is important for mental health care providers working with the family as a unit to be comfortable managing family members' differing opinions, agendas, ways of coping, and emotions, while finding ways to maintain a relationship with the family unit as a whole.

Manifestations of Respeto in Mental Health Care

Respeto can be expressed in mental health care settings through various behaviors. For instance, family members may show deference to authority by not openly questioning recommendations made by providers. Additionally, families may expect providers to know, understand, and adhere to preexisting hierarchical relationships within the family. Lastly, Latinos/as might prefer and insist on using formal titles when referring to their provider as a sign of respect.

Respeto: Strategies for Mental Health Providers

1. Mental health care providers should communicate respectfully and empathically with clients and all members of the family.
2. It is recommended that providers be mindful of their role within the family and respect the family's cultural preferences, which may include rituals, prayers, and other cultural beliefs. For instance, Latino/a families may consult with traditional healers regarding the concern(s) that brought them to therapy, which can include folk healers (e.g., *curanderas/os, santero/as, hueseros/as, shamanes, naturistas, sobadores/as*).
3. When communicating with the patient and his or her family, providers are encouraged to use formal titles to show *respeto* and establish a more hierarchical relationship. Titles including *doctora/doctor* (doctor), *señorita* (Ms.), *doña/señora* (Mrs.), *dama* (lady), and *señor/caballero* (Mr.) are encouraged.

Manifestations of Confianza in Mental Health Care

Building and establishing *confianza* with Latino/a clients and their families is often complicated. Experiences of discrimination, prejudice, and oppression can have a detrimental effect on the establishment of *confianza* (Smith, Sudore, & Perez-Stable, 2009). In fact, clients and families may be cautious with the information they initially disclose to their mental health care provider. Such cultural suspicion is normal, expected, and healthy, and it is considered a resiliency factor resulting from strategies employed by ethnic minorities to cope with a long-standing history of oppression and discrimination (Boyd-Franklin, 2006; White & Cones, 1999). Mental health care providers may begin to notice a change in the clients' behaviors toward them once *confianza* has been developed. For instance, clients and family members may attempt to deepen their *confianza* by asking providers questions related to their personal life.

Confianza: Strategies for Mental Health Providers

1. Given the complexity regarding the establishment of *confianza* for Latino/a clients, mental health care providers are encouraged to be aware that building *confianza* will take time and patience.
2. The development of a relationship based on *confianza* will depend on the provider's ability to demonstrate respect and empathy toward the client and his or her family. Thus it is essential for mental health care providers to consistently follow through with promises made to the client.

3. Providers can demonstrate their own *confianza* by spending additional time with the client and his or her family. Providers can engage in *platicas* (personable small talks) with the client before and after each session.
4. Mental health care providers are highly encouraged to assess their own level of racial and ethnic identity development in order to understand the experiences of Latinos/as and other ethnic minority clients and families. Such work will enable providers to engage in open dialogues with clients about issues of discrimination and prejudices, which will likely have a significant positive impact in the establishment of *confianza*.
5. It is recommended that information regarding confidentiality be provided in a clear and respectful manner to ensure that the client understands the type of information that is recorded in his or her chart/record, who has access to it, and where the files are maintained.

Manifestations of Dignidad in Mental Health Care

Given the inherent challenges and fears likely to surface during psychotherapy, clients may exhibit a number of behaviors. For instance, as clients grapple with anxieties evoked by the need to disclose their private narratives to a stranger, they may experience *vergüenza* or the fear of being judged. This can be particularly evident among clients who are survivors of sexual abuse. Such experiences may lead clients to feel vulnerable and physically exposed. Clients may also worry about being ridiculed for their experience, mental health diagnosis, or difficulties completing activities of daily living. Experiences of racism and discrimination (e.g., when clients are called derogatory names, harassed by law enforcement, bullied in the workplace) may have further impact on a client's sense of *dignidad*, as they may feel that their worthiness, self-esteem, and self-concept are jeopardized. Lastly, family members may attempt to protect their loved ones' sense of *dignidad* by minimizing the event(s) along with associated signs and symptoms that led the client to seek mental health services. For instance, family members may communicate that the client's symptoms will go away on their own and suggest that the client seek alternative methods of healing (e.g., prayer, traditional healing, natural remedies such as *jarabes* [natural syrups made from herbs] and teas) where perhaps the client may feel less exposed and vulnerable.

Dignidad: Strategies for Mental Health Providers

1. It is recommended that mental health care providers have an open conversation with the client and his or her family regarding the etiology and prognosis of the mental health diagnosis (if one was given), while allowing the client and the family to exercise as much autonomy as they wish regarding course of treatment.
2. Mental health care providers are encouraged to take time to assess what "humane care" looks like for each client and his or her family and incorporate such humane attention into treatment.

3. In some instances, collaboration with traditional healers in the treatment of Latinos/as may contribute to client's development of *confianza* and facilitate the maintenance of their *dignidad*.
4. In order to honor a client's sense of *dignidad*, mental health care providers can assign the client to the same clinician who conducted the intake (some agencies have different professional staff conducting clinical interviews and treatment). Although this may be difficult given the realities of staffing at various mental health care agencies, we must find solutions to these challenges if we are truly dedicated to compassionate, culture-centered, and humane treatment.

Conclusion

In order to truly craft and deliver the best quality of culturally congruent mental health care possible, clinicians are encouraged to consider the role that cultural values have on service delivery. This can be accomplished by integrating cultural values into the treatment of Latinos/as while taking into account differences in ethnic identity, racial identity, and level of acculturation. Although culture-centered mental health care may be an arduous and complex task, this process is necessary if indeed we are committed to providing an environment in which the client and his or her family can live and function with dignity. Culture, when uniquely honored and integrated into mental health care, serves to demonstrate the therapist's commitment to social justice and culturally responsive treatment.

References

Adames, H. Y., Chavez-Dueñas, N. Y., Fuentes, M. A., Salas, S. P., & Perez-Chavez, J. G. (2014). Integration of Latino/a cultural values into palliative healthcare: A culture centered model. *Journal of Palliative & Supportive Care, 12*(2), 149–157. doi:10.1017/S147895151300028X

Allende, I. (2000). Isabel Allende, a life of extreme. *BBC World News.* Retrieved from http://www.bbc.co.uk/worldservice/arts/highlights/allende.shtml

Añez, L. M., Silva, M. A., Paris, M., & Bedregal, L. E. (2008). Engaging Latinos through the integration of cultural values and motivational interviewing principles. *Journal of Professional Psychology: Research and Practice, 39*(2), 153–159. doi:10:1037/0735–7028.39.2.153

Ani, M. (1994). *Yurugu: An African centered critique of European cultural thought and behavior.* Trenton, NJ: African World Press.

Arredondo, P., Gallardo-Cooper, M., Delgado-Romero, E. A., & Zapata, A. L. (2014). *Culturally responsive counseling with Latinas/os.* Alexandria, VA: American Counseling Association.

Boyd-Franklin, N. (2006). *Black families in therapy: Understanding the African American experience.* New York, NY: The Guilford Press.

Bracero, W. (1998). Intimidades: Confianza, gender, and hierarchy in the construction of Latino–Latina therapeutic relationships. *Cultural Diversity and Mental Health, 4,* 264–277.

Carter, R. T. (1991). Cultural values: A review of empirical research and implications for counseling. *Journal of Counseling & Development, 70*(1), 164–173. doi:10.1002/j.1556-6676.1991.tb01579.x

Carteret, M. (2012). *Cultural values of Latino patients and families.* Retrieved from http://www.dimensionsofculture.com/2011/03/cultural-values-of-latino-patients-and-families/

Castro, F. G., Stein, J. A., & Bentler, P. M. (2009). Ethnic pride, traditional family values, and acculturation in early cigarette and alcohol use among Latino adolescents. *The Journal of Primary Prevention, 30*(3–4), 265–292. doi:10.1007/s10935-009-0174-z

Chandler, C. (1979). Traditionalism in a modern setting: A comparison of Anglo- and Mexican-American value orientations. *Human Organization, 38*(2), 153–159.

Chavez-Dueñas, N. Y., Adames, H. Y., & Organista, K. C. (2014). Skin-color prejudice and within-group racial discrimination: Historical and current impact on Latino/a populations. *Hispanic Journal of Behavioral Sciences, 36*(1), 3–26. doi:10.1177/0739986313511306

Chochinov, H. M. (2002). Dignity-conserving care—a new model for palliative care: Helping the patient feel valued. *Journal of the American Medical Association, 287*(17), 2253–2260.

Cohen, L. (1979). *Culture, disease and stress among Latino immigrants.* Washington, DC: Smithsonian Institution.

Coohey, C. (2001). *The relationship between familism and child maltreatment in Latino children and their families in the United States: Current research and future directions.* Westport, CT: Preager.

Falicov, C. (1998). *Latino families in therapy: A guide to multicultural practice.* New York, NY: Guilford.

Gallardo, M. E., Yeh, C. J., Trimble, J. E., & Parham, T. A. (2012). *Culturally adaptive counseling skills: Demonstrations of evidence-based practice.* Thousand Oaks, CA: Sage Publications.

Germán, M., Gonzales, N. A., & Dumka, L. (2009). Familism values as a protective factor for Mexican-origin adolescents exposed to deviant peers. *The Journal of Early Adolescence, 29*(1), 16–42. doi:10.1177/0272431608324475

Gil, A. G., Wagner, E. F., & Vega, W. A. (2000). Acculturation, familism and alcohol use among Latino adolescent males: Longitudinal relations. *Journal of Community Psychology, 28*(4), 443–458.

Gonzales, N. A., Germán, M., Kim, S. Y., George, P., Fabrett, F. C., Millsap, R., & Dumka, L. E. (2008). Mexican American adolescents' cultural orientation, externalizing behavior and academic engagement: The role of traditional cultural values. *American Journal of Community Psychology, 41*(1–2), 151–164. doi:10.1007/s10464-007-9152-x

Helms, J. E., & Cook, D. A. (1999). *Using race and culture in counseling and psychotherapy: Theory and process.* Needham Heights, MA: Allyn & Bacon.

Horevitz, E., & Organista, K. C. (2013). The Mexican health paradox: Expanding the explanatory power of the acculturation construct. *Hispanic Journal of Behavioral Sciences, 35*(1), 3–34. doi:10.1177/0739986312460370

Inclan, J. (1985). Variations in value orientations in mental health work with Puerto Ricans. *Psychotherapy: Theory, Research, Practice, Training, 22*(2S), 324–334. doi:10.1037/h0085511

James, S. A. (1993). Racial and ethnic differences in infant mortality and low birth weight: A psychosocial critique. *Annals of Epidemiology, 3*(2), 130–136.

Kalibatseva, Z., & Leong, F. L. (2014). A critical review of culturally sensitive treatments for depression: Recommendations for intervention and research. *Psychological Services*, *11*(4), 433–450. doi:10.1037/a0036047

Kaplan, C. P., Napoles-Springer, A., Stewart, S. L., & Perez-Stable, E. (2001). Smoking acquisition among adolescents and young Latinas. The role of socioenvironmental and personal factors. *Addictive Behaviors*, *26*(4), 531–550. doi:10.1016/S0306- 4603(00)00143-X

Kluckhohn, F. R., & Strodtbeck, F. L. (1961). *Variations in value orientations*. Evanston, IL: Row Peterson.

Lawton, K. E., Gerdes, A. C., Haack, L. M., & Schneider, B. (2014). Acculturation, cultural values, and Latino parental beliefs about the etiology of ADHD. *Administration and Policy in Mental Health and Mental Health Services Research*, *41*(2), 189–204. doi:10.1007/s10488-012-0447-3

Lewis-Fernandez, R., & Kleinman, A. (1994). Culture, personality, and psychopathology. *Journal of Abnormal Psychology*, *103*, 67–71.

Lorenzo-Blanco, E. I., Unger, J. B., Baezconde-Garbanati, L., Ritt-Olson, A., & Soto, D. (2012). Acculturation, enculturation, and symptoms of depression in Hispanic youth: The roles of gender, Hispanic cultural values, and family functioning. *Journal of Youth and Adolescence*, *41*(10), 1350–1365. doi:10.1007/s10964-012-9774-7

Ma, M., Malcolm, L. R., Diaz-Albertini, K., Klinoff, V. A., Leeder, E., Barrientos, S., & Kibler, J. L. (2014). Latino cultural values as protective factors against sexual risks among adolescents. *Journal of Adolescence*, *37*(8), 1215–1225. doi:10.1016/j.adolescence.2014.08.012

Mannino, F. V., & Shore, M. F. (1976). Perceptions of social supports by Spanish-speaking youth with implications for program development. *Journal of School Health*, *46*(8), 471–474. doi:10.1111/j.1746-1561.1976.tb02037.x

Marin, G., & Marin, B. V. (1991). *Research with Hispanic populations*. Thousand Oaks, CA: Sage.

Miller, W. R., & Rollnick, S. (2013). *Motivational interviewing: Helping people change* (3rd ed.). New York, NY: Guilford Press.

Miranda, A. O., Estrada, D., & Firpo-Jimenez, M. (2000). Differences in family cohesion, adaptability, and environment among Latino families in dissimilar stages of acculturation. *The Family Journal*, *8*(4), 341–350. doi:10.1177/1066480700084003

Organista, K. C. (2007). *Solving Latino psychosocial and health problems: Theory, practice, and populations*. Hoboken, NJ: John Wiley & Sons.

Pabon, E. (1998). Hispanic adolescent delinquency and the family: A discussion of sociocultural influences. *Adolescence*, *33*, 941–955.

Parham, T. A., Ajamu, A., & White, J. L. (2010). *Psychology of Blacks: Centering our perspectives in the African consciousness* (4th ed.). Upper Saddle River, NJ: Prentice Hall.

Parham, T. A., White, J. L., & Ajamu, A. (1999). *The psychology of Blacks: An African centered perspective* (3rd ed.). Upper Saddle River, NJ: Prentice Hall.

Perez, G. K., & Cruess, D. (2014). The impact of familism on physical and mental health among Hispanics in the United States. *Health Psychology Review*, *8*(1), 95–127. doi:10.1080/17437199.2011.569936

Romero, A. J., Cuellar, I. C., & Roberts, R. E. (2000). Ethnocultural variables and attitudes toward cultural socialization of children. *Journal of Community Psychology*, *12*, 79–89.

Ruiz, J. M., Steffen, P., & Smith, T. B. (2013). Hispanic mortality paradox: A systematic review and meta-analysis of the longitudinal literature. *American Journal of Public Health*, *103*(3), e52–e60. doi:10.2105/AJPH.2012.301103

Santiago-Rivera, A. L., Arredondo, P., & Gallardo-Cooper, M. (2002). *Counseling Latinos and la familia: A practical guide.* Thousand Oaks, CA: Sage Publications.

Saetermoe, C.L., Beneli, I., & Busch, R.M. (1999). Perceptions of adulthood among Anglo and Latino parents. *Current Psychology, 18*(2), 171–184.

Scribner, R., & Dwyer, J.H. (1989). Acculturation and low birthweight among Latinos in the Hispanic HANES. *American Journal of Public Health, 79*(9), 1263–1267.

Sitaram, K. S., & Haapanen, L. W. (1979). The role of values in intercultural communications. In M. K. Asante & C. A. Blake (Eds.), *The handbook of intercultural communications* (pp. 147–160). Beverly Hills, CA: Sage.

Smith, A. K., Sudore, R. L., & Perez-Stable, E. J. (2009). Palliative care for Latino patients and their families: Whenever we prayed, she wept. *Journal of American Medical Association, 301*(10), 1047–1057.

Sommers, I., Fagan, J., & Baskin, D. (1993). Sociocultural influences on the explanation of delinquency for Puerto Rican youths. *Hispanic Journal of Behavioral Sciences, 15*(1), 36–62. doi:10.1177/07399863930151002

Szapocznik, J., Scopetta, M. A., & King, O. E. (1978). Theory and practice in matching treatment to the special characteristics and problems of Cuban immigrants. *Journal of Community Psychology, 6*(2), 112–122. doi:10.1002/1520- 6629(197804) 6:2<112::AID-JCOP2290060203>3.0.CO;2-R

Triandis, H. C., Marin, G., Lisansky, J., & Betancourt, H. (1984). *Simpatia* as a cultural script of Hispanics. *Journal of Personality and Social Psychology, 47*, 1363–1375.

Unger, J. B., Ritt-Olson, A., Teran, L., Huang, T., Hoffman, B. R., & Palmer, P. (2002). Cultural values and substance use in a multiethnic sample of California adolescents. *Addiction Research & Theory, 10*(3), 257–280. doi:10.1080/16066350211869

Unger, J. B., Shakib, S., Gallaher, P., Ritt-Olson, A., Mouttapa, M., Palmer, P., & Johnson, C. (2006). Cultural/interpersonal values and smoking in an ethnically diverse sample of Southern California adolescents. *Journal of Cultural Diversity, 13*(1), 55–63.

Valle, R., & Martinez, C. (1980). Natural networks among Mexicano elderly in the United States: Implications for mental health. In M. R. Miranda & R. A. Ruiz (Eds.), *Chicano aging and mental health* (pp. 87–117). Washington, DC: Government Printing Office.

Vega, W. A., Gil, A. G., Warheit, G. J., Zimmerman, R. S., & Apospori, E. (1993). Acculturation and delinquent behavior among Cuban American adolescents: Toward an empirical model. *American Journal of Community Psychology, 21*(1), 113–125. doi:10.1007/BF00938210

Villar, M. E., & Concha, M. (2012). Sex education and cultural values: Experiences and attitudes of Latina immigrant women. *Sex Education, 12*(5), 545–554. doi:1 0.1080/14681811.2011.627733

Villarruel, F. A., Carlo, G., Grau, J. M., Azmitia, M., Cabrera, N. J., & Chahin, T. J. (2009). *Handbook of U.S. Latino psychology: Development and community-based perspectives.* Thousand Oaks, CA: Sage Publications.

White, J. L., & Cones, J. H., III. (1999). *Black man emerging: Facing the past and seizing a future in America.* New York, NY: W. H. Freeman.

Zuñiga, M. E. (1992). *Dichos* as metaphorical tools for resistant Latino clients. *Psychotherapy, 28*, 480–483.

9 Culturally Responsive and Racially Conscious Mental Health Approaches With Latinos/as

Healing is therapeutic, but not all therapy is healing.

–Parham, 2002, p. xxiv

Having focused on specific content that helps clinicians understand the sociohistorical context which has shaped the lives of Latinos/as, in this chapter, we will now focus our attention on how such material can be integrated into mental health treatment. When considering the unifying theme of this book—that is, within-group Latino/a differences—clinicians can begin to understand the lack of attention that has been paid to particular differences within this community such as race, skin color, and physiognomy. More specifically, research integrating these factors into clinical practice is severely lacking. However, the few available studies suggest that skin color, physiognomy, and colorism (a form of within-group racial discrimination) can negatively affect interpersonal relations, mental health, educational attainment, and income for Latinos/as (e.g. Arce, Murgia, & Frisbie, 1987; Montalvo, 2004; Montalvo & Codina, 2001; Ramos, Jaccard, & Guilamo-Ramos, 2003; Telzer & Vazquez-Garcia, 2009). Consequently, considering factors such as skin color, physiognomy, and racial identity in the general well-being and mental health treatment of Latinos/as may not only foster rapport building in therapy but also improve treatment outcomes for individuals across the color gradient. Integrating such factors may also contribute to the provision of culturally responsive and racially conscious services to individuals of this racially heterogeneous community. In this chapter, we address this gap by briefly reviewing the literature on psychotherapy and the different practices, interventions, and models used to assess and improve treatment effectiveness. Specifically, the chapter begins with a brief review of the literature on Empirically Supported Treatments (EST), Evidence-Based Practice (EBP), and Culturally Adapted Psychotherapies (CAPs), with a particular focus on the congruence of those modalities with Latinos/as of diverse racial and ethnic backgrounds. The chapter also discusses a number of existing interventions designed specifically for Latinos/as that lack an explicit consideration of the role that race plays for members from this ethnic group. The chapter concludes with a treatment framework to assist mental health practitioners working with Latinos/as deliver interventions rooted in a culturally responsive and racially conscious ethos and praxis.

Brief History of Empirically Supported Treatments and Evidence-Based Practice

A focus on the integration of empirical science and clinical practice has dominated the field of mental health for the past three decades. The approach of using scientific findings to provide the most effective psychotherapeutic treatments to individuals has been influenced by two major movements: *Empirically Supported Treatments* (ESTs), also known as Empirically Validated Treatments (EVTs), and the *Evidence-Based Practice in Psychology* (EBPP) movement. The following section provides a brief history of these two approaches to the treatment of mental health conditions.

Empirically Supported Treatments

The ESTs movement, led by Division 12 (Clinical Psychology) of the APA, outlined the criteria required for interventions to be classified as ESTs (Task Force on Promotion and Dissemination of Psychological Procedures, 1995). In order for an intervention to meet the standards set forth by the EST task force, two criteria are required: one, the outcome should be superior in the treatment group in comparison to the no treatment/control group and two, the intervention should be manualized so providers and researchers can follow the treatment and replicate the study. Further, it requires that the treatment is equivalent to other established interventions designed to address the same symptomatologies. It is interesting to note that the philosophy followed by the ESTs movement was modeled after the United States (U.S.) Food and Drug Administration (FDA) guidelines for approving new medications (Wampold, Lichtenberg, & Waehler, 2002). Following guidelines established to meet the needs of different fields (i.e., FDA), the ESTs may miss the particular complexities inherent in the etiology and treatment of mental health conditions.

While some applaud the systematic methods employed in ESTs, others have critiqued and cautioned against the perils of utilizing a positivistic philosophy (e.g., empiricism) to guide knowledge production and objectivity in mental health interventions (Chwalisz, 2003). For instance, the level of rigor required to meet randomized control trials coupled with the criteria outlined by the task force are said to compromise the generalizability and ecological validity of ESTs (Carter & Goodheart, 2012; Chwalisz, 2003; Franklin, DeRubeis, & Westen, 2006; Wampold, Lichtenberg, & Waehler, 2002). Others critique ESTs' emphasis on manualized treatments and their focus on short-term symptom relief rather than considering their long-term effects (e.g., Wampold, 2007). Lastly, a number of scholars posit that ESTs are not suitable for individuals with varying personality types or those from oppressed racial and ethnic communities (La Roche & Christopher, 2009; Sue et al., 2006; Wampold, 2007; Westen, Novotny, & Thompson-Brenner, 2004). Despite these criticisms, the underlying philosophy of ESTs continues to be the prevailing paradigm that drives most of the current research in psychotherapy (Sternberg, 2006).

Evidence-Based Practice

The Evidence-Based Practice (EBP) movement in the field of mental health arose out of the many criticisms of ESTs. In 2006, a policy statement titled, *Evidence-Based Practice in Psychology* (EBPP), was published by the APA. The document provides practitioners and researchers with a framework that identifies the components that constitute "evidence" in the treatment of mental health. Overall, EBPP is defined as the "best available research with clinical expertise in the context of patient characteristics, culture, and preferences" (APA Presidential Task Force on Evidence-Based Practice [APA], 2006, p. 273). EBP can be visualized as the framework of a three-legged stool that consists of three equally important domains: 1) *Evidence*, referring to the best available research on interventions regarding the mental health condition(s) of interest; 2) *Clinical Expertise*, referring to practitioners' training and competence with the particular symptoms being addressed; and 3) *Client Characteristics*, pertaining to individuals' race, ethnicity, gender, socioeconomic status, cultural values, and the like. La Roche and Christopher (2009) discuss how the definition proposed by the EBP movement aligns better with the Institute of Medicine's view of evidence, which is influenced by a socio-constructivist paradigm (Sackett, Straus, Richardson, Rosenberg, & Haynes, 2000) unlike ESTs, which, as previously stated, are guided by a positivistic philosophy.

Culturally Adapted Psychotherapies

Although most mental health practitioners may agree that little to no quarrel exists on whether or not there is a need to identify interventions that are effective, the EBP approach becomes more complicated when considering the interplay between evidence, culture, and context (Bernal & Rodriguez, 2012; La Roche, 2013). Hence when considering the pivotal question of "evidence for whom," while critically thinking about how evidence is situated within a particular socio-political context, some scholars have focused on creating frameworks to address the complexities and challenges of integrating evidence, culture, and context. These frameworks are formally referred to as *Culturally Adapted Psychotherapies* (CAPs). CAPs have been defined as "the systematic modification of an evidence-based treatment or intervention protocol to consider language, culture, and context in such a way that it is compatible with the client's cultural patterns, meanings, and values" (Bernal, Jimenez-Chafey, & Rodriguez, 2009, p. 362).

Culturally Adapted Psychotherapy Frameworks

A number of CAPs are used by clinicians who seek to integrate clients' cultures into their service delivery. Although these approaches are diverse, they have predominantly included 1) matching client and therapist on race and ethnicity, 2) providing treatment in the client's preferred or native language, 3) incorporating traditional cultural values into treatment, and 4) using any combination of the previously discussed practices. In an effort to provide some structure to the way in which CAPs are delivered, a number of frameworks and models have been proposed in the literature.

The Ecological Validity Framework (EVF) developed by Bernal, Bonilla, and Bellido (1995) is one of the first and most cited cultural adaptation frameworks. The EVF is based on Bronfenbrenner's (1977) ecological systems theory, which aims to explain how human development is impacted by a set of complex interconnecting systems (i.e., microsystem, mesosystem, exosystem, macrosystem, chronosystem). In other words, individuals encounter and are embedded in different environments throughout their life span, which influences how they think, behave, and what they ultimately value. The EVF is designed to take into account a client's cultural experiences when designing a mental health treatment plan. Hence, "if the criteria of ecological validity are met, then one can assume that the treatment is aligned with the culture, language, and worldview of the client" (Rodriguez & Bernal, 2012, p. 25).

In an effort to integrate the client's culture into mental health treatment, the EVF describes eight dimensions that need to be addressed. These eight broad areas are outlined in Bernal et al. (1995) and include the following:

1. *Language*–inclusive of both oral and written communication, regionalisms, and slang
2. *Persons*–referring to the therapeutic dyad, the client's expectation of therapists, and ethnic matching
3. *Metaphors*–incorporating folk sayings, *dichos*, and visual objects into interventions
4. *Content*–integrating the client's cultural values, customs, and traditions into treatment
5. *Concepts*–using concepts that are consonant with the client's culture
6. *Goals*–constructing treatment plans that are aligned to the client's cultural context
7. *Methods*–making cultural adjustments to interventions and including genograms, rituals, and *cuento* therapy
8. *Contexts*–focusing on how social and political contexts at the time of treatment may impact engagement and treatment outcome

A number of scholars have applied the EVF to a number of diverse clinical settings, including parent-child interaction therapy with families of Puerto Rican descent whose children have been diagnosed with attention deficit/ hyperactivity disorder (AD/HD) (see Matos, Bauermeister, & Bernal, 2009), cognitive and interpersonal treatment for Latino/a adults with depression (see Rosselló & Bernal, 1996), treatment interventions with Black Caribbean youths (see Nicolas & Schwartz, 2012), and Latina women suffering from trauma (see Wallis, Amaro, & Cortés, 2012). Although an in-depth review of the literature on CAPs is beyond the scope of this chapter, exemplars of other culturally adapted frameworks and models can be found in Bernal and Rodríguez's (2012) text titled *Cultural Adaptations: Tools for Evidence-Based Practice with Diverse Populations*.

The Evidence in Culturally Adapted Psychotherapies

In the last decade, a number of meta-analyses have been conducted to ascertain the effectiveness of interventions created for specific cultural groups (i.e., CAPs). In general, effectiveness in the social sciences is often reported as the mean difference between comparison groups (e.g., CAPS, EBPs, treatment as usual) and statistically symbolized as "d" in research reports. In other words, in studies focusing on treatment effectiveness, "d" refers to the number of standard deviations that help to differentiate the two treatment groups. Hence psychotherapy researchers are more interested in assessing the difference in effect size (i.e., d) rather than just the significance level of such difference (i.e., p value). Cohen (2001) provides guidelines to assist in the interpretation of "d," including 0.8 = a large effect size, 0.5 = a medium effect size, 0.2 = a small effect size, and anything below 0.2 is often not considered worthy of further analyses.

One of the first meta-analyses ($N = 76$) that focused on culturally adapted mental health interventions was conducted by Griner and Smith (2006). Their results indicated that cultural adaptation consisted of a multitude of practices. For instance, in their review, they found that the majority of studies (84%) incorporated cultural language and traditional cultural values into the mental health intervention. Another significant portion of studies matched client and clinician according to ethnicity (61%) and language (74%). Lastly, a small portion of studies engaged in practices that involved training their staff on cultural competence (17%). Overall, Griner and Smith's (2006) meta-analysis found CAPs to have moderately strong benefits ($d = 0.45$).

In 2011, Benish, Quintana, and Wampold conducted another meta-analysis where they compared a total of 21 published and unpublished studies on 1) "culturally adapted psychotherapy" or interventions that integrated cultural beliefs about illness and health into mental health treatment with 2) "bona-fide psychotherapy," or interventions with established evidence of effectiveness that were not culturally adapted. Overall, the meta-analysis found that culturally adapted interventions were more effective than nonadapted "bona-fide" treatments ($d = 0.32$). In addition, culturally adapted interventions were more effective than control groups or treatment as usual ($d = 0.33$).

Lastly, another meta-analysis conducted with ethnic minority youths (i.e., African American, Latino/a, and mixed/other minority youths) was done by Huey and Polo (2008). This study compared the effectiveness of EBPs versus treatment as usual and CAPs versus treatment as usual. Overall, their analysis ($N = 25$) focused on EBPs for anxiety, depression, AD/HD, and conduct disorders. The results of their first comparison revealed a medium effect of $d = 0.44$, pointing to evidence that EBPs were more effective than treatment as usual (i.e., control group). Their second comparison (i.e., CAPs vs. treatment as usual) showed no difference between CAPs and treatment as usual. Interestingly, out of all of the meta-analyses reviewed, Huey and Polo (2008) were the only group to report results indicating that CAPs was not more statistically effective than standard treatment for ethnic minority youths. Their findings were discussed by Helms (2015), who outlined a number of important and valid critiques regarding Huey and Polo's meta-analysis, including 1) the researchers failed to discuss the cultural or racial socialization components of their samples; 2) the cultural congruence or appropriateness of measures was not examined, including whether they were normed for culturally and racially minoritized youths; 3) this study lacked explicit descriptions of the treatment protocol besides simply stating that they engaged in "culturally adapted interventions"; and 4) the researchers failed to describe important characteristics of service providers that can have an impact on treatment outcomes (e.g., race, ethnicity, native language).

Problematizing the Evidence in Culturally Adapted Psychotherapies

Overall, most of the meta-analyses conducted on the effectiveness of CAPs (e.g., Benish, Quintana, & Wampold, 2011; Griner & Smith, 2006) provide evidence suggesting that they are better than standard treatments for ethnically and racially minoritized people. Exceptions to these findings include a study that found no difference between CAPs and treatment as usual (e.g., Huey & Polo, 2008), which has been criticized by experts in the literature on race and culture (see Helms, 2015). Although two of the meta-analyses reviewed in this chapter found a positive difference between CAPs and treatment as usual (i.e., Benish et al., 2011; Griner & Smith, 2006), all of these studies reviewed thus far can benefit from further examination of their methodology, operationalization of variables, and overall meaningfulness of the results. For instance, none of the three meta-analyses explicitly discussed nor operationalized the complexity embedded in what was considered as evidence. This can be clearly observed in the way in which the construct of "ethnicity" was loosely assessed, as well as in the researchers' lack of consideration for the pivotal role of internalized racial socialization (Helms, 2015). Hence lack of focus on these important factors generates three important questions: What was exactly considered as evidence of treatment effectiveness? What is the role of the service provider's characteristics (e.g., race, ethnicity, stage/status of racial and ethnic identity) on treatment effectiveness? How useful are the results of the available meta-analysis on CAPs for specific members of minoritized racial and ethnic groups?

Solutions: Considering Cultural and Racial Equivalent Frameworks

Identifying solutions to the problematization of what is considered "evidence" in CAPs requires researchers and practitioners to develop and embrace practices congruent with the complexities inherent in the cultural and racial experiences of People of Color. Hence complex cultural and racialized problems require complex and explicitly racialized solutions. These efforts can tremendously benefit from *cultural equivalence frameworks*, which help provide some parameters and operationalizations for cultural and racial evidence in CAPs (Helms, 2015). Cultural equivalence frameworks include *functional equivalence, conceptual equivalence, linguistic equivalence*, and *psychometric equivalence* (Helms, 2015; Lonner, 1985). CAPs and outcome studies that do not consider the four types of cultural equivalence outlined by Lonner (1985) "places one at risk of [developing], measuring, and interpreting meaningless artifacts as if they were meaningful" (Helms, 1992; 2015, p. 17). Table 9.1 provides some exemplars on ways psychotherapists and researchers can address the *functional* and *conceptual* equivalence of racially and culturally responsive interventions and outcomes. In the table, racially and culturally equivalent interventions are compared using examples of Latinos/as.

Existing Latino/a-Specific Interventions: A Call for Racially Equivalent Frameworks

Mental health professionals working with Latinos/as are encouraged to consider the following set of important questions. How do you know what has the potential to alleviate the ailments of your racially and ethnically minoritized clients? What do you do to learn who your Clients of Color are? What are the pieces of information that you would need to know in order to help your clients achieve their goals? Unfortunately, many of these questions may not be at the forefront of many clinicians' thoughts given the day-to-day work and the complexity of concerns they encounter. When they do consider them, some may answer these questions in a very matter-of-fact way, leading to some regurgitating responses rooted in Eurocentric values, beliefs, and practices similar to the traditional practices outlined in the first column in Table 9.1. Others may consider the complexities embedded in the

Table 9.1 Culturally and Racially Responsive Evidence-Based Practice: Treatment and Assessment Equivalence Assumptions With Latino/a Exemplars

	Traditional Intervention	Racially Conscious Intervention	Culturally Responsive Intervention
Functional Equivalence	• Symptoms are treated the same regardless of the client's cultural and racial dynamics.	• Symptoms may be interpreted or expressed according to racial stereotypes.	• Nature of symptoms may be dependent on ethnic cultural norms, which may be misinterpreted.
	Assessment • Standardized self-report measures, normed on predominately White samples, are interpreted in the same way, regardless of race/ethnic cultural dynamics of the client.	*Assessment* • Effects of racism (e.g., experiences of discrimination) should be intentionally measured.	*Assessment* • Ethnic cultural norms may determine whether items describe functional behaviors in client's environments.
	Example • The same cutoff scores developed on predominately White samples are used to determine symptomatology in Latino/a samples.	*Example* • Client may hide or not reveal depression symptoms to avoid being racially stereotyped.	*Example* • Client may respond to items according to what is socially desirable in his or her cultural environment.
Conceptual Equivalence	• The service provider determines the meaning of behaviors.	• Clients' racial life experiences shape their behavior in treatment including responses to questions, assessments, and measures.	• Clients respond to treatment and assessment techniques in ways that are culturally congruent.
	Assessment • If an assessment measure or technique has been used successfully with other samples, then it measures the same symptoms in the current sample.	*Assessment* • Select questions and measures that allow clients to share experiences that may be analogous to how the symptom(s) would look in their group.	*Assessment* • Develop or interpret assessment techniques and measures according to what is culturally normative in the client's culture.

Traditional Intervention	Racially Conscious Intervention	Culturally Responsive Intervention
Example • Symptoms are expressed the same way regardless of race/ethnicity.	*Example* • Relative to Whites, Afro-Latinos/as may express depression as anger, while Latinos/as of Indigenous descent may express depression as withdrawal.	*Example* • Latinos/as may show symptomatology (e.g., depression) through responses to items about relationships rather than moods.

Note: From "An Examination of the Evidence in Culturally Adapted Evidence-Based or Empirically Supported Interventions," by J. E. Helms, 2015, *Transcultural Psychiatry, 52*(2), p. 174–197. Copyright 2015 by Sage Publications. Adapted with permission.

questions and may seek ways to align their services with all aspects of the client's culture and race. Regardless of where one may fall on this spectrum, our overall ethical obligation as mental health providers is to provide clients with the most effective intervention available (Trimble, Scharrón-del-Río, & Hill, 2012; Vasquez, 2012) and one that is grounded in the client's cultural (Arredondo & Toporek, 2004) and racial experiences (Chavez-Dueñas, Adames, & Organista, 2014; Helms & Cook, 1999). In fact, empirical studies report that culturally and racially diverse clients consider their therapists' cultural responsiveness and understanding of their worldview as more relevant than ethnic matching (Ancis, 2004; Knipscheer & Kleber, 2004). The following section describes two Latino/a-specific frameworks that can help mental health providers to understand the worldview of their Latino/a clients.

Latino/a-Specific Interventional Frameworks

Multidimensional Ecosystemic Comparative Approach (MECA)

A number of frameworks have been proposed to assist clinicians in aligning their services to the culture, values, and beliefs of their diverse Latino/a clients. One of the first frameworks developed was the *Multidimensional Ecosystemic Comparative Approach* (MECA; Falicov, 1998). MECA is designed to meet the following three goals: 1) help clinicians understand the various components that make up an individual's culture (e.g., gender, nationality, immigration status, sexual orientation) and use this information to address the client's presenting concerns and worldview; 2) underscore how a client's values evolve and change as a result of context within different systems, institutions, and agencies (e.g., school, child protective services, courts, political circles), which provide clients with varying degrees of access, resources, and power/powerlessness; 3) provide a method for meaningfully comparing and understanding similarities and differences (e.g., history of immigration, political status, host perception) across cultures (e.g., Mexicans vs. Puerto Ricans vs. Dominicans; gays vs. lesbians vs. bisexuals) to better understand the unique experiences of individuals and families. Overall, MECA was designed to be used with any theoretical orientation and at any stage of treatment.

Latino/a Skills Identification Stage Model (L-SISM)

At the turn of the century, the *Skills Identification Stage Model* (SISM), a framework designed to help therapists identify core issues that facilitate the therapeutic process, was developed specifically for people of African descent by Parham (2002). Overall, SISM focuses on the *what* and *how* of providing culturally responsive mental health treatment and centers on two main questions: What is important for clinicians to achieve therapeutically with their clients? How can clinicians reach this goal using culturally congruent techniques? (Parham, 2002). The SISM is nonlinear and grounded within a culturally explanatory model (CEM; Kleinman, Eisenberg, & Good, 1978), which assists clinicians with understanding the ways in which clients think about their illness, wellness, etiology, signs, symptoms, prevention, treatment, and prognosis. Cultural explanations are often dynamic, have emotional meaning, and are embedded in the person's sociocultural context (Gallardo, 2012; Parham, 2002). Overall, the SISM consists of six domains: 1) *Connecting with Clients*, 2) *Assessment*, 3) *Facilitating Awareness*, 4) *Setting Goals*, 5) *Instigating Change*, and 6) *Feedback and Accountability*. More recently, Gallardo, Yeh, Trimble, and Parham (2012) expanded the SISM by applying it to ALANAs (African Americans, Latinos/as, and North American Indians and Alaska Natives) and MENAs (Middle Eastern and North Africans).

Similar to the SISM, the *Latino/a Skills Identification Stage Model* (L-SISM; Gallardo, 2012) focuses on the six domains with special attention in assisting practitioners to develop culturally responsive interventions with Latino/a clients. The first domain (*Connecting with Clients*) of L-SISM focuses on *personalismo*, making small talk, using *dichos* (proverbs), music, and poetry as ways to connect with clients and educate them about the psychotherapeutic process. The second domain (*Assessment*) focuses on the evaluation of generational status, ethnic identity, level of acculturation, language usage, trauma and environmental factors. The third domain (*Facilitating Awareness*) pays close attention to clients' strengths and existing resources as a way on facilitating awareness regarding the social-political forces and reframe how they may be thinking about their problems. In addition, the third area focuses on traditional ways clients can cope with their presenting problems (e.g., community-specific narratives, assigned readings). The fourth domain (*Setting Goals*) focuses on the development of treatment goals with particular attention to how the provider's own belief system about Latinos/as may impact the therapeutic process. In this domain, the importance of incorporating clients' level of education, socioeconomic status, community groups, and expanded role of the family in helping clients achieve treatment goals is also underscored. The fifth domain (*Instigating Change*) speaks to the importance of culturally adapting existing interventions and having the practitioner connect to Latino/a communities and to serve as a cultural broker for clients. Lastly, the sixth domain (*Feedback and Accountability*) highlights the need to understand and evaluate treatment outcomes in a Latino/a-specific context.

The Need for New Conceptual Frameworks in Latino/a Mental Health

A Call for Culturally Responsive and Racially Conscious Interventions

Despite the recent increase in literature focusing on the need to design culturally responsive mental health treatments for Latinos/as (e.g., Falicov, 1998; Gallardo, 2012; Santiago-Rivera, Arredondo, & Gallardo-Cooper, 2002), there continues to be a lack of attention given to interventions that explicitly address within-group differences (e.g., race) among this population (Adames, Chavez-Dueñas, & Organista, 2016; Chavez-Dueñas et al., 2014). As discussed throughout this book, most of the literature on Latino/a mental health uses pan-ethnic labels such as "Latino/a" and "Hispanic." These terms gloss over the diverse experience of Latinos/as who come from distinct nations (see Chapter 3), have different levels of acculturation (see Chapter 5), are within varying stages of racial and ethnic identity (see Chapter 6), identify with different genders (see Chapter 4), and represent various generational and socioeconomic statuses, religions, forms of spirituality, and race/skin-color gradients (see Chapters 1 and 2). Although pan-ethnic terms have political relevance and often provide a sense of unity among individuals who have experienced a shared history of oppression, discrimination, and invisibility in the U.S. (Chavez-Dueñas et al., 2014), they also obscure within-group differences and their implications. This practice is vividly observed in the current theories and empirical research on Latino/a identity, which tend to focus on ethnicity while neglecting the role of race in the lives of Latinos/as (Adames et al., 2016; Chavez-Dueñas et al., 2014). This pattern also becomes clear when noting the disproportionate number of studies on Latinos/as, which solely focus on ethnic identity development to the exclusion of racial identity (Cokley, 2007). The pattern of neglecting race extends to the literature on interventional frameworks, including those explicitly designed to consider culture such as CAPs for Latinos/as (Adames et al., 2016). These practices offer an incomplete picture of Latinos/as who are ethnically and racially diverse, as extensively discussed throughout this volume. Table 9.2 provides a list of interventional strategies and their effectiveness and usefulness when considering both culture and race in psychotherapy research and practice with Latino/a populations.

Table 9.2 A Place for Culture and Race in Psychotherapy Research and Practice With Latinos/as

Interventions	Effectiveness & Usefulness with Latino/a Population
ESTs or EVTs: Empirically Supported Treatments or Empirically Validated Treatments	• **Ineffective/No Use** when differences between Latinos/as and all other cultural and racial groups are treated the same. • **Questionable Effectiveness and Use** when ESTs/ EVTs are normed on and designed for Latinos/as given that such an approach most likely treats all Latinos/as as a homogenous group without considering within-group differences (e.g., skin color, racialized experiences, acculturation level).
EBPs: Evidence-Based Practices	• **Questionable Effectiveness and Use** of EBPs designed for Latinos/as given that such an approach most likely treats all Latinos/as as a homogenous group without considering within-group differences (e.g., skin color, racialized experiences, acculturation level).
CAPs or CATs: Culturally Adapted Psychotherapies or Culturally Adapted Treatments	• **More Effective and Useful** compared to EBPs and ESTs/EVTs; however, most CAPs/CATs are likely to treat all Latinos/as as a homogenous group without considering how skin color impacts Latino/a racialized dynamics.
C2R-EBPs Culturally *and* Racially Responsive Evidence-Based Practices	• **Most Useful** approach with Latinos/as since it includes both the cultural norms, values, and practices with racialized dynamics, which can be different based on the skin color of Latinos/as. Thus clients' cultural *and* racial lives are equally pivotal in molding the behaviors, thoughts, and affects of Latinos/as. There is a need to evaluate the effectiveness of C2R-EBPs with Latinos/as.

CREAR-CE-Treatment Approach: Culturally Responsive and Racially Conscious Ecosystemic Treatment Approach

Overall, the need to consider the role of race, skin color, and physiognomy in conjunction with culture when treating Latinos/as has been established in this chapter and throughout this volume. However, the role of race can be easily overlooked and, in some instances, avoided by clinicians given the exclusive focus on ethnicity and culture in the Latino/a mental health literature. In order to assist clinicians in beginning the process of cultural and racial competence, a training and treatment approach titled CREAR-CE (*Culturally Responsive AND Racially Conscious Ecosystemic Treatment Approach*) was designed. CREAR (pronounced *kre'ar*) is a verb in Spanish that means to form, to create, or to build anew, which is at the core of the psychotherapeutic process—that is, to help and guide clients as they build new possibilities for themselves. In this section, a treatment approach explicitly devoted to assisting clinicians in the integration of race and culture into treatment is described. The CREAR-CE Treatment Approach can be used with any theoretical orientation employed by the treating clinician. The components of the approach are described in the following section in detail.

The CREAR-CE Treatment Approach is divided into three phases that include various domains within each phase (see Figure 9.1). Phase I focuses on

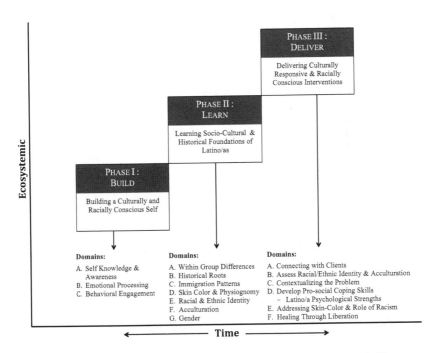

Figure 9.1 Culturally Responsive AND Racially Conscious Ecosystemic Treatment Approach (CREAR-CE)

CREAR (pronounced kre'ar) is a verb in Spanish that means to form, to create, to build anew, which is at the core of the psychotherapeutic and liberating process.

the complexity inherent in the process of clinicians developing self-knowledge and awareness. To achieve this goal, Phase I includes three domains: a) *Complexity of Self-Knowledge and Awareness*, b) *Emotional Processing*, and c) *Behavioral Engagement*. Phase II emphasizes content clinicians need to know in order to have an in-depth understanding of the sociocultural and sociohistorical foundations of the Latino/a experience, such as within-group differences, immigration process, skin color and physiognomy, racial and ethnic identity in the lives of Latino/a clients, acculturation, and gender. Lastly, Phase III focuses on specific strategies that can help providers guide clients through the process of connecting with their personal and collective healing powers.

Phase I: Building a Culturally Responsive and Racially Conscious Self

Domain A: The Complexity of Self-Knowledge and Awareness

The first domain emphasizes the importance of developing knowledge and awareness of the self as both a cultural and racial being. As such, this domain focuses on the clinician's conceptual/theoretical/intellectual learning, which includes gaining factual knowledge and information about his or her own ethnic and racial group. Overall, scholars have posited that the role of the healer is to heal thyself, to remember the past, to access the spirit, and to confront his or her history (Fu-Kiau, 1991; Hilliard, 1997). Thus we argue that developing conceptual knowledge of the self is necessary for providers to establish a therapeutic relationship with Latino/a clients as well as to develop culturally congruent and racially conscious treatment plans. This information can be obtained from a variety of sources and training approaches that may include textbooks, lectures, courses, journals, and films/documentaries.

Domain B: Emotional Processing

The second domain focuses on assisting clinicians in learning how to become aware of and process emotional responses evoked by content encountered in Domain A. Emotional change can be attained via four interrelated processes. One, clinicians become attuned to the various emotions they may experience when exposed to information that challenges their views about themselves. Two, clinicians reflect on the meaning of those emotions. Three, clinicians express their feelings and thoughts with others via dialogues with similar and diverse others. Four, clinicians focus on the emotions that surface while engaging in dialogue. The following are a number of alternative options available for providers to engage in emotional processing.

- Attend conferences that have dialogues as part of the program design, such as the "Difficult Dialogues" at the National Multicultural Conference and Summit.
- Review available resources that may assist with starting dialogue groups, such as the Presidential Initiative on Race ("One America Dialogue Guide:

Conducting a Discussion on Race," 1998) and visiting the *National Coalition for Dialogue and Deliberation* website for resources.
- Use stimulating documentaries and training videos such as the *Color of Fear* (Wah, 2004), *The Way Home* (Butler, 1998), *Rape in the Fields* (Bergman & Cediel, 2013), *Mirrors of Privilege: Making Whiteness Visible* (Butler, 2006).

Domain C: Behavioral Engagement

In the third domain, clinicians are encouraged to seek and engage in interactions with individuals who are in advanced stages/statuses of racial and ethnic identity development (Chapter 6 in this volume provides an overview of racial and ethnic identity theories and behavioral exemplars that can help individuals assess where others may be in their stages/statuses of racial and ethnic identity development). Such engagement may assist in the development of self-knowledge in four ways: 1) raise awareness about the implicit biases and prejudices that clinicians may hold but are not conscious of, 2) help providers recognize the role that they play in perpetuating systems of oppression, 3) challenge providers to abandon racist ideologies (i.e., for White clinicians) and abandonment of internalized racism (i.e., for clinicians for color), and 4) hold clinicians accountable for using their areas of privilege to help others cope with a complex racist and oppressive world. Progressing through the behavioral engagement domain involves clinicians getting out of their comfort zones and having meaningful interactions with people of similar and different backgrounds (White & Henderson, 2008). In other words, providers are encouraged to spend time with people who are both similar and different from themselves by getting out of their professional offices, labs, and spaces.

Phase II: Learning Social-Cultural and Historical Foundations of Latinos/as

As discussed throughout this volume, knowing and understanding a client's sociohistorical context, level of acculturation, stage/status of both racial and ethnic identity development, and traditional cultural values and worldview is critical when providing culturally responsive and racially conscious treatment. These important components of clinical intervention are addressed in Phase II of the CREAR-CE Treatment Approach, and the content for this phase is included in Chapters 1 through 8 of this book, *Cultural Foundations & Interventions in Latino/a Mental Health* (Adames & Chavez-Dueñas, 2017).

Phase III: Delivering Culturally Responsive and Racially Conscious Treatment

The third phase of the CREAR-CE Treatment Approach focuses on areas that help clients connect with their personal and collective healing powers, including

1) *Connecting with Clients*, 2) *Assessing Clients' Racial-Ethnic Identity and Acculturation*, 3) *Contextualizing the Problem*, 4) *Developing Prosocial Coping Skills*, 5) *Addressing Skin Color and the Role of Racism*, and 6) *Healing Through Liberation*. The CREAR-CE Treatment Approach is intended to assist clinicians in delivering culturally conscious interventions while explicitly focusing on the ever-present role of race in the lives of Latino/a clients. The domains included in Phase III are identified as therapeutic tasks and strategies grounded in culturally based assumptions and anchored in the Latino/a experience with an explicit focus on race.

Although we believe cultural and racial socialization have impacted all Latino/a clients, race- and culture-related factors may not always be the sole reason why they are seeking treatment. However, incorporating these two important factors can assist clinicians in understanding how race and culture may be interwoven within the presenting problems and contribute to their etiology. When all aspects that have shaped clients' experiences are taken into account, therapy can become a transformative force that can begin to change "a frown into a smile, a cry into laughter, self-doubt into self-confidence, personal isolation into social connectedness, mistrust into trust, and responsible risk taking, and even silence and hesitation into articulate words" (Parham, 2002, p. 102). This treatment approach is not intended to be exhaustive; moreover, the CREAR-CE Treatment Approach is not linear, despite being presented as such in the following section.

Domain A: Connecting with Latino/a Clients

As discussed in Chapter 8 in this volume, *confianza* (trust) is a traditional cultural value characteristic of Latino/a culture, where individuals are invested in establishing relationships that are based on reciprocal trust. *Confianza* is exemplified when someone expresses his or her deeper feelings only to an inner circle of familiar confidants. Overall, *confianza* connotes that the other person(s) in the relationship have their best interest in mind (Adames, Chavez-Dueñas, Fuentes, Salas, & Perez-Chavez, 2014; Bracero, 1998; Lewis-Fernandez & Kleinman, 1994). Given the central role of this traditional value in Latino/a culture, it is essential that therapists learn to effectively establish *confianza* with their Latino/a clients.

Building and establishing *confianza* with Latino/a patients and their families is often complicated. Experiences of discrimination, prejudices, and oppression can have a detrimental effect on establishing *confianza* (Adames et al., 2014; Smith, Sudore, & Perez-Stable, 2009). In fact, families may be cautious with the information they disclose to health-care providers initially. Such cultural suspicion is normal, expected, and healthy, and it is considered a resiliency factor resulting from strategies employed by minoritized ethnic and racial groups as a way to cope with a long-standing history of oppression and discrimination (Boyd-Franklin, 2006; White & Cones, 1999). The establishment of a relationship based on *confianza* will depend on the practitioner's ability to integrate other traditional cultural values into therapy, such as *personalismo* (personalism), a value that places emphasis on warm and supportive interactions with others. Thus practitioners need to listen, demonstrate care and empathy, and be open and affirming of their Latino/a clients' cultural and racial experiences.

Latinos/as tend to be relationship-centered and prefer formal and supportive interactions to informal interactions (Carteret, 2012). When establishing relationships with professionals, Latinos/as require rapport building that includes warmth, formality, and regard. A significant emphasis is placed on professional relationships where the "means" to the professional care is as important as the treatment received (Adames et al., 2014). Thus, with regard to communication style, Latino/a individuals have a preference for exchanges that are pleasant, free of conflict (Añez, Silva, Paris, & Bedregal, 2008), and conducive to the maintenance of harmonious relationships (Adames et al., 2014). As a result, Latino/a families may engage in a number of unique and culturally congruent behaviors. For instance, Latinos/as are likely to engage in indirect forms of communication by speaking through metaphors known as *dichos* (Zuñiga, 1992).

In addition to the establishment of *confianza* and *personalismo*, other traditional elements of the Latino/a culture can assist therapists in connecting with their clients. For instance, clinicians can use the vast array of Latino/a musical genres to connect with the ways in which Latinos/as express a variety of emotions (e.g., joy, pride, sorrow, longing, loss) and cope with life's challenges. Moreover, the effective use of *dichos* (proverbs) by clinicians can help to strengthen clinicians' cultural credibility (see Aviera, 1996; Comas-Diaz, 2006; Falicov, 1998 to obtain more specific information on how to use *dichos* in psychotherapy with Latinos/as).

Domain B: Assessing Latino/a Clients' Racial Identities and Level of Acculturation

Developing culturally responsive and racially conscious treatment for Latinos/as can be an arduous and complex task for most mental health professionals. Domain B focuses on helping clinicians to understand their Latino/a clients' distress from a cultural and racial frame of reference. In order to acquire such understanding, two areas are important to consider and assess, including a) racial identity and b) level of acculturation (Note: level of acculturation is associated with ethnic identity, hence our focus on acculturation.). First, clinicians are encouraged to assess their clients' level of acculturation, which will assist in determining the degree to which clients are connected to their Latino/a roots. For instance, clients who are highly acculturated may not adhere to traditional Latino/a cultural values. These individuals are likely to respond better to more Eurocentric psychotherapeutic interventions. Alternatively, clients with low levels of acculturation and those who are bicultural may benefit from and prefer treatment approaches that integrate traditional Latino/a cultural values such as those described in Chapter 8 of this volume.

Besides level of acculturation, assessing clients' stage/status of racial identity development is essential to the development of effective treatment approaches. Chapter 6 provides an in-depth discussion of these two concepts and how they are assessed. Overall, clinicians working with Latinos/as are encouraged to assess their clients' racial identities. Integrating this important component into the assessment process may assist providers in determining how Latino/a clients perceive the world and interact with others who are racially similar or different. A thorough assessment of clients' racial identity development can assist in developing treatment plans tailored to Latinos/as across the color gradient and across the statuses/stages of their racial identities. There is an abundance of empirical literature (e.g., Caldwell, Kohn-Wood, Schmeelk-Cone, Chavous, & Zimmerman, 2004; Ponterotto & Park-Taylor, 2007; Seaton, Scottham, & Sellers, 2006) indicating that a strong/advanced racial identity can serve as a protective factor for People of Color from oppressed communities navigating hostile and racist terrains. We highly encourage clinicians, when appropriate, to help clients foster a strong racial identity in therapy. This goal can be achieved by customizing treatment plans to include specific ways for clients to become familiar with their racial roots.

Domain C: Contextualizing the Problem

In Domain C, clinicians help clients understand the etiology of their presenting problem, while explicitly addressing how clients' race and culture may be contributing to their symptoms. To meet this goal, clinicians can assist clients in contextualizing their problems. The process of externalization can be particularly effective with Latino/a clients and other oppressed communities who are often socialized to internalize and blame themselves for the challenges they face. Thus this strategy can serve as a way to give clients permission to not blame themselves for experiencing symptoms as a consequence of living in abnormal, oppressive, and racist environments. In other words, contextualizing the problem helps clients to put the blame where it belongs—that is, on the system and not on themselves. Through this process, clients begin to learn about the role of systemic oppression and its effect on their sense of *self-concept* (how I think about myself) and *self-worth* (how much value I place on myself).

Domain D: Integrating Latino/a Psychological Strengths Into Mental Health Interventions and Developing Prosocial Coping Skills

The CREAR-CE Treatment Approach is based on the principle that problems in living result from individuals' disconnection from their culture, their racial roots, and other social and biological factors that make them unique. The provision of culturally responsive and racially conscious treatment requires clinicians to both acknowledge and use the strengths (e.g., personal, cultural, racial) that have helped Latinos/as persist in the face of adversity.

Consequently, interventions that help Latino/a clients become aware of and reconnect with their culture of origin and with their unique self can promote healing. Thus, in Domain D, clinicians are invited to focus on helping clients identify the traditional cultural values (i.e., *familismo, respeto, dignidad, confianza, personalismo/simpatía, vergüenza, amabilidad, lealtad, obediencia, responsabilidad, ser trabajador, honestidad, humildad*; see Chapter 8 in this volume) as well as personal and cultural strengths they utilize in their everyday lives. A review of the *Seven Psychological Strengths of Latinos/as* (i.e., determination, *esperanza* [hope], adaptability, strong work ethic, connectedness to others, collective emotional expression, and resistance) is provided in Chapter 1 of this text. Overall, cultural and racial strengths "allow individuals to successfully meet the challenges and demands placed on them by the larger social context" (Parham, 2002, p. 111) and thus help serve as a buffer from internalizing the social diseases of society.

When clinicians are assisting their Latino/a clients to generate prosocial skills, it is important for the provider to first assess what clients have already done in an attempt to address their presenting problem. Some useful questions that can assist clinicians in meeting this goal include the following: How have you dealt with the problem before? What has worked in the past to alleviate the problem? Who has helped you cope with the problem? Are there any reasons why you are not using these ways of coping now? In an effort to avoid redundancy and decrease helplessness, clinicians are then encouraged not to suggest or recommend any solutions that the client has used in the past. There are a wide array of culturally congruent Latino/a prosocial skills that clinicians can encourage their clients to use to cope with their distress, including dancing, singing, praying, going to church/mosque/temple, using art (e.g., spoken word, humor, painting, drawing, acting), playing and/or watching sports, socializing, and connecting with spiritual guides (e.g., curandera/os, santero/as, priests, pastors).

Domain E: Explicitly Addressing and Integrating the Role of Skin Color and Racism in Treatment

As discussed in Chapters 1 and 2, Latinos/as have a rich history of ancestral traditions that traces its roots to three distinct racial groups (i.e., Black, Indigenous, and White). The mixing of these groups, referred to as *mestizaje*, resulted in Latinos/as having a wide variety of skin colors and phenotypic characteristics.

Unfortunately, Latinos/as have been socialized to deny, deflect, and minimize the social hierarchy where individuals with lighter skin and more European-looking phenotypes have higher power and status than individuals with darker skin and more Indigenous and/or African-looking phenotypes (Adames et al., 2016). These beliefs are referred to as *Mestizaje Racial Ideologies (MRIs)*. In Domain E, clinicians are called to explicitly identify, acknowledge, and address the impact of skin color, physiognomy, and MRIs on their Latino/a clients' family dynamics and access to opportunities. This goal can be achieved in a number of ways, including 1) using information obtained in Domain B regarding clients' racial identity development to understand how clients view themselves racially, 2) paying attention to how skin color and physiognomy may be impacting the presenting problem, 3) helping clients become aware of their MRIs and helping them to address such beliefs in therapy, and 4) validating, affirming, and providing a space for clients with darker skin and Indigenous/African phenotypes to discuss, reflect on, and process their experiences of colorism and racism.

Domain F: Healing Through Liberation

The last domain in Phase III aims to promote a social justice orientation among Latino/a clients. Engagement in social justice work has been associated with positive mental health for minoritized ethnic individuals (e.g., Peck, Kaplan, & Roman, 1966). Having an understanding of how power operates to maintain systems of oppression can help clients recover faster from their presenting problems (Comas-Diaz, 2015; Landrine & Klonoff, 1997). Moreover, assisting Latino/a clients in integrating a social justice orientation into their lives may help them create a sense of purpose and hope as they make meaningful contributions to their communities, a praxis that is well aligned with the traditional cultural value of Latino/a collectivism. To help develop a social justice orientation, clinicians and clients can explore causes that the client is passionate about and identify ways in which clients can engage to help make systemic change. There are a variety of activities and roles that clients can participate in, such as volunteering, becoming a *promotora/o*, and running for different leadership positions within their communities (e.g., parent-teacher association, public office). Overall, helping clients develop a social justice orientation allows them to heal by using their individual and collective voices to create changes that better the lives of themselves and others.

Conclusion

In this chapter, we have provided an overview of the psychotherapy literature and underscored the necessity for new models and frameworks on Latino/a mental health that integrate the role of race, skin color, and physiognomy. Overall, as outlined in this chapter, the ability to provide culturally congruent and racially conscious mental health services for Latino/a clients is a complex task that requires an advanced level of skills and cultural competence (Parham, 2002). Such a level of competence may be unusual in the field, not just because of the low percentage of Latinos/as who are mental health providers but also because many of those Latinos/as lack the training and knowledge necessary to meet this goal. Nevertheless, we hope that this chapter can serve as a call to action for practitioners to integrate these important elements into their clinical practice with Latino/as, and for scholars to begin exploring the effect that these variables have on treatment outcome.

References

Adames, H. Y., Chavez-Dueñas, N. Y., Fuentes, M. A., Salas, S. P., & Perez-Chavez, J. G. (2014). Integration of Latino/a cultural values into palliative healthcare: A culture centered model. *Journal of Palliative & Supportive Care, 12*(2), 1491–157 doi:http://dx.doi.org/10.1017/S147895151300028X

Adames, H. Y., Chavez-Dueñas, N. Y., & Organista, K. O. (2016). Skin color matters in Latino/a communities: Identifying, understanding, and addressing Mestizaje Racial Ideologies in clinical practice. *Professional Psychology: Research and Practice*. doi:http://dx.doi.org/10.1037/pro0000062

Ancis, J. R. (2004). Culturally Responsive practice. In J. R. Ancis (Ed.), *Culturally responsive interventions: Innovative approaches to working with diverse populations* (pp. 3–21). New York, NY: Brunner-Routledge.

Añez, L. M., Silva, M. A., Paris, M., & Bedregal, L. E. (2008). Engaging Latinos through the integration of cultural values and motivational interviewing principles. *Journal of Professional Psychology: Research and Practice, 39*(2), 153–159. doi:10:1037/0735–7028.39.2.153

APA Presidential Task Force on Evidence-Based Practice. (2006). Evidence-based practice in psychology. *American Psychologist, 61*(4), 271–285. doi:10.1037/0003–066X.61.4.271

Arce, C. H., Murgia, E., & Frisbie, W. P. (1987). Phenotype and life chances among Chicanos. *Hispanic Journal of Behavioral Sciences, 9*, 19–22. doi:10.1177/073998638703090102

Arredondo, P., & Toporek, R. (2004). Multicultural Counseling Competencies = Ethical Practice. *Journal of Mental Health Counseling, 26*(1), 44–55.

Aviera, A. (1996). 'Dichos' therapy group: A therapeutic use of Spanish language proverbs with hospitalized Spanish-speaking psychiatric patients. *Cultural Diversity and Mental Health, 2*(2), 73–87. doi:10.1037/1099–9809.2.2.73

Benish, S. G., Quintana, S., & Wampold, B. E. (2011). Culturally adapted psychotherapy and the legitimacy of myth: A direct-comparison meta-analysis. *Journal of Counseling Psychology, 58*(3), 279–289. doi:10.1037/a0023626

Bergman, L., & Cediel, A. (2013). *Rape in the fields*. Boston, MA: WGBH Educational Foundation.

Bernal, G., Bonilla, J., & Bellido, C. (1995). Ecological validity and cultural sensitivity for outcome research: Issues for the cultural adaptation and development of psychosocial treatments with Hispanics. *Journal of Abnormal Child Psychology, 23*(1), 67–82. doi:10.1007/BF01447045

Bernal, G., & Domenech Rodríguez, M. M. (2012). Cultural adaptation in context: Psychotherapy as a historical account of adaptations. In G. Bernal, M. M. Domenech Rodríguez, G. Bernal, M. M. Domenech Rodríguez (Eds.), *Cultural adaptations: Tools for evidence-based practice with diverse populations* (pp. 3–22). Washington, DC: American Psychological Association. doi:10.1037/13752–001

Bernal, G., Jiménez-Chafey, M. I., & Rodríguez, D. M. M. (2009). Cultural adaptation of treatments: A resource for considering culture in evidence-based practice. *Professional Psychology: Research and Practice, 40*(4), 361–368. doi:10.1037/a0016401

Boyd-Franklin, N. (2006). *Black families in therapy: Understanding the African American experience.* New York, NY: The Guilford Press.

Bracero, W. (1998). Intimidades: Confianza, gender, and hierarchy in the construction of Latino— Latina therapeutic relationships. *Cultural Diversity and Mental Health, 4,* 264–277.

Bronfenbrenner, U. (1977). Toward an experimental ecology of human development. *American Psychologist, 32*(7), 513–531. doi:10.1037/0003–066X.32.7.513

Butler, S. (1998). *The way home.* Oakland, CA: World Trust Educational Services.

Butler, S. (2006). *Mirrors of privilege: Making whiteness visible.* Oakland, CA: World Trust Educational Services.

Caldwell, C. H., Kohn-Wood, L. P., Schmeelk-Cone, K. H., Chavous, T. M., & Zimmerman, M. A. (2004). Racial discrimination and racial identity as risk or protective factors for violent behaviors in African American young adults. *American Journal of Community Psychology, 33*(1/2), 91–105. doi:10.1023/B:AJCP.0000014321.02367.dd

Carter, J. A., & Goodheart, C. D. (2012). Interventions and evidence in counseling psychology: A view on evidence-based practice. In N. A. Fouad, J. A. Carter, & L. M. Subich (Eds.), *APA handbook of counseling psychology, Vol. 1: Theories, research, and methods* (pp. 155–166). Washington, DC: American Psychological Association. doi:10.1037/13754–006

Carteret, M. (2012). *Cultural values of Latino patients and families.* Retrieved from http://www.dimensionsofculture.com/2011/03/cultural-values-of-latino-patients-and-families/

Chavez-Dueñas, N. Y., Adames, H. Y., & Organista, K. C. (2014). Skin-color prejudice and within-group racial discrimination: Historical and current impact on Latino/a populations. *Hispanic Journal of Behavioral Sciences, 36*(1), 3–26. doi:10.1177/0739986313511306

Chwalisz, K. (2003). Evidence-based practice: A framework for Twenty-First-Century Scientist-Practitioner Training. *The Counseling Psychologist, 31*(5), 497–528. doi:10.1177/0011000003256347

Cohen, B. H. (2001). *Explaining psychological statistics* (2nd ed.). New York, NY: John Wiley & Sons.

Cokley, K. (2007). Critical issues in the measurement of ethnic and racial identity: A referendum on the state of the field. *Journal of Counseling Psychology, 52,* 224–239.

Comas-Diaz, L. (2006). Latino healing: The integration of ethnic psychology into psychotherapy. *Psychotherapy: Theory, Research, Practice, Training, 43*(4), 436–453. doi:10.1037/0033–3204.43.4.436

Comas-Diaz, L. (2015). Bienestar: A Latina grounded healing approach to trauma. *Latina/o Psychology Today, 2*(1), 6–11.

Falicov, C. J. (1998). *Latino families in therapy: A guide to multicultural practice.* New York, NY: Guilford Press.

Franklin, M. E., DeRubeis, R. J., & Westen, D. (2006). Are efficacious laboratory-validated treatments readily transportable to clinical practice? In J. C. Norcross, L. E. Beutler, & R. F. Levant (Eds.), *Evidence-based practices in mental health* (pp. 375–401). Washington, DC: American Psychological Association.

Fu-Kiau, K. K. (1991). *Self healing power and therapy: Old teachings from Africa.* New York, NY: Vantage Press.

Gallardo, M. E. (2012). Therapists as cultural architects and systemic advocates: Latina/o Skills Identification Stage Model. In M. E. Gallardo, C. J. Yeh, J. E. Trimble, &

T. A. Parham (Eds.), *Culturally adaptive counseling skills: Demonstrations of evidence-based practice* (pp. 77–112). Thousand Oaks, CA: Sage Publications.

Gallardo, M. E., Yeh, C. J., Trimble, J. E., & Parham, T. A. (2012). *Culturally adaptive counseling skills: Demonstrations of evidence-based practice.* Thousand Oaks, CA: Sage Publications.

Griner, D., & Smith, T. B. (2006). Culturally adapted mental health intervention: A meta-analytic review. *Psychotherapy: Theory, Research, Practice, Training, 43*(4), 531–548. doi:10.1037/0033–3204.43.4.531

Helms, J. E. (1992). Why is there no study of cultural equivalence in standardized cognitive ability testing? *American Psychologist, 47*(9), 1083–1101. doi:10.1037/0003-066X.47.9.1083

Helms, J. E. (2015). An examination of the evidence in culturally adapted evidence-based or empirically supported interventions. *Transcultural Psychiatry, 52*(2), 174–197. doi:10.1177/1363461514563642

Helms, J. E., & Cook, D. A. (1999). *Using race and culture in counseling and psychotherapy: Theory and process.* Needham Heights, MA: Allyn & Bacon.

Hilliard, A. G. (1997). *SBA: The reawakening of the African mind.* Gainesville, FL: Marare Press.

Huey, S. J., & Polo, A. J. (2008). Evidence-based psychosocial treatments for ethnic minority youth. *Journal of Clinical Child and Adolescent Psychology, 37*(1), 262–301. doi:10.1080/15374410701820174

Kleinman, A., Eisenberg, L., & Good, B. (1978). Culture, illness, and care. *Annals of Internal Medicine, 12*, 83–93.

Knipscheer, J. W., & Kleber, R. J. (2004). A need for ethnic similarity in the Therapist-Patient Interaction? Mediterranean migrants in Dutch mental-health care. *Journal of Clinical Psychology, 60*(6), 543–554. doi:10.1002/jclp.20008

Landrine, H., & Klonoff, E. A. (1997). *Discrimination against women: Prevalence, consequences, remedies.* Thousand Oaks, CA: Sage Publications.

La Roche, M. J. (2013). *Cultural psychotherapy: Theory, methods, and practice.* Thousand Oaks, CA: Sage Publications.

La Roche, M. J., & Christopher, M. S. (2009). Changing paradigms from empirically supported treatment to evidence-based practice: A cultural perspective. *Professional Psychology: Research and Practice, 40*(4), 396–402. doi:10.1037/a0015240

Lewis-Fernandez, R., & Kleinman, A. (1994). Culture, personality, and psychopathology. *Journal of Abnormal Psychology, 103*, 67–71.

Lonner, W. J. (1985). Issues in testing and assessment in cross-cultural counseling. *The Counseling Psychologist, 13*(4), 599–614. doi:10.1177/0011000085134004

Matos, M., Bauermeister, J. J., & Bernal, G. (2009). Parent-child interaction therapy for Puerto Rican preschool children with ADHD and behavior problems: A pilot efficacy study. *Family Process, 48*(2), 232–252. doi:10.1111/j.1545–5300.2009.01279.x

Montalvo, F. F. (2004). Surviving race: Skin color and the socialization and acculturation of Latinas. *Journal of Ethnic and Cultural Diversity in Social Work, 13*(3), 25–43. doi:10.1300/J051v13n03_02

Montalvo, F. F., & Codina, G. E. (2001). Skin color and Latinos in the United States. *Ethnicities, 1*(3), 321–341. doi:10.1177/146879680100100303

Nicolas, G., & Schwartz, B. (2012). Culture first: Lessons learned about the importance of the cultural adaptation of cognitive behavior treatment interventions for

Black Caribbean youth. In G. Bernal, & M. M. Domenech Rodríguez (Eds.), *Cultural adaptations: Tools for evidence-based practice with diverse populations* (pp. 71–90). Washington, DC: American Psychological Association. doi:10.1037/13752-004

One America Dialogue Guide: Conducting a discussion on race. (1998). *One America in the 21st century: The President's initiative on race*. Washington, DC: U.S. Government Printing Office. Retrieved from https://www.ncjrs.gov/pdffiles/173431.pdf

Parham, T. A. (2002). Counseling models for African Americans: The what and how of counseling. In T. A. Parham (Ed.), *Counseling persons of African descent: Raising the bar of practitioner competence* (pp. 100–118). Thousand Oaks, CA: Sage Publications.

Peck, H. B., Kaplan, S. R., & Roman, M. (1966). Prevention, treatment, and social action: A strategy of intervention in a disadvantaged urban area. *American Journal of Orthopsychiatry, 36*(1), 57–69. doi:10.1111/j.1939-0025.1966.tb02290.x

Ponterotto, J. G., & Park-Taylor, J. (2007). Racial and ethnic identity theory, measurement, and research in counseling psychology: Present and future directions. *Journal of Counseling Psychology, 54*(3), 282–294. doi:10.1037/0022-0167.54.3.282

Ramos, B., Jaccard, J., & Guilamo-Ramos, V. (2003). Dual ethnicity and depressive symptoms: Implications of being Black and Latino/a in the United States. *Hispanic Journal of Behavioral Sciences, 25*(2), 147–173. doi:10.1177/0739986303025002002

Rodríguez, D. M. M., & Bernal, G. (2012). Frameworks, models, and guidelines for cultural adaptation. In G. Bernal, & M. M. Domenech Rodríguez (Eds.), *Cultural adaptations: Tools for evidence-based practice with diverse populations* (pp. 23–44). Washington, DC: American Psychological Association. doi:10.1037/13752-002

Rosselló, J., & Bernal, G. (1996). Adapting cognitive-behavioral and interpersonal treatments for depressed Puerto Rican adolescents. In E. D. Hibbs, & P. S. Jensen (Eds.), *Psychosocial treatments for child and adolescent disorders: Empirically based strategies for clinical practice* (pp. 157–185). Washington, DC: American Psychological Association. doi:10.1037/10196-007

Sackett, D. L., Straus, S. E., Richardson, W. S., Rosenberg, W., & Haynes, R. B. (2000). *Evidence-based medicine: How to practice and teach EBM* (2nd ed.). New York, NY: Churchill Livingstone.

Santiago-Rivera, A. L., Arredondo, P., & Gallardo-Cooper, M. (2002). *Counseling Latinos and la familia: A practical guide*. Thousand Oaks, CA: Sage.

Seaton, E. K., Scottham, K. M., & Sellers, R. M. (2006). The status model of racial identity development in African American adolescents: Evidence of structure, trajectories, and well-being. *Child Development, 77*(5), 1416–1426.

Smith, A. K., Sudore, R. L., & Perez-Stable, E. J. (2009). Palliative care for Latino patients and their families: Whenever we prayed, she wept. *Journal of American Medical Association, 301*(10), 1047–1057.

Sternberg, R. J. (2006). Evidence-based practice: Gold standard, Gold plated, or fool's gold? In C. D. Goodheart, A. E. Kazdin, & R. J. Sternberg (Eds.), *Evidence-based psychotherapy: Where practice and research meet* (pp. 261–271). Washington, DC: American Psychological Association. doi:10.1037/11423-011

Sue, S., Zane, N., Levant, R. F., Silverstein, L. B., Brown, L. S., Olkin, R., & Taliaferro, G. (2006). How well do both evidence-based practices and treatment as usual satisfactorily address the various dimensions of diversity? In J. C. Norcross,

L. E. Beutler, & R. F. Levant (Eds.), *Evidence-based practices in mental health: Debate and dialogue on the fundamental questions* (pp. 329–374). Washington, DC: American Psychological Association. doi:10.1037/11265–008

Task Force on Promotion and Dissemination of Psychological Procedures. (1995). Training in and dissemination of empirically validated treatments: Report and recommendations. *The Clinical Psychologist, 48*(1), 3–23.

Telzer, E. H., & Vazquez-Garcia, H. A. (2009). Skin color and self-perceptions of immigrant and US born Latinas: The moderating role of racial socialization and ethnic identity. *Hispanic Journal of Behavioral Sciences, 31*(3), 357–374. doi:10.1177/0739986309336913

Trimble, J. E., Scharrón-del-Río, M. R., & Hill, J. S. (2012). Ethical considerations in the application of cultural adaptation models with ethnocultural populations. In G. Bernal & M. M. D. Rodríguez (Eds.), *Cultural adaptations: Tools for evidence-based practice with diverse populations* (pp. 45–67). Washington, DC: American Psychological Association. doi:10.1037/13752–003

Vasquez, M. T. (2012). Psychology and social justice: Why we do what we do. *American Psychologist, 67*(5), 337–346. doi:10.1037/a0029232

Wah, L. M. (2004). *Color of fear*. Berkeley, CA: Stirfry Productions.

Wallis, F., Amaro, H., & Cortés, D. E. (2012). Saber Es Poder: The cultural adaptation of a trauma intervention for Latina women. In G. Bernal & M. M. Domenech Rodríguez (Eds.), *Cultural adaptations: Tools for evidence-based practice with diverse populations* (pp. 157–178). Washington, DC: American Psychological Association. doi:10.1037/13752–008

Wampold, B. E. (2007). Psychotherapy: The Humanistic (and Effective) Treatment. *American Psychologist, 62*, 857–873.

Wampold, B. E., Lichtenberg, J. W., & Waehler, C. A. (2002). Principles of empirically supported interventions in counseling psychology. *The Counseling Psychologist, 30*(2), 197–217. doi:10.1177/0011000002302001

Westen, D., Novotny, C. M., & Thompson-Brenner, H. (2004). The Empirical Status of Empirically Supported Psychotherapies: Assumptions, Findings, and Reporting in Controlled Clinical Trials. *Psychological Bulletin, 130*(4), 631–663. doi:10.1037/0033- 2909.130.4.631

White, J. L., & Cones, J. H., III. (1999). *Black man emerging: Facing the past and seizing a future in America*. New York, NY: W. H. Freeman.

White, J. L., & Henderson, S. J. (2008). The browning of America: Building a new multicultural, multiracial, multiethnic paradigm. In J. L. White & S. J. Henderson (Eds.), *Building multicultural competency: Development, training and practice* (pp. 17–49). New York, NY: Rowman & Littlefield Publishers.

Zuñiga, M. E. (1992). *Dichos* as metaphorical tools for resistant Latino clients. *Psychotherapy, 28*, 480–483.

Part IV

The Impact of Latino/a Psychology on Racially and Ethnically Diverse Students and Professionals

10 The Impact of Latino/a Psychology on Racially and Ethnically Diverse Students and Professionals

> *Mentoring to transgress is about authenticity, connection, and waking students' sense of humanity while learning to be comfortable with the discomfort.*
>
> –Adames and Chavez-Dueñas

In this chapter, a group of ethnically and racially diverse students and professionals describe their journeys through their ethnic and racial identity development, which were impacted by the content of this book. Their experiences highlight growth stemming from knowledge gained about themselves as cultural and racial beings. The Students and Professionals of Color share how their experiences of self-discovery, although painful at times, were the catalysts to self-healing and liberation. The White students and professionals reflect on how the process of acknowledging and challenging their complicit roles in the system of oppression, which characterizes the United States (U.S.) society, allowed them to develop more genuine relationships with others while seeing themselves in more authentic ways. All students and professionals describe how learning the content of this book began as pure academic training but evolved into a transformative journey of acceptance, strong racial and ethnic identity, and a deep sense of personal responsibility to continue working and engaging in social and racial justice work both in their personal and professional lives.

Ultimately, we believe the nine narratives offered in this chapter will incite similar self-reflections and growth, and they will provoke dialogue on the topics of Latino/a history, race, immigration, acculturation, and within-group differences. We hope that mental health practitioners, researchers, and students working with Latino/a populations who read this book and these nine narratives will begin or continue on their own journeys toward Latino/a cultural competence. Overall, our goal is for readers of this book to become thinkers and doers who see themselves as both cultural and racial beings motivated to produce excellence when studying and working with Latino/a communities and other Communities of Color after reading these closing pages.

Essay One

Standing Strong: Latinos/as Sustained by Roots of
Connectedness, Knowledge, and Wisdom

> Silvia P. Salas-Pizaña, Jessica G. Perez-Chavez, and Robert L. Mendez
> *Every great dream begins with a dreamer.*
> –Harriet Tubman, n.d., para. 1

In this essay, we, three Latinos/as, speak about our journeys of identity development and self-discovery. Our experiences of growth, stemming from our knowledge about Latina/o psychology, are discussed. Reflecting on our own personal journeys of struggle, perseverance, and hope, we discuss how our intersecting immigrant, racial, and ethnic identities have shaped the course of our lives. More importantly, we discuss how our journeys of self-discovery, although painful at times, were the catalysts to self-healing and enhancements to our resilience.

Jessica

My name is Jessica y soy indocumentada. I call myself a DREAMer, but the reality is that I am living the dream dreamed many moons ago by the original DREAMers, my immigrant parents. I became an immigrant in a foreign land before I had any awareness of how it would shape my future. I was only a toddler when my parents, my sister, and I crossed the U.S.–Mexican border.

Life in the U.S. began in Pilsen, a predominately immigrant neighborhood in Chicago where my *abuelita* lived. I remember very little of those first few years, but I know that my parents took on factory jobs, sometimes more than one at a time, in order to provide for us. Their courageous decision to immigrate to this country afforded my sister and me with countless opportunities that they themselves never had. Although in some ways, my story as an undocumented Latina is different from my parents', learning about Latina/o psychology has given me the language and context to understand how my life is deeply rooted in their immigrant narratives. I had to understand and embrace their stories in order to understand and embrace my own.

During my childhood, I attended predominantly low-income Latino schools where I easily identified and connected with my peers. The stressors I experienced then were not entrenched in the pressures to fit into mainstream culture, but rather in the constant fear and anxiety my parents experienced as a result of living in a country that benefits from their labor but expects that they live in the shadows of society. It manifested in the tension that built inside our car when a police car would drive behind us and in their reluctance to go to hospitals and airports. That tension, which I felt and knew so well at a young age, was anxiety and fear over the possibility of being separated from my family. It is a fear that I struggle to put into words because it continues to exist in my life today.

As I grew older, I began to understand this fear and the limits imposed by my status. As an undocumented person, I was unable to travel, drive, obtain a valid form of identification, work, and qualify for financial aid. But the most difficult part was witnessing and feeling my parents' fear, loss, and *desesperacion* (desperation) from being undocumented. Although I have an Ivy League college degree, nothing has changed for my family. Knowing this is at times debilitating and emotionally and physically exhausting. Still, I understand that my struggles are small in comparison to those my parents are forced to overcome, and I appreciate that I was able to go to school and study while they worked excruciating jobs where they were treated with little dignity. Their strength to endure in this anti-immigrant country gave me the courage to "come out" in high school as an undocumented Latina. Soon thereafter, I became involved in the DREAMers movement. At a young age, I became an activist for my community and myself. For the first time, I felt I had a voice.

When it was time to go to college in New York, I was thrilled that I was about to begin the dream long dreamed by my parents. However, when the school year started, I quickly became aware of the invisibility of undocumented students on campus and of the small number of Students of Color in my classes; to add to that culture shock, for the first time I realized that I came from a very poor family. All of these realizations made me feel inadequate and different. My confidence and self-esteem plummeted as I constantly began to compare myself to my White peers. During class discussions, I did not participate because I was afraid I would sound inarticulate or unintelligent. This fear came true when I mispronounced a word during a class presentation. My professor corrected me after class and advised me to "work on my English." I remember feeling humiliated, unintelligent, and ashamed of myself. That experience became all too frequent while in college. Soon my shame and self-doubt began to impact my grades and my ability to speak to professors. I went from being an outspoken activist to being the quiet Latina whose voice had been muted. I often wondered if my parents had experiences like those, where they felt so estranged to the space they occupied and to the unfamiliar faces that surrounded them.

I do not know how my mentors sensed that I was struggling, but they did, and I am grateful to them for it. I found comfort in their *consejos* and words of encouragement. Like me, they are from similar backgrounds: Latina/o immigrants and first-generation college students. They provided me with countless opportunities to learn about Latina/o psychology outside of the classroom setting. As they guided me through my very first research poster titled "When the American Dream is Out of Reach: Clinical Implications of Undocumented Status in Latino/a Youth," I began to make more sense of my identity as an undocumented Latina. Through this research project,

I found visibility, validation, and meaning. I began to understand that my feelings of shame were a product of a world that constantly devalues and dehumanizes the people that I represent and not a reflection of my ability and self-worth. Learning about theories of ethnic identity development was key to understanding my story and embracing all the strengths, values, and wisdom that come from my family and community. Through Latina/o psychology, I also learned that I should not compare myself to my White and documented classmates, because our experiences are not the same.

To this day, I continue to heal through the power that comes from the love, support, and wisdom of my family and community. Now, more than ever, I can clearly see the undeniable beauty in our struggles as immigrants. I see this beauty in my parents' work ethic, through my mentors' inner strength, and in my grandmother's invincible spirit. I have inherited these strengths from them and my ancestors. It is through their sacrifices, tears, blood, and sweat that I have the privilege to write in this space about how my path changed by learning about Latina/o psychology. I have learned that my dreams belong to the original courageous DREAMers, who dared to dream and who continue to show me that all it takes is one dream to make many more possible.

Silvia

In the U.S., my achievements are owed to so many Latina/o immigrants who struggled and dared to create a path that is easier to endure today and to those who entered my life and gave me hope—to you all I owe my accomplishments. Although the pursuit of my parents' dreams included giving my siblings and me access to formal education, I never imagined that as a first-generation college student and immigrant with dark skin and Indigenous features from rural Aguascalientes, Mexico, I would survive and thrive in the ivory halls of academia. Today, as a Ph.D. student in counseling psychology, I realize that my imagination was limited compared to the dreams of my *mamá y papá* and mentors. From them I learned that dreams are not made out of thin air, but out of hard work and determination. Part of the arduous process has included learning about *mi cultura* (my culture) through the study of Latina/o psychology.

Latina/o psychology has taught me many lessons that validate my existence as a woman, immigrant, and Person of Color. Learning about the rich spectrum of skin color in Latin America helped me find a space to contextualize my experiences as a dark-skinned Mexican. While living in Mexico, I understood my dark skin's negative associated value from personal experience and a story my mother often shared. This story is of the visit *mi mama Cuca* (maternal grandmother Cuca) made when I was born. Upon reaching to uncover my blanket, she discovered that my dark skin resembled hers and remarked ¡*Oh, es prietita!* (She is dark!); *mama Cuca* was saddened by the discovery. My mother shared that *mama Cuca* immediately reassured her that by age 15 I would be *una señorita bella* (a beautiful young lady). At six years old, unable to grasp *mama Cuca's* disappointment that I did not have white skin, I focused on my hatred of being called *prieta* and my desire to be light skinned like my family. Latina/o psychology taught me how that night, *mama Cuca* tried to convey her wisdom about race and how her granddaughter's dark skin would likely be a source of pain, a reality *mama Cuca* knew all too well.

With age, *mama Cuca's* wisdom began to resonate after my family and I immigrated to the U.S. 18 years ago. We settled in a predominately White rural town in Indiana where I witnessed my family struggle to survive both economically and morally and internalized the negative way others treated us. In school, my skin color and background were a reminder of my status; my desire to be White increased. I dealt with these feelings by trying to change things I had control over (e.g., changing clothes, straightening my hair). However, my skin color and cultural heritage made me a visible target for rejection. Thus my early lessons in the U.S. reinforced what *mama Cuca* already knew: that this White world was not made for a dark-skinned person like me.

My mentors, whom I met while studying Latina/o psychology, helped to reinforce the early life lessons of *mama Cuca*. They were the first brown Latina/o psychologists I met in a sea of White faces within the ivory spaces of academia. Thus their mentoring became pivotal in instilling hope that I, too, could become a psychologist. They saw in me the strengths I thought I lacked, challenged me to grow, and stood beside me when I shared my pain. No professor had done that for me before.

After many years of lacking the words to explain my experiences and believing I was not capable of succeeding in academia, my mentors introduced me to my culture again through Latina/o psychology. I did not realize how deeply the racism I experienced affected me; it made me forget *mama Cuca's* strength. I learned of the corrosive nature of the use of derogatory words (e.g., *prieta)* concerning my dark skin and its impact on my self-concept. I was made to believe I was weak and forced to reject what gave me strength: my dark skin and culture. I became angry and pained. It was painful to realize that the White culture I sought to value had made me an alien to myself.

Prior to Latina/o psychology, I was easily pushed and bruised by the currents, which made me feel like I was drowning in the saltiness of the U.S. sea. I never imagined the difficult path that I would have to walk as a result of having dark skin. The arduous process of finding value and strength in my dark skin and culture gave me the anchor that now supports me. Never in a million years would I have imagined that I could say I am in a Ph.D. program fulfilling my family's dreams. Although my experiences due to racism and discrimination have not changed, my ancestors, my family, and my mentors have taught me that perseverance is a power that lies within; we just have to find it through our culture while avoiding quenching our thirst by seeking validation from White and oppressive cultures. Although it was a hard lesson, I have learned that as Latinos/as, we cannot rely on an oppressive culture to define a path for us. Instead, we must be grounded in and guided by our cultural roots, which ultimately create paths for future Latina/o generations.

Robert

When I began studying Latina/o psychology, I was honestly and mistakenly worried about being put into a "box" as a "Latino therapist." I was completely confused in my racial/ethnic identity. I still thought that if I could please, mimic, and make enough money to be accepted by Whites, I would be immune to discrimination, injustice, and pain. I was afraid of my last name. I was afraid that my last name would keep me out of certain opportunities.

Little did I know, I would not be completely wrong about being put into a box. However, today I welcome and find it an honor to be in that box. My perception of myself is not at all uncommon for many Latinos/as. This is one of the gifts of studying Latina/o psychology and culture. It is essential for clinicians to have a thorough and clear understanding of not only the history of Latinas/os but also of how that history has impacted this resilient, resourceful, and intelligent community. As I began and continued studying Latina/o psychology and culture, I found myself feeling angry, enlightened, inspired, sad, and any other feeling one can think of. This is how education should make us feel. If we can have these feelings, it may mean that our hearts were touched which is a good thing. I was learning so much. I was learning about the other side of Latina/o and American history. I was learning about my socialization as a Latino male into American society and its impact on me. I learned that much of my apprehension in believing that I too could participate in society and make a change for my community and for others came from not seeing anyone whom I could identify with doing those things.

As I began studying the content in this book and learning about the struggles and triumphs of Latinas/os, specifically for me, the history Puerto Ricans have gone through, I began to feel empowered. It was the beginning of seeing myself as worthy, resilient, intelligent, compassionate, and strong. I began to recognize and take pride in all that my grandparents, parents, and ancestors had gone through so that I could be sitting in a graduate school program working on my master's degree. They put their lives on the line so that I could learn and be afforded opportunities that unfortunately they were not. They sacrificed so that I could be. I would have never gained this gift if it were not for the content covered in this book. Moreover, the material inspired me to begin creating who I want to be instead of who I think I should or society thinks I should be. It helped me to begin taking a thorough analysis of who I am as a cultural being, clinician, scholar, and human. It encouraged me to take notice of how I, too, can participate in oppression without meaning to (whether meaning to or not, I still did). I recognized my privileges as a male, light-skinned Latino who is able-bodied, educated, and heterosexual and also how I could use those privileges to help those who are not afforded the same. Unless I share and use my privileges to help others, I will continue to uphold the dominant culture's superiority and oppressive actions.

Learning about ethnic identity inspired me to take inventory of myself as a cultural being and to learn how it has impacted my life thus far, as well as how it could possibly affect my future patients. I grew up thinking that my anger, shame, sadness, and feelings of inferiority were shameful and had to be hidden. I felt anger because of previous experiences with discrimination, but I did not feel I could or should be angry or hurt. I was told by my teacher and authority figures growing up that my anger was intimidating and immature. Expression of my anger could get me labeled a "thug," "irrational," "immature," or "violent and dangerous." However, my mentors encouraged me to allow myself to feel those feelings. They actually told me it could be a healing and powerful experience. They were right. I was angry, hurt, ashamed, and sad that I let negative images, stories, and lies about my culture affect me and keep me playing small. After some kicking and screaming on my part, I came to believe that these feelings were justified and normal. Finally, the healing could begin and my life has never been the same.

I owe my life to my ancestors, grandparents, parents, mentors, and, especially, Jailyn Isla Méndez, my daughter. Without these people before me and next to me telling me that I can, I would not be able to continue clearing the path and opening the doors for those who are to come after me. One of the gifts of studying Latino/a psychology is that I now know that the example I set, my achievements, and the legacy I leave behind are no longer about me. It is all bigger than me. It is for those who have sacrificed their lives and everything they had for me to have many fortunate and powerful experiences and opportunities.

Essay Two

Our Separate Struggles are Connected: The Impact of Latina/o Psychology on the Lives of African American and South Asian Graduate Students

Minnah W. Farook, Danielle Alexander, and Shanna N. Smith
Education is the passport to the future, for tomorrow belongs to those who prepare for it today.

–Malcolm X, 1964, p. 223

Minnah

Growing up in Bangladesh as the eldest of three sisters, I was constantly reminded of my responsibility to a family that had no sons and came from a highly patriarchal society. In a country where women's rights were restricted and economic opportunities were limited, my parents taught me that education was the only way for a woman to have self-determination. In order to make my parents proud, I focused on my studies when my parents immigrated to the U.S. to ensure my siblings and I had the opportunities they did not have in Bangladesh.

As a child growing up in the suburbs of Detroit where I often was the only Person of Color in my classes at school, I was keenly aware that I was different. I was constantly reminded that I was a foreigner, an English-language learner, and not White. I often heard my peers complain about how the area was "becoming like the south of 8 Mile Road (in Detroit)," where the residents are primarily African American and other People of Color. However, it took some time to understand that they were talking about me. I felt ashamed and angry with my parents for bringing us to a place where we were unwanted. I tried to distance myself from my Bengali Muslim community and felt embarrassed when my mother picked me up from school in her *selwar kameez* and hijab. In an effort to be accepted, I tried to highlight how I was more like my White peers. I was happy when my peers paid attention to me. For a moment, I was not invisible.

In college, I experienced difficulties finding my place among peers at a predominantly White institution. I questioned whether I was capable of being successful, particularly when I struggled to keep up with the coursework that my White peers seemed to have little difficulty with. I felt ashamed when I thought about how hard my parents worked to make sure I could have the opportunities that they did not have in Bangladesh. I wondered what was wrong with me and why I was not like my peers.

I felt even more disconnected from the larger society after the events of 9/11. My family and I were among those "randomly selected" for additional security screenings at airports and the U.S.–Canada border. I sought to understand why people suddenly looked at my Muslim community with suspicion. The more I learned when I researched the history of Islam and the contributions of Muslims to civilization, the more difficult it was to understand the negative perceptions others have about Muslims. I saw the beauty of Islam, and I saw its purpose and its strength in my community. For the first time in my life, I felt truly connected to my Muslim identity.

Despite some setbacks in college, I graduated and went on to pursue my master's degree. I was once again in a similar environment where my White peers seemed smarter, more sophisticated, and more confident than I was. However, this time I had the privilege of meeting two Latina/o psychologists who helped me contextualize my experience as a South Asian immigrant, a Muslim woman, and a Person of Color. I was introduced to the content of this book, and for the first time, I was able to reframe my own experience of acculturating to U.S. American culture. Studying about the history of Latinas/os encouraged me to research and appreciate the rich history of Bangladesh and South Asia.

In the content of this book, learning about the stereotypes, prejudices, and discrimination that many Latinas/os face helped me understand the historical and political context that has shaped my life as a Bengali Muslim immigrant woman. I discovered parallels between how Latinas/os are portrayed in the U.S. and the orientalist representations of Islam and Muslims in Western media. I felt angry about the system of oppression that works by taking away power from People of Color and other minoritized communities. I felt ashamed for distancing myself from people who look like me and share a collective experience of marginalization. With the support of my mentors, and the knowledge I gained from Latina/o psychology, I became determined to increase my awareness. With this new wealth of knowledge gained, I strive to be a vessel from which the voices of the silenced, those who have had similar experiences, can be heard.

The journey of understanding my own identity has been a difficult one, as I had internalized many negative stereotypes about People of Color. I had lower expectations from myself and other People of Color, and I measured myself from a standard that was created by and for the benefit of White individuals. Through this process, I started understanding how racial socialization impacted me as an individual, my community, and the larger society. I did not expect to learn so much about myself in the course of studying Latina/o psychology. With the content of this book, I found strength in my difficult experiences as a Person of Color and my voice. Today, I lift my voice for others and myself.

As I continue my studies as a doctoral student in counseling psychology, I continue working on my racial and ethnic identity. I find strength from the support of my family and feel determined to make them proud. I remind myself that I can no longer internalize the false narratives that others create about who I am and what I am capable of. Because I will continue to live in a society that denigrates and rejects people who look like me, it is essential that I liberate my mind and accept myself so I can stay awake and help others free themselves of mental colonization.

Danielle

Before beginning my narrative, I would like to proudly state that I am a Black woman. This is a phrase I have affectionately grown to love and use to define myself. It is an identity I have fought hard to discover.

I honestly do not remember a time when I did not know I was Black; those features were clearly defined by the color of my skin and the texture of my hair. However, I never felt connected to my Black identity. My parents never explicitly talked about race with my young brother and me; we were taught that, "we are all just people." Although they never shared any negative feelings about being Black, I did not grow up being proud to be Black. I remember wishing that I were Asian, Latina, and even White . . . anything besides Black. Those other races and ethnicities had such unique cultural heritages to be proud of. To me, being Black did not seem that special.

Even though I did not fully understand what it meant to be Black in the U.S., my environment made it abundantly clear to me that I was different. I grew up in the northwest suburbs of Atlanta in predominately White neighborhoods that were sparsely populated by African Americans and Latinas/os. It was not rare to find that I was the only Black kid in class. Some of the kids liked me because I was Black, some disliked me because I was Black. For others, it did not seem to matter.

As a kid, all I wanted was to fit in. But even at seven years old, I understood that my skin color kept me from completely "fitting in," and I grew incredibly frustrated because of that. Soon enough, I started to hate every physical aspect of myself. From the texture of my hair to the dark color of my eyes, my round nose, and dark complexion—I simply hated everything that reminded me of my Blackness. Since I could not change my physical features, I worked hard to separate myself from my Black identity. I subscribed to the fashion trends of my White peers, I tried talking more like them, and began chemically altering my hair so I could wear it straight. It was a compliment whenever I heard someone say, "You don't act, talk, look . . . like other Black people." Those phrases meant that I was "fitting in." I felt I was part of the crowd, until I was not, and I became part of a stereotypical comment or joke about Black people. These comments reminded me where I really stood.

Around the time I went to college, my dad moved to the south side of Atlanta. This was the first time I was in an environment where the majority of the population was Black, and I remember feeling very uncomfortable. I had believed the media's negative messages that most Black people were "ghetto," loud, slang talking, and ignorant. In spite of my Black peers being nothing like how I had imagined them to be, it was still different from the world I was used to. I felt disconnected and out of touch when trying to navigate the new Black environment I had been tossed into. I knew that I was not White, but I also felt like I would never know what it meant to be Black.

The ideas I had about Blackness and my Black identity were challenged when I entered graduate school. After I introduced myself in one of my classes during my first year, the professor commented on how I failed to list the most obvious fact about myself: I am Black. I was struck by his comment because no professor had ever asked me to identify myself as a racial being. His comment challenged me to do something I was actively avoiding: to think of my Blackness. I tried to dismiss the uncomfortable feeling that his comment had stirred in me, but his words continued to echo in my mind.

I was further challenged to think about my racial identity when I began to study Latina/o psychology. As it turned out, learning about Latina/o psychology was one of the most difficult experiences I ever had to endure. The many ways that learning about culture, racial identity, and oppression challenged me extended beyond academic readings by forcing me to reflect and process information emotionally and not just intellectually. As my cultural understanding of Latinas/os broadened, my understanding of my own racial/cultural identity flourished. In the process, I reclaimed my racial identity and proudly called myself a Black woman. I say Black woman because "African American" does not invoke the same pride that "Black" does for me. Calling myself Black reminds me of the 1960s' Black Power movement. Proclaiming Black feels powerful since the word has had so many negative connotations, not only for me but also for the general U.S. American culture.

In claiming my Blackness, I took on a spirit of relief, pride, and self-love, but also sadness. While I finally connected to a piece of my identity that I have been detached from for so long, I blamed myself because it took me over 23 years to finally make that connection. However, the concepts and theories illustrated in this book ultimately helped me overcome my feelings of self-blame.

I feel proud of the fact that I became more conscious and proud of my Blackness. I am grateful to my mentors, two Latina/o professors, and to Latina/o psychology, which have been the catalysts for such personal growth and self-love. As I continue on my own cultural journey, I feel well prepared to enter the mental health field and to utilize the skills I learned to address the multiple problems within all Communities of Color. I hope people see from my story that growth is painful, change is painful, yet it is only through growth and change that we will be able to navigate through these difficult journeys.

Shanna

It is impossible to weave together the quilt of my story without integrating the beautiful cloths that created me—my great-grandmother's wisdom, my grandmother's heart, my grandfather's strength, my mother's resilience, my father's soul, my sister's laughter—along with the friends I have met along the road, and the ancestral spirits who have guided me to where I am today: a graduate student pursuing a master's degree. All have worked to renew the spirit of hope within me in the face of adversity. My prayer is to channel some semblance of their voices, to return to them what they continuously give to me: hope and strength despite shattered knees. Everything I have and will come to gain later is owed to them.

Even as a young Black girl, I always knew there was something different about my skin color; it was easy to see I was brown skinned. Yet growing up there was nothing unusual or out of place about my skin color. I was blessed to have a family who possessed the experience, knowledge, and resources to make sure I internalized from a very young age that being Black is beautiful. The wisdom of my family instilled pride in me about my race, my skin color, and my people. I would never want to be anything aside from who I am today: a proud Black woman. Graduating from a historically black university only deepened my understanding of myself, and as an adult, I felt grounded and cemented in my identity.

What I remained unaware of for a very long time was the extent to which systematic oppression, racism, and societal disdain against my people would bleed into all areas of my own life. For the majority of my life, I lived around Black people, my people, where my life was not in danger because of the color of my skin. My exposure to White people, and by extension my knowledge of whiteness itself, was heavily limited outside of "extreme" instances of racism. It was not until I began a graduate program in counseling psychology at the age of 22 that I was fully exposed to a largely White world at a predominantly White institution.

It was a jarring experience; immediately, I felt like an impostor. For the first time, I was the only Black person in the classroom. Everywhere I went, I was hypervisible yet invisible at the same time to my classmates and professors. My professors and classmates expressed genuine shock and awe when I did well on assignments, projects, and exams, while some accused me of plagiarism on papers. Before long, I felt alienated, rejected, and alone. Isolated, I feared trusting anyone. I stopped speaking in classes because I was exhausted from the anxiety of representing my whole Black community. Somehow I knew what was happening without possessing the language to describe it, yet there were moments where I felt I was losing my mind.

Toward the end of that semester, I met my mentors, two Latina/o professors and psychologists, who reached out to me. With their encouragement and support, I began studying Latina/o psychology, and it was through this process that I was challenged to explore my own identity in ways I had never consciously done before. The content of this book opened the door for me to discover much more about myself. In Latina/o psychology, I learned about racial/cultural identity development, where I found sincere validation in my lived experiences and was able to process through my emotions, which were very much justified. In learning about the multiple nuances of oppression and racism, I discovered I was not paranoid or going crazy, but developing healthy cultural suspicion while experiencing the horrifying effects of racism. My own levels of power and privilege were brought to the forefront, which I had never considered. Equally shocking was that I was seeking validation from the oppressor as a result of socialization I had no idea I had experienced.

The most important piece that changed me while studying Latina/o psychology was the realization of my own ignorance concerning other Communities of Color, specifically Latinas/os. For the first time, I realized I had never reached beyond an intellectual level of understanding when it came to other Communities of Color. Becoming aware of my ignorance touched a powerful chord within me, provoking feelings of guilt and shame. How could I have been so blind? In researching U.S. history, how did I bypass the integral history of the Aztecs? Why did I not think to learn of the narratives and struggles of undocumented immigrants? How had I come to grips with the issue of colorism in the Black community, yet had not applied how the implications could affect any other Community of Color? When I came to understand the damaging implications of identifying Afro-Latinas/os only as Black, I reflected on friends I had growing up, plenty of whom were Afro-Latinas/os who I simply assumed were Black because of their dark skin.

Throughout this process of learning and growing, I have been able to step outside of my guilt and develop a spirit of determination to become conscious about not only the issues within and outside of my Black community but also the oppression faced by all Communities of Color, and I have made a commitment to the healing and advancement of all marginalized communities. But in order to accomplish this, I understand that the process of growth is impossible without the effort of self-discovery. Studying the content of this book has left me with an instrumental lesson: the fight for a world where we can all live and thrive is not isolated to any one community. As the cords of the dream catcher, our experiences as People of Color traveling the muddy landscapes of a bitterly oppressive world are all woven together. As we fight together for justice, and for the realization of a beautiful world, we must also fulfill our obligation to fight for the sake of one another. In turn, we must share our spaces with one another and look toward a better tomorrow.

Essay Three

White European American Clinicians: Rediscovering Our Humanity by Resisting a Socialization of Ignorance, Silence, and Denial

Leah Hirsch, Mackenzie T. Goertz, and Chelsea L. Parker
My humanity is bound up in yours, for we can only be human together.
–Archbishop Desmond Tutu, 1989, para. 7

As three White, non-Latinas who were introduced to Latina/o psychology upon entering our graduate programs in counseling psychology, we believe the material in this book has helped us become competent clinicians and scholars by cultivating our humanity through an increased ability to challenge our White socialization of silence and denial about racism and social inequity. The study of Latina/o mental health redefined our interpersonal approach, both personally and professionally, and we learned that we need to go deeper into our understanding of both ourselves and others if we want to be affirming and effective forces in society. Additionally, we realized that to apply White, Eurocentric values and theories as generally as we had been taught is an unethical, ineffective, and harmful practice. Exposure to this material has been an emotionally draining, yet stimulating experience that helped set us on our paths toward becoming critical race theorists striving to intervene beyond the individual level so as to promote change within the systems of inequality that define society.

Leah

I chose to study psychology because I wanted to learn about cultures different than my own and join an altruistic field that would benefit humanity. I was born to Jewish immigrant parents whose family remained in South Africa, which resulted in almost yearly trips to their native country and exposure to cultural practices that differ greatly from those of the dominant, White culture of the U.S. As a Jew, I grew up learning about the hardships and oppression my people have endured and was proud of our resiliency. I naively believed that my unique background made me more open-minded and knowledgeable about diverse communities than my White peers.

This was my attitude when I started my graduate program at 24 years old and decided to focus my studies on Latina/o psychology. I met one of my mentors, who first introduced me to the term White privilege—a reality that I had lived my entire life but never recognized or put a name to. As is common for Whites in the early stages of their racial identity development, I found myself feeling defensive and resistant to the fact that I had enjoyed what scholars describe as "unearned privileges" due to my race. I vividly remember my visceral reaction when my mentor challenged my resistance and tried to help me understand this concept. The anger was all-consuming and caused blood to rush to my cheeks, my face to feel hot, and what felt like a fire to brew in the pit of my stomach. My initial reaction of anger derived from an unwillingness to recognize reality—that is, the White privilege I had enjoyed and the racism I had been implicitly and explicitly socialized to perpetuate. I had the false belief that my unique background made me immune to the prejudiced socialization of Whites in the U.S., and I thought that to admit that I was in fact a racist was equivalent to admitting that I was a bad person who consciously engaged in oppressive thoughts, beliefs, and actions. I did not understand the subtleties of racism or recognize the microaggressions I was committing each and every day. Admittedly, I am still working to understand myself as a White racial being, which I know is going to be a lifelong journey.

Anger can sometimes precipitate a more intense emotional response or, in my case, a series of emotions. At first, I was angry because I felt misjudged and misunderstood, but eventually I could not ignore the facts. My anger then shifted toward my family, teachers, media, and all those who I had learned from growing up because I was frustrated with only learning about White privilege at age 24. This anger transitioned into a deep sadness, disappointment, and shame in myself as I started to recognize my reality and acknowledge the hypocrisy I lived. I struggled with self-hatred as I looked at the history of oppression and violence for which my community was responsible. I had learned about this history in the past, but maintained an intellectual, surface-level understanding and was now developing a more personal knowledge. I still struggle to accept that I am a part of a community that continues to perpetuate horrific cruelty, but this struggle pales in comparison to those of the oppressed. Additionally, I have internalized the idea that it is my responsibility as a student, clinician, researcher, and human being to not continue to be complicit in the systemic oppression and inequalities of today by pretending that the past does not impact the present.

My experience has led me to believe that it is imperative that Whites learn about cultures different from their own in a way that allows us to both challenge the lens with which we view the world and highlight the strengths and resiliencies within different communities. We cannot accurately understand or appreciate other cultures if we maintain our White, Eurocentric ideologies, and, unfortunately, we have been given an unfair amount of power that makes the need for more flexible thinking a necessity. Regardless of profession, Whites continue to be at the top of our racially driven sociopolitical hierarchy; for this reason, we have a responsibility to combat this oppressive system.

Latina/o psychology reintroduced me to my humanity, a humanity shaped by reality, humility, and purpose. I want to continuously work to no longer be complicit in the oppression of others by doing nothing or claiming ignorance. I do not have all the answers, and I am only at the start of my lifelong journey, but I am certain that the study of Latina/o psychology opened my eyes to a beautiful multicultural and multiracial world to which I was previously blind.

Mac

I came to this material by happenstance, knowing very little about Latinas/os. Two Latino/a psychologists introduced me to the concentrated study of Latina/o mental health, and while I liked the idea of such in depth training, I was concerned that this concentration would limit me from working with other populations. I remember asking myself why I would want to invest so much in learning to connect with and serve a community I had never been interested in before. The responses I received from family and friends were similar; they asked with confusion, "But why Latinos?" Many asked me why Latinas/os could possibly need their own study of psychology because, "Wasn't psychology the same for all people?" To be honest, I really did not know the answers to these questions at the time. I did not understand that Latinas/os are in fact not a homogenous group, or that the field of psychology has largely been developed by and for Whites of European descent, or that Latinas/os, like other marginalized groups, face unique challenges to mental health and lack access to resources that result directly from their historic and contemporary experiences of racism and oppression. The reality is that it took much convincing before I was able to commit to the study of Latina/o mental health. Had I had the understanding of the world that I have today, I would have leaped forward into this training without hesitation. Little did I know, this decision would be the start to my journey in multicultural psychology, as well as a journey in self-discovery that grounds me in purpose, responsibility, and direction.

In the beginning, my beliefs about the Latina/o community were based almost exclusively on depictions provided through the lens of White America, including the media, in which individuals of Latina/o descent are often demoralized, criminalized, and/or exoticized. These representations molded distinct biases that I internalized into personal attitudes and behaviors that served to support the existing sociopolitical hierarchy, which places White individuals like myself at the top. In other words, I embraced the idea that my own White, European American cultural values were a global norm. Studying Latina/o mental health began to challenge my biases and cultivate a multicultural worldview by one, immersing me in the cultural values, norms, and historical narratives of Latinas/os; two, provoking me to consider the impact of my socialization as a White person on my current ways of thinking, feeling, and acting in this world; and three, highlighting the unearned privileges and power embedded in my White identity that ultimately characterize the lens I use to conceptualize racial and ethnic groups, including Latinas/os.

As you learned in the early pages of this book, to begin to understand something one must first learn the history that shapes it. In the process of doing that, I was overwhelmed by the degree to which studying Latina/o history made me feel uncomfortable in my White skin. From the colonization of ancient civilizations in Latin America to the present-day dehumanization of immigrants, I was confronted with the legacy of my own people as tireless oppressors. I did not anticipate the study of another ethnic group to be so deeply entrenched in my own history. This was an emotionally intense and deeply painful experience. Seeing people that were just like me perpetrating such intense and long-standing acts of human degradation shook the core of who I thought I was, and I fiercely resisted the notion that I could be like them. I felt a need to demonize and characterize them as the other in order to separate myself from such a legacy. How could I be a part of this too? I fought adamantly to believe that I was somehow exempt from perpetuating such oppression.

Overtime, I was able to move through this resistance as I began to understand what it meant to be socialized as a White person. Inherent in our socialization are deep-seated levels of racism, including a preference for White ideologies and an unwavering, false belief that opportunities are afforded to individuals on the sole basis of merit and virtue (i.e., the myth of meritocracy). This understanding highlighted for me that I am in fact very much a part of the oppressive legacy of my ancestors and that I have been both complicit in and explicitly supportive of its continuation today. Accepting this fact has not been easy. My early reactions were hot with anger and feelings of betrayal. I felt as if everything I had been taught was a lie. As time passed, the anger morphed into feelings of guilt, shame, and embarrassment that made it difficult to keep moving forward with the material. Fortunately, my immersion in the material of this book, and the relationships I have come to have with others doing this work, have helped me to lean into the discomfort and keep moving forward in this critical journey.

I recall feeling an overwhelming sense of hypocrisy when I considered the fact that I was seeking to promote healing among individuals whose very problems I was helping to create. It became clear to me then that in order to become a competent provider, I needed to expand my role far beyond the helping relationship. Specifically, I now understand that I have both a personal and professional responsibility to actively work at combating racism and other forces of oppression that threaten the lives and health of all people, but more importantly those of oppressed communities. I believe my journey with this material has armed me with the skills, knowledge, and awareness necessary to become an agent of social change and justice. My original concerns about the study of Latina/o mental health being too narrow in scope and limiting me from working with other populations seem largely ironic now, because the result has been the exact opposite. Additionally, this journey has taught me that in doing this work, I must be fiercely committed to respecting and privileging the perspectives of People of Color and folks with other marginalized identities so as to avoid repeating the very dynamics that constitute the ongoing systems of oppression.

Chelsea

For Whites, color blindness is much more comfortable and easier and yet so much more deadly than consciousness. When I began learning about Latina/o psychology, I never imagined that I would learn so much about who I am and my own identity as a White woman. Never could I have guessed that I would experience so many emotions in the process or that my core values would change. Every inch of my being wondered when I would finally reach a state of awareness where feelings of discomfort, anger, sadness, guilt, shame, isolation, and confusion would no longer consume me.

I chose to attend a graduate program in counseling with a concentration in Latina/o psychology mostly due to my experiences working and volunteering within communities throughout the Caribbean and South and Central America. Because of these experiences, I thought I had some notion of what Latino culture as a whole included. After all, I had built houses and sidewalks alongside community members in Peru and the Dominican Republic. I had taught English to Ecuadorian children and their parents. I had lived in their homes for months, eaten their food, and witnessed their trials and tribulations first hand. Of course I knew Latino culture, or so I thought.

While reflecting on my journey, there is one specific memory that constantly replays in my head. In fact, I can still feel my face becoming red and anger surging throughout my entire body in the moment when a professor's words shook the core of my beliefs. As a class, we were asked to give reflections on an emotionally charged film, and my reflection was that it was difficult to look past the poor acting. "You can look at the acting in that movie rather than the emotions behind it because you are White," my professor responded, pointing out a typical reaction of someone who is from the dominant White culture. Looking back, my anger was in reaction to feeling as though the professor was questioning who I am as a person, and for the first time in my life, someone blamed my race for my response. My head swirled with defense. "That's not because of my race. I'm a good person." Then I used the crutch of unaware White individuals everywhere, "I'm not racist." My anger was a single speck of what occurs in the everyday lives of People of Color as a result of racism.

Although defensiveness continued to impact my interactions with others, at that point, I was drowning in a sea of discomfort that I had never known before. I suddenly found myself questioning everything I had been taught in schools, the messages I had been exposed to via the media, and, for the first time, my own racial identity. I was unaware that I had been socialized to believe in the myth of meritocracy and did not understand that I had been afforded unearned privileges due to the color of my skin. Everything in me wanted to fight it, to find some other explanation. I was in the early stages of my White racial identity development, where I remained for a while, experiencing intense emotions and a sense of hypervigilance toward any sign of racism or discrimination.

With this first realization of my own White privilege, I found myself with what I thought was "newfound knowledge" of oppression and racism in our society. I tried to educate other Whites around me and became angry when friends, colleagues, and loved ones demonstrated continued ignorance. Aligning with my non-White friends and classmates and seeking out Mentors of Color mediated some of the guilt I was feeling, especially when People of Color appeared to accept me and promote my growing awareness. However, as I look back, I question how much time I spent listening in these relationships, as I recognize I was often more focused on how to fix things rather than really trying to understand the experiences of People of Color. When I finally began to actually listen to the experiences of minoritized ethnic individuals and made an effort to validate rather than trying to save or fix situations, things began to change.

Studying Latina/o psychology brought me face-to-face with my biases, prejudices, and the stereotypes I held as truths. I began, for the first time, to realize how racism impacts the lives of People of Color and of White people too. I learned how my own beliefs, attitudes, and actions support the current system of oppression and what I can do to begin challenging these beliefs. Over time I have learned that as a White woman, I must learn about oppression by listening to those who are most negatively impacted by it. In fact, I can never stop listening, and if I really want to change, I must take responsibility and utilize my privilege to work toward contributing to the development of anti-racist society. I must also understand that I will continue to commit errors and apologize when I do so, while attempting to not make such errors again. I additionally have to be humble and continue to work on myself, as well as work within my White community by serving as a role model for future generations.

The lessons that I continue to learn from studying Latina/o psychology point to one overarching fact: racism continues to plague our society and harms everyone in it. Those of us from the dominant culture come from a legacy of generations that have strategically crafted this mess. Therefore, we have an obligation to clean it up. Every day there continues to be People of Color who are jailed, mistreated, and murdered for their race. There are children growing up in unsafe neighborhoods, surrounded by violence and poverty, with limited access to resources and without positive role models. We need to work together toward developing an anti-racist society for the benefit of all. Awareness cannot be an afterthought anymore.

References

Malcolm, X. (1964). *Malcolm X collected speeches, debates, and interviews*. US: Malcolm X Files. Retrieved from http://malcolmxfiles.blogspot.com/p/malcolm-x-e-book.html

Tubman, H. (n.d.). *Harriet Tubman quotes*. Retrieved from https://www.goodreads.com/author/quotes/59710.Harriet_Tubman

Tutu, D. (1989). *Desmond Tutu peace foundation: Quotable Desmond Tutu*. Retrieved from http://www.tutufoundation-usa.org/exhibitions.html

Index